Praise for the best-selling *Motley Fool UK Investment Guide*

"(The book) is geared entirely to the UK market and it is difficult to see how anyone could fail to benefit." *Mail on Sunday*

". . . a thoroughly entertaining read . . . It shows the novice investor and the expert alike how to take full control of their investing future and how to have fun doing it." *The Investor*

"This book may not save you a fortune, but it could just make you one." *amazon.co.uk*

"As a guide for the novice the book is an excellent starting point" *Computer Shopper*

"I can thoroughly recommend *The Motley Fool UK Investment Guide* . . . which shows how to successfully invest your money in an easy-to-understand manner, spiced with a bit of fun as well." *Weekly News*

Praise for the *Motley Fool UK* web site: Winner 1998 *Creative Freedom* Best Electronic Media Site. Winner 1999 *New Media Age* Best Personal Finance web site

" . . . provides a good grounding in the share-dealing basics for investors who are new to the stock market game." *The Daily Telegraph*

"The brilliant Motley Fool achieves just the right balance between humour and hard-nosed research to make playing the market fun as well as, hopefully, profitable." *The Sun*

"The site is written in wonderful plain English . . . its highly targeted content is utterly empowering people searching for personal finance answers." *New Media Age*

"The financial future is bright and easier to understand, thanks to The Motley Fool." *Business Age*

"What the Motley Fool says can have an impact on the biggest stock markets in the world." *The Scotsman*

"Cool. Actually quite hip." *Wired Magazine*

"It stands out as an ethical oasis in the area that is fast becoming home to charlatans." *The Economist*

"The Motley Fool site offers excellent information in an irreverent and friendly style." *Computeractive*

The following Motley Fool books are also published by Boxtree:

The Motley Fool UK Investment Guide
The Fool's Guide to Investment Clubs
The Fool's Guide to Online Investing (available soon)

THE MOTLEY FOOL UK INVESTMENT WORKBOOK

David Berger and Bruce Jackson

BOXTREE

First published 1999 by Boxtree
an imprint of Macmillan Publishers Ltd
25 Eccleston Place, London, SW1W 9NF
Basingstoke and Oxford

www.macmillan.co.uk

Associated companies throughout the world

ISBN 0 7522 1787 9

3 5 7 9 8 6 4

A CIP catalogue record for this book is available from
the British Library.

Typeset by SX Composing DTP, Rayleigh, Essex
Printed by Butler & Tanner Ltd, London and Frome

Contents

'I'm a Fool, not a mug.'
George Row,
Community Producer and Foolish Metrics Wizard,
Motley Fool UK

Preface

These days, like it or not (and we hope you will like it by the time you finish this book), we all need to know a little about investing. And we really mean 'a little'. This stuff isn't particle physics. It's basic, easy, rewarding stuff, which, if you give yourself the chance, may make you very wealthy over time, with remarkably minor effort. The hard truth is that no-one else apart from you has the same interest in your future wealth and security. Not the government, not a financial adviser, not a pensions company. No-one.

When faced with someone giving you a hard sell for anything, financial or not, remember this useful saying as they weep crocodile tears, imploring you to *just buy* their pleasingly priced endowment/pension/unit trust/car:

'It's your life. It's only *their* job.'

And that's the crucial difference. By buying this book, you've already taken a huge mental step towards assuming control of your life and influencing it for the better in a way no-one else could ever do for you. That counts for a lot before you even turn the next page.

We hope you'll finish this workbook with a feeling that you can do it and that it is possible for you to make practical sense of your finances, invest your own money and secure your long-term financial future. We can't guarantee it, naturally, but that's what we hope. And even if you don't come away with that feeling of confidence, even if you come away with just a little more knowledge, feeling able to ask your financial adviser a few relevant questions, then that's a positive result too.

Of course, if at one or two points in what follows the faintest glimmer of a smile crosses your lips, if the cares and worries of your day-to-day life vanish for the most fleeting of moments, we'll be even happier.

In fact, so embarrassingly desperate are we to take credit for any value at all you may have gained from this purchase that you will even find a wan glimmer of a smile on our faces as you throw your oversized £9.99 briquette on to next Sunday's barbecue.

The majority of the first half of the book, up to Chapter 7 'How Do I Start Looking for Individual Stocks?', was written by David Berger and most of the second half by Bruce Jackson, which may account for any slight differences in style. Alan Oscroft, senior writer at the Fool UK, contributed significantly to the two USA chapters.

Gushing praise for the book may therefore be sent directly to both of us at **UKWorkbook@ fool.co.uk** Naturally, comments leaning towards the darker end of the Good-Naff continuum may be usefully directed to **TheRubbishBin@fool.co.uk**, where you may rest assured they will receive our fullest attention.

Be Foolish!

David Berger
Bruce Jackson

Who's the Fool?

'Be friends, you English fools, be friends. . .'
Henry V, Act IV, scene 1, Bates speaking

A TALE OF FOOLISHNESS IN 14 MINUTES 38 SECONDS

What is Foolishness, why is it and how can it help you? In 14 minutes 38 seconds, the average time it took a random selection of the British public and their pets[1] to flip through this section, we hope you'll have the answer. At the end of it, you may already be thinking of yourself as a Fool. Or it may take a bit longer. Or it may never happen. Any of these options is alright by us, although the first two strike us as preferable because we think taking a Foolish attitude revolutionizes how you sort out your finances and get on and invest your savings for your future. Strangely, being a bit of a Fool (with a capital 'F') can make a lot of things seem much, much clearer than they did before. It also makes them more fun.

Intrigued? Baffled? Don't put the book down yet, we beseech thee!

___
[1] As expected, they were inseparable.

A Little Bit of History

There is a jester character in most countries. When we're explaining what the Motley Fool is to someone from another culture not rooted in the Shakespearean tradition of the Fool, the pattern is usually one of a prolonged period of furrowed browing, followed by a broad, spreading smile and the illumination of a cartoon lightbulb above their heads. This signifies that the person concerned has made a deep connection with the predominant Fool character from their own history. If they're German, they expostulate: 'Ach, you mean Till Eulenspiegel!' If they're from Chad, they say 'Ah, you mean Haraz-Djombo!' Meanwhile, if they're from Laos, they say, 'Ah, you mean Sop Pong!'

Actually, if truth be told (and the Fool is all about honesty), we've never tried to explain the Motley Fool to anyone from Laos or Chad and have just made up those names for the local jester characters. However, so confident are we that those countries will have Fools as a rich part of their cultural heritage, that we are offering a super-deluxe, FOOL T-shirt to anyone who writes in with the real names for the jesters in Laos and Chad. You'll have to provide proof, but if you think you know, this is the email address: UKWorkbook@fool.co.uk. We have a stack of T-shirts put by, so don't be shy!

In our own tradition, our model is the Fool from *As You Like It*. I'm not going to comment any further on this, beyond to say that it's a jolly inspiring and rather funny read. The reason for this unwonted reticence is that in the introduction to *The Motley Fool UK Investment Guide* I waxed somewhat lyrically and, as it turns out, somewhat wrongly, on the Fool from *As You Like It*. How do I know this? A former General Manager of the Royal Shakespeare Company, former trustee and guardian of Shakespeare's birthplace, current advisory director of the RSC and a member of the Arts Council of England emailed to tell me so in a very gentle and polite manner. What does this tell us? Firstly, this tells us that I am an idiot who should check his facts a little more carefully at times. However, it also tells us that this online medium allows you to neither run nor hide and that this is one of its most powerful attributes. This immediacy keeps those publishing in the medium sensitive to the needs and wants of those they are writing for. It also lends it a vibrancy and connection with the reader unmatched anywhere else.

Back in 1993, reckoning that Fools were everywhere and before most people had heard of the Internet, two American brothers, David and Tom Gardner, set up the Motley Fool as a print (yes, on actual paper) investment newsletter. They found the whole basis of the professional investment industry, hereinafter called 'The Wise', to be so flawed as to be laughable. But not

laughable in a hale-fellow-well-met-we're-all-chums-here way, but laughable in an incredible way, in a how-can-we-all-have-believed-this-stuff-for so-long way.

While promising superior investment returns, 90 per cent of professional fund managers were underperforming the stock market index, an average standard of investment performance which even the know-nothing investor can mimic at little cost, as we shall see. Meanwhile, the newspapers and the conventional media were screaming deafeningly about short-term movements in the stock market and imminent collapse. This stuff sells newspapers, but again, as we shall see, it is not an accurate reflection of the nature of the stock market, which is the most reliable investment vehicle over time. On top of this, stockbrokers were cold-calling customers and hard-selling duff penny shares, which were much more likely to go down to zero than provide the crushing returns the salesmen were promising. All this, and more, combined to create an alarmist atmosphere of imminent disaster and danger which threatened to annihilate the individual investor, while an illusion of safety and security wafted down from the professionals. 'We'll look after you in this shifting, uncertain world of investing. You can trusssst us, my preciousss. . .' came the Gollum-like and none too convincing reassurance.

The truth, of course, was the inverse. While the stock market, if approached on a reasonably informed basis, was the most reliable way for individual investors to grow their long-term wealth, many of the professionals and financial services companies were in business to suck out much of that wealth and were providing precious little in return.

The time was ripe for two Fools with a pig's bladder on a stick to start beating the heads of the industry and provide an alternative which helped individuals – Fools – to figure out for themselves what to do with their money. As Fools should, they did it with humour and a sense of humility, which oft fazed the Wise, working them up into paroxysms of anger, indignation and outrage. This kind of reaction is often seen in cornered beasts who know they have nowhere to run.

From its original print incarnation, the Fool moved to the online medium in 1994. Since then, it has grown and grown and grown. Sometimes the rate of growth has almost been frightening. The US Motley Fool web site (www.fool.com) now has millions of visitors a month, there are over one million US Fool books sold, a national radio show, a syndicated newspaper column and big, big plans.

The Fool was introduced into the UK in 1997 and has experienced similar, rapid growth at the Fool UK web site (www.fool.co.uk). The Internet is pretty well the only environment where growth of 25 to 30 per cent a month can be achieved. *The Motley Fool UK Investment Guide*, published by Boxtree in November 1998, has been a best-seller and we hope complements this book well. Currently, the Fool UK now also has a newspaper column, many thousands of loyal users and is gaining wide exposure in the traditional media. Beware, purveyors of Wise investment blather in Britain, the Fool has come to town.

VOT IS FOOLISHNESS? ZIS IS FUNNY, JA?!

One of the things I like about the Motley Fool, both as a company and as an online being (I can't think of any better way to describe it), is that it encourages open, constructive debate. That means that if you ask a hundred Fools what precisely Foolishness is, you're likely to get at least two hundred answers in reply. That said, there are unifying ideas and an ethos floating around and the Fool most definitely has a point of view. It is that point of view which many find so attractive and which sets it apart from an otherwise rootless investment world, obsessed with the short term and without the customer at its heart. What follows is my own attempt to put some of these Foolish sentiments down on paper. If you have any comments on these, you are cordially invited to visit our web site at **www.fool.co.uk** and chat about them on our message boards. If you work for the Fool UK or the Fool US and are reading this, then stop by the message boards too and put in your two penn'orth.

Enjoy Life

It is too short to get terribly serious about. It really is. So, while we love investing, that doesn't mean it has to be a dreadfully serious, worthy and – this was coming, you knew it was – *Wise* undertaking. Kick back, relax, have a laugh, be Foolish, for this is the Age of the Fool!

Part of enjoying life is resting assured that you are providing adequately for your future. If, however, that becomes all-consuming, obsessive and to the detriment of other aspects of your life, then halt! You've got the balance wrong. Live well and enjoy life. If you have no room for a sense of ease, if your endeavours to grow your wealth have taken over everything – if you've missed the point of it all – then that's troubling and definitely not Foolish.

Nurture a Foolish Approach to Investing

You could call this a rational approach, but it wouldn't quite hit the spot. There's common sense and rationality in it, but also a slightly head-on-one-side, contrary, skittish way of looking at things. As a Fool, you will also grow to be self-confident, comfortable in your own abilities and not cowed by the tactics of the financial services Mafia, aka 'The Wise'. Above all, our approach is long-term and aims to build wealth steadily and effectively over time. There are no get-rich-quick schemes to be found here. Begone, hypesters and Johnny-come-latelys!

Sort Out Your Own Goals and Risk Tolerances

No-one knows you like you. Except your psychoanalyst. Your psychoanalyst, though, is unlikely to be involved in your investment decisions . . . Well, hang on just one minute, there's a business in this! A Fool-certified, online investing psychoanalyst: you can't invest or make money until you can laugh. It was your mother, wasn't it? She never tickled you. The harlot. Now, for a light £85 an hour our online Foolish analyst will be pleased to help give your psyche the wash and brush-up it has needed for so long. Just email FoolishTrickCyclist@fool.co.uk with your credit card number and a summary of your problems and the Foolish analyst will contact you *right* back . . .

. . .

OK, agreed, maybe this is one Internet business plan which will need a bit of reworking. Perhaps we'll just agree for the moment that it has potential and leave it at that?

But in the meantime, until we can get our Foolish psychoanalytical service up and running, no-one knows you like you do. That means that no financial adviser, no matter how 'independent' they may call themselves, can understand what your goals and ambitions and life philosophy are. Further on in this book, we'll be helping you to look at yourself and sort out those priorities in your own life.

The Best Things in Life are Free

The velvet caress of a summer's evening. A joke shared with a stranger. Ideas and philosophy and the heady aroma of true liberation. *Der* Fool! *Der* Fool *ist* free! Or at least, pretty well free. You've paid for this book, possibly, but in some ways this is a 'value-added' service. The kernel of the Motley Fool's philosophy, a plethora of daily articles, a range of data services and the Motley Fool's thriving online community are available free to anyone with access to the Web. Crucially for us, that means we don't see ourselves as having a conflict of interest with the people who visit the site. We don't sell any financial services ourselves and currently have no plans to.

In many ways, the Internet is the 'Land of the Free', with Internet access now increasingly coming free and a huge range of outstanding services available gratis. Just because something is free doesn't mean you can't create a business out of it, however, and the Motley Fool is mainly funded by advertising carried at our site. This means that there is now a request coming up: if you enjoy the Fool, find it useful and want to keep it free, please click on any ads you see at our site, pass through to the advertisers' own web sites and see what they have to offer. It's this traffic from the Fool to our advertisers and back which keeps us in business. One word of caution: just because we carry an advertiser at our site doesn't mean we endorse the products they sell, but it does mean that we think they may be worth a look. In other words, we don't knowingly permit what we consider to be out and out, unmitigated sharks to advertise with us, but we still encourage you to use your Foolish discriminatory powers in selecting which product best suits you and represents the best value.

Get Out of Debt

Short-term, high interest rate debt in the form many of us carry it – on credit cards – is pernicious and nasty. It must be avoided at all costs. We talk about debt when we go on to fill out our own balance sheet and ways of getting out of it in chapter 3.

The Power of Time and the Miracle of Compounding

One of the most popular chapters of *The Motley Fool UK Investment Guide* was entitled 'The Miracle of Compounding'. In it we followed the fortunes of a variety of characters who saved different amounts over different periods of time. The conclusions are truly extraordinary and we give a brief recap of them in Chapter 2, 'Getting Started'. If you're just browsing this book on the shelf and are on the brink of putting it back and walking away, do yourself the favour of flipping to page 23 first. Odds on, it'll make you reverse your decision.

The Power of the Stock Market

Over time, the stock market is the most reliable accumulator of long-term wealth available to us. There are many preconceptions and fallacies about it, but it is the place for Fools to grow their long-term money. No doubt at all. Again, Chapter 2, 'Getting Started', has the gen.

The Power of the Individual

The average individual can indeed understand what investing is all about and can make investing decisions for themselves. Mostly, they do not need 'financial advice' and can learn to select their own investments with far less specialised knowledge than is generally reckoned. The mythology, fostered in large part by the financial services industry, that they *cannot* do so is a major contributor to the high level of ignorance and misconception about investing. This book and the Motley Fool aim to dispel this myth, enabling and enobling many ordinary people in the process.

The Power of Community

One of the major driving forces behind the success of the Motley Fool has been the community of people who use the site and post on its message boards. By their own contributions and the collective force that they represent, Fools using the site – that potentially means you – are as important in the day-to-day running of the Fool and shaping its future direction as are employed Fools. The Motley Fool only works because it touches people and helps them steer their lives for the better. That makes them want to give back to others and keeps the phenomenon surging forward. There's much more on this in the next section, along with a rather tidy little analogy with Deep Blue, IBM's chess-playing, Kasparov-beating supercomputer.

The Ability to Get a Seat in a Crowded Restaurant by Proclaiming Yourself a Fool

Er, actually, we've tried it. It doesn't work.

To recap, here's that list of key Foolish ideas once more, minus the last, somewhat facetious one:

- Enjoy Life
- Nurture a Foolish Approach to Investing
- Sort Out Your Own Goals and Risk Tolerances
- The Best Things in Life are Free
- Get Out of Debt
- The Power of Time and the Miracle of Compounding
- The Power of the Stock Market
- The Power of the Individual
- The Power of Community

Sound OK? Nothing too dodgy?

. . .

Yes?

. . .

Sure?

. . .

Onward!

CHAPTER I
Getting the Best Out of this Book and the Fool Online

The Book

It's a workbook. If you were smart, you picked that up straightaway from the title. Being a workbook means that it's been designed with the image of you sitting over it at midnight, sucking a pen or pencil, sweating, gripped in mortal terror as you realise you don't know the answer to the P/E ratio question and *your homework has to be handed in tomorrow*!

Is this what workbooks mean to you? If it is, don't worry, calm down, shed those images of yourself in primary school, at turns awed and terrified by Miss Treece, your first and most mysterious, most moustachioed form teacher.

It's not like that here. Miss Treece retired long ago.

You don't *have* to fill in the gaps or answer all the questions. You don't even have to get any of them right (although they're mostly pathetically easy), but wielding a pen or pencil does help keep you focused and involved. It's easy to drift off while reading any book on investing – perhaps, even, this one – and getting your brain working makes this less likely to happen. Writing the answers in, rather than simply filling them in mentally, is much better for this and may even present you with a few surprises as you realise that you don't know the answer to a question you thought you did.

Read and work through the book in whatever sequence you like. Although it is written with a definite order and progression, doing things out of synch can sometimes make them 'stickier' and easier to learn and is some people's style. By the end of it, our aim is that you will have a thorough grounding in the basic principles of Foolish investing and be so familiar with the important jargon that you'll never feel intimidated or baffled again.

You don't need to do this, but what may help this book come alive is if you combine reading it with visits to the Motley Fool online area relevant for the section you're reading at the time. And that's what comes next . . .

The Fool Online

Some people, people who don't know much about either field, seem to think that the Internet poses a threat to books and newspapers. They think they are going to become obsolete, that no-one will buy them. From where we're sitting, it really doesn't feel so. Let's remember that one of the most successful commerce sites on the Internet is a book retailer (**Amazon.com / Amazon.co.uk**) and that Motley Fool European HQ in London is generally awash with pink, paper copies of *The Financial Times*, despite the whole text being available free online.

Instead, the printed word you can feel and the printed word you can only see complement each other and this book has been written with that in mind. Much of what you will read here is complemented in the content areas you will find at the Motley Fool UK web site (**www.fool.co.uk**), where you'll find articles that are hopefully readable, informative and which may give you the odd giggle. It won't take much surfing at the UK site before you find yourself facing one of the Fool's message boards. We have mentioned these message boards several times now and anyone who has never visited them or never been online will be wondering what on Earth they really are. Actually, the answer's very simple. They're all about intercourse.

Quick and Incessant Intercourse: The Motley Fool Message Boards

Many things have changed in the last 200 years or so, but often you find that things have changed more in superficial appearance than in substance. On 2 July 1999 (two days after the submission date for this manuscript), the local paper for

North Devon, the *North Devon Journal*, celebrated 175 years of existence and naturally reprinted the front page of their first ever edition. On Friday, 2 July 1824, Mr J. Avery of Joy Street, Barnstaple, the proprietor, addressed his readers, outlining the ethos behind his ground-breaking newspaper:

> 'Friends and Fellow Countrymen,
> It certainly is a truism that we live in times when the interchange of ideas takes place with unparalleled rapidity – a rapidity equally unknown to the polished Greek of the days of Alcibiades; or to the cultivated Roman, when the voice of Cicero delighted and astonished the Senate of the Mistress of the World; a rapidity which no time, age or place has ever before witnessed; we however repeat this truism, because we believe that it is one of the most powerful causes of bringing our *Journal* into existence. It is this desire for a quick and incessant intercourse that has arisen in this kingdom within the last half a century, that has tended so much to increase our power as a nation.'

Change the classical references, which we frankly haven't a clue about, sharpen up the prose a bit, substitute 'half a decade' for half a century' and you could be reading a piece from *The Guardian* or the *Telegraph*. Back then the revolution was not the Internet, of course, but the weekly regional newspaper:

> 'Without attempting to disparage other periodical works, we may be allowed to state our conviction that a WEEKLY NEWSPAPER is much the most desirable for the convenience of the Public.'

And on the subject of readers' letters, Mr Avery was quite clear:

> 'He will endeavour to adhere to the motto "*Open*

to all parties, influenced by none," while those parties do not overstep modesty, and make that a vehicle for personal slander and detraction . . .'

Throughout the entire piece, he could have been writing about the Internet and the quick, incessant intercourse taking place today amongst parts of its community. That intercourse has now reached a degree of quickness and incessance which he could never have imagined in his newspaper, but he would have certainly applauded it were he alive today.

How are the Motley Fool message boards, literally electronic cork boards on which message can be posted for others to see and respond to, such an advance? Why are they so powerful that we are devoting so much space here to discussing something which many people dismiss as 'mere chatter'?

Well, the best analogy I've heard for the Fool's message boards I shall credit to David Gardner, co-founder of the Motley Fool, from whom I first heard it. He gleaned the basic idea from a business book and went on to apply it to the Fool. You remember Deep Blue? This was the IBM supercomputer which 'beat' Garry Kasparov, the world chess champion, in a chess match in 1997. "Machine Beats Man" read the headlines around the world. Except, they were wrong. Machine didn't beat man. Lots of people working together beat man. Let me explain. Deep Blue didn't come into existence on its own, it was created through the expenditure of millions of dollars by IBM and the collective endeavours of many people over a long period, lead by project manager Chung-Jen Tan. Bill Gates, Chairman of Microsoft, said this after the first Deep Blue – Kasparov match in 1996, which Deep Blue in fact lost:

'In a very real sense, the recent chess match was between one person, Kasparov, and an opposing committee of people employing a tool to execute collective strategies. The tool was a computer.'

When Deep Blue won in 1997, he had this to say:

The computer that was used to beat Kasparov didn't figure out how to play chess; it was told by people to do some mechanical, numeric comparisons. The machine didn't recognize any patterns; it didn't gain any knowledge by playing those chess games in any way, shape or form. It just performed rote calculations blindingly fast.

Humans gave Deep Thought algorithms that let it evaluate different chess positions, a knowledge of book openings and the ability to try out billions of possible chess moves each minute.

Deep Blue was the tool by which the creativity and expertise of many different people was organised into a form in which it could challenge Kasparov.

By aggregating the expertise and experience of many different people on a huge variety of subjects, the Motley Fool message boards act in a similar way to Deep Blue. Whereas previous to the Internet and the Motley Fool one person alone had little hope of finding their way through a morass of misinformation and fragmented information, let alone to challenge the might of the Wise, now they can do that in a quite unprecedented fashion. Thinking of selling your endowment policy? Ask a question on the Endowments and Mortgages message board and a host of people will come back to share their own experiences and opinions. Excited by Vodafone's profits? So are a group of other people on the Vodafone message board. Not a clue what type of

ISA you want? Put it to the people who visit the ISAs and PEPs message board.

Having your question answered in a useful fashion on a message board is immensely powerful. In fact, here is a Foolish Challenge: you are hereby challenged not to say "Wow!", accompanied by a prolonged exhalation of breath and a sense of wonderment, when you first have a question answered by someone else on a Motley Fool message board. (Note, it is other Fool users who do most of the answering, not Fool staff.)

Pretty soon, once you have gone through a particular financial experience yourself, you'll be wanting to help other people out with their problems. In the next section, you can see how to go about posting a message.

The real power of the Internet, as we've mentioned, lies in the way it brings together and organises people and resources scattered all over the network. Another graphic example of this is the "SETI at Home" project, run by the University of California, Berkeley, which is searching for extra-terrestrial intelligence. This aims to turn the Internet into a giant supercomputer, making use of all the under-utilised processing power on our personal computers. You go along to the site – http://setiathome.ssl.berkeley.edu – and download a program which becomes your computer screensaver. This analyses blocks of radio data from the farthest reaches of the universe when you're not doing anything in particular with your computer but it happens to be switched on. When it has analysed the results, your computer sends them back to the site, where they are aggregated into the bigger picture and if your computer does discover a pattern indicating intelligent life, your name will be listed on the research paper announcing it to the world. In this way, a massive amount of data is analysed for free

through the collective endeavours of the community of Internet users, a task which would otherwise require mammoth processing power and be barely practicable. So far, the number of intelligent life forms discovered rests at precisely zero, but by the time you read this one Horace Smith from Rochdale may be famous as the co-discoverer of the Googly-Spink race of beings from the environs of Popper IV. (Don't know about you, but our fingers are firmly crossed, hoping they're friendly or else if they're not, that it will take them 5000 years of interstellar travel to get here. Yikes!)

Many of the most creative and inspiring uses of the Internet make use of this property of aggregating collective expertise or resources in some way and so, we humbly propose, we would like to lump the Motley Fool up there with the best of them. That's what we meant earlier on when when we referred to the 'Power of Community'.

Posting a Question at the Fool Online

There are hundreds of message boards on an extraordinary variety of topics at the Motley Fool UK (there are thousands at the Motley Fool US) and it can feel an intimidating experience for a first-timer. Never fear. Brush those thoughts away, new-found Internet Jockey, you won't come to any harm here. Fire up your computer, type in www.fool.co.uk and hop along to our homepage. We hope the look and feel of our site is welcoming to newcomers and if you have any comments on it yourself, send them to UKWorkbook@fool.co.uk and we'll pass them along to Keith Pelczarski and Shannon Zimmerman, our two Foolish DesignMeisters. They work like blazes on our behalf and deserve far more than we habitually give them (the odd raw hunk of beef tossed down into the darkened cellar where we have them chained).

Once you've had a look around the rest of the site – go on, click on anything you like, it won't bite – click on the 'Messages' tab at the top. That takes you to the main messages page. There you'll see a series of links which lead to the individual message boards. The first thing we'd ask you to do is click on the link which says 'Read this first'. This contains important information about posting and various disclaimers. Now, go back one page and then click on 'The Information Desk'. As you can see, this takes you to a page which displays a number of individual message boards. Click on 'Ask a Foolish Question' and see what people are discussing on that board, our most general board.

It's often a good idea to read messages and not to post for a while (to cyber-geeks this is known as 'lurking'), just so you can get a feel for the atmosphere and kind of things being discussed. That way you'll get comfortable with the way it all works. Click around many of the other boards to get the feel for what is happening on them too. Do explore each of the main folders on the message board main page (there are about seven) to see what message boards they contain: you will almost certainly find one at least which grabs you.

When you have seen enough and want to ask a question or respond to someone else's, then it is easy to do so. To do the first, hit 'Post New' and in the second 'Post Reply'. What's this? It's telling you that you're not registered? To post messages, but not only to read them, you do have to register with us, so go ahead and click the link to do so. It's a dead simple, free process, which takes a very short time and allows you to choose your personal username. Please note: we do not pass email

addresses of Motley Fool users on to anyone else, so you won't be getting junk email from anyone trying to sell you a porcelain figurine of Margaret Thatcher, a snip at £89.99, or an unforgettable once-in-a-lifetime offer of a musical bathing costume, £19.49, inc. P+P. Also, no-one else, apart from Fool staff, will be able to see your email address when you post on the message boards.

What if no-one answers your question? Well, then we're sorry but it means you're an evil person, an ugly soul, whom everyone despises and can't wait to see the back of. No, you're not really, but that is how it can feel. If you ask a perfectly sensible, polite question and no-one replies, but seems to be busy replying to everyone else's questions, you can feel pretty affronted. Don't worry, though, sometimes that's even how we feel and we've been posting on the message boards since the whole shebang started.

The reason no-one has replied, however, is probably because it has got lost in the general hubbub of the message board, rather than that you have a bad case of cyber-odour. Do try again, or try with a slightly different question. You will get an answer and it will almost certainly be a valuable experience. You're not a bad person. We know you're not.

As you'll see when you look at the message boards, there are a number of other facilities they offer. One of these is the 'Good post/bad post' facility. This allows you to nominate an excellent post for 'Post of the Day' and to bring to the attention of Fool staff members posts which may be inappropriate, such as those soliciting business, those which attempt to move a share price just by rumour alone (known as 'ramping') or which are unpleasant in some other way. Compared with many message board facilities on the Internet, the Fool's boards are extraordinarily well behaved, civilized, welcoming and pleasant and that is because they are fundamentally self-policing through the efforts of the users in highlighting when things are going awry. Remember, though, that not everyone online is your friend and not everyone has your best interests at heart, even at the Motley Fool. Don't act simply on the urging of others and don't make any investments simply on the basis of a share 'tip'. If you always make up your own mind, on the basis of your own research, you will never be led astray.

What you will find after a short period of lurking is that you have indeed stumbled upon a community of Fools, or rather many sub-communities of Fools. Message boards, particularly the busier ones, have a life of their own with major and minor characters, major and minor dramas and act as a social meeting place. They are about as far from anti-social geekery, which is still a common misconception about the Internet, as it's possible to get and also have the capacity to help you make informed decisions about your life and your finances which was previously unimaginable.

Er, sorry, what if I'm not online and have no intention of becoming so?

No matter! The book will stand alone. It is merely *complemented* by the online area. That said, not being online could just be one of your biggest mistakes going forward, as you will be missing out on a host of relevant information and help which just isn't available to you in any other place or in any other way. Hopefully, this chapter has shown you a little of why this may be so and for more on this, see *The Motley Fool UK Investment Guide* which has a whole chapter on online and how revolutionary the environment is. (I mean, if you're not going to come and visit our site, you can at least buy our other books.)

Don't forget too, if the cost of buying a computer is beyond your reach, then most public libraries these days offer Internet access at very reasonable rates and there is a growing number of cybercafés. The way things are going, can you really afford *not* to be online?

CHAPTER 2

Getting Started

If a man shall begin with certainties, he shall end in doubts; but if he will be content to begin with doubts, he shall end in certainties.
Francis Bacon, *The Advancement of Learning* (1605)

WHY ARE YOU HERE?

You've probably asked yourself this already. If you haven't already got a firm answer, we hope by the end of this section you'll have a clearer idea and also be aware of how this book may be able to help you. For the moment, though, limber yourself up, shed your preconceptions and consider this next question. What is the difference between this view of the future -

The mood of optimism in London is under pressure. With the FTSE 100 index (6350) drifting down to test the 10-week moving average, this is not a time for being brave. I have placed my stop limit at 6250 for the December 6400 calls (550p). Conservative traders should exit the market if that breaks.

But what are the chances of a bounce out of this area? Markets are driven by perceptions. In the immediate future, it will require takeovers in some of the leaders to lift the mood of caution that has developed.

And the following one?

You must make so many rapid-fire decisions around late May's Sagittarius Full Moon that as June begins you're catching up on other events. This is important because some choices (indicated by aspects to the planet of renewal, Pluto, in your sign) could transform certain pivotal relationships. Keeping up remains a challenge all month; just do what you can, relying on instinct to steer you correctly.

Well, one was from the 14 May 1999 edition of *Investors Chronicle*, price £2.95, not glossy at all, and one was from the June 1999 edition of *Vogue*, price £3.00 and very glossy indeed.

Does this help draw a distinction between them?

Nope.

How about attempting to summarise the sentiments expressed in each one?

That doesn't really help either.

Do either of these forecasts give you any

worthwhile guidance on how you should act in the coming months?

This final question, as they say, answers itself.

The first example above comes from the world of traded options, a type of investment you can rest assured you will not find dealt with here. The second is, of course, a horoscope (Cancer, since you ask).

What we're trying to do in this book is to give an everyday basis to the whole business of investing, to make it a bit less like consulting a soothsayer, a bit less of a mystical and unknowable undertaking, and bring it down to more concrete levels. You might think that taking investment out of the rarified realms of astrology and rooting it firmly in the real world means that we'll be attempting to feed you exercises like this in the course of this book:

> For this exercise, we construct a quadrotree, which is a two-variable version of a CRR (Cox-Ross-Rubinstein) binomial tree. But first let's look at a single lognormal stochastic variable, X_t, with $x_t \equiv \log X_t \ldots$

Actually, let's *not* look at a single lognormal stochastic variable. Not before lunch, anyway. That came from a publication on a type of investment called convertible bonds and is most definitely not the kind of thing this book is about. You'll find some very simple arithmetic here, yes, but only things which will help you see the wood for the trees. And just to prove how important seeing the wood for the trees is, consider for a moment the Long Term Capital Management Hedge Fund. You may remember the furore around the middle of 1998 when it went belly up. And my gosh, did it do so with style!

Based on some fancy and highly abstract

mathematical wizardry developed by two Nobel laureates, Merton and Scholes, the fund took its $2.2 billion in assets and borrowed a further $125 million (is that all?) in other investments. They then leveraged this $125 million for a total market exposure of $1.25 *trillion*. That's like putting your £100,000 house up as security in a poker game where the stakes are £50 million. Unfortunately, by late September 1998, following a series of disastrous short-term bets on the direction of European interest rates, loans into Russia and more, the fund had lost 90 per cent of its value and had to be bailed out by a consortium of banks under the direction of the US Federal Reserve (similar to our Bank of England).

If you like, what the professionals at the LTCM hedge fund were trying to do was apply the kind of mathematics we read in the third quote to the kinds of situations in the first two quotes, with the risk of losing 500 times what they were worth if they got it wrong. Crazy.

Is it any wonder that most of us don't believe we can handle investing on our own when the professionals get it so horrifically wrong? There is good news, though, and that's that you have something the experts at LTCM most definitely did not: common sense. For all their genius, they were utterly unable to see that Long Term does not mean creating computer models to race after hourly profit. David and Tom Gardner classed the strategy of the LTCM in their book *Rule Breakers Rule Makers* as being similar to a dog chasing flies up a railway track.

PAFF!

'Long term' to most ordinary people means five, ten or twenty years. All you have to do is be an ordinary person and you will never make the same kinds of mistakes as the managers of the LTCM hedge fund made. In fact, you won't make them anyway because no-one is ever going to lend you five hundred times what you're worth. You'll be doing well if you manage to get a mortgage three times the size of your salary. In other words, there are safeguards to prevent you being one hundredth as stupid as the managers of the LTCM hedge fund.

Despite how intimidating investing may seem from the outside, it doesn't have to be so. In fact, more people than ever before are now getting interested in it and never before has information and guidance been so accessible, due to that extraordinary medium changing our lives, the Internet.

In our lifetimes, most of us would like to save and invest enough to buy our house, enjoy a suitable lifestyle, perhaps buy a small holiday home or a boat and eventually fund someone to wipe the dribble and semolina pudding from our collars when we can sadly no longer do it ourselves. It doesn't often occur to us, however, to think that it may be fun too. (Investing, that is, not the business with the dribble and the semolina, which really, really isn't.)

The way to invest in Britain has always been through investment advisers, often so-called 'Independent Financial Advisers'. If you still think 'Independent' advice is always the way to go after reading what comes next, then you've probably wasted the price of the book, for which we're sorry, but not *quite* sorry enough to give your money back. On with the story . . .

One of the regular contributors to our site signed up for a pension plan with a well known, a very well known, pension provider. After he read our first book, *The Motley Fool UK Investment Guide*, he decided to check through the pension plan which he had set up several years before, looking at both its charges and its performance. Here is what he found:

5 per cent initial charge on the investment fund. **Uh huh . . .**
£5 per month management fee.
Right . . .
1 per cent per year management fee.
This is getting worse . . .
23 month 'Reduced Allocation Period' for contributions, meaning that 65 per cent of the contributions for the first 23 months are eaten up in charges.
OK, this is starting to look very bad . . .
Whenever contribution amounts are changed (i.e. you put more in each month, as his adviser was urging him to do on a yearly basis), the 'Reduced Allocation Period' *restarts for the whole contribution amount.*
Fishier and fishier, as fishy as a three-week-old haddock . . .
But the plan is index-linked, meaning your direct debit contributions go up automatically in line with inflation.
At last, something that's good!
Oh, hang on . . .
The 'Reduced Allocation Period' applies to the increased contributions each time they're adjusted for inflation. In other words, 2/3 of the yearly increase will be eaten in charges for a further 23 months.
Can it get worse?
Yes, if you look at the performance of the underlying investment. Over the last four years it had been hammered by the stock market index, which it would have been possible to mimic using a very simple type of investment known as an index tracker and with *total* charges as low as 0.5 per cent of the investment per year.

Not surprisingly, the question which was playing more and more on our correspondent's mind was this: 'So I can see what's in it for them, but what's in it for me?' He is currently exploring the issue with the company involved and there are hints of pension mis-selling in the air, which may result in compensation for him, so we won't intrude into his private grief anymore here.

It's starting to look at this point as if we're assembling a few reasons for why you're *not* here. Since those can be as useful to examine as why you are here, take a shufti at these and put a tick in the box of all those which apply to you. This also happens to be the first part of the book where you have to get out a pencil:

Why You're Not Here

☐ a) To invest for your future using short-term forecasts which read like horoscopes

☐ b) To get involved in incomprehensible mathematics

☐ c) To put yourself at risk of losing 500 times what you own

☐ d) To set yourself up with investments which take 65 per cent in charges

☐ e) To find new and rewarding chat-up lines

Here's hoping you ticked all five boxes. If the only one you failed to tick was box (e), then please report to Fool Central, where we'll plug you in for one of our free courses, entitled 'Human Relationships: Beyond the Numbers. Love in the Internet Era!'

Now that we've got that sorted out, let's explore some of the reasons why you may in fact be here. Do any of these apply to you:

☐ a) I want to learn a bit more about investing

☐ b) I want to save enough money to retire one day

☐ c) I want to save enough money to retire *as*

soon as humanly possible

☐ d) I want to save enough money to blow it all in one senseless, yet magnificent, gesture[1]

☐ e) I am the kind of person who's prepared to make a little effort on my own behalf

☐ f) I am totally humourless and I am hoping you can teach me something

☐ g) You are totally humourless and I am hoping I can teach *you* something

☐ h) Guiding my own life gives me a bit of a thrill and quite a lot of satisfaction

If you only ticked one of these, any one of them, then you have reason enough to be here. Somewhere, buried in this volume, is something for you. At a minimum we hope you'll come away with the feeling that

I can do this
It will require a little diligence
I can reap substantial rewards if I'm patient

And with that, we'll move on. If we stay around here for too long, we're going to start asking why we're here, meaning *here*, the Earth, Putney, Eastbourne, Abu Dhabi, No. 48 Cross Street, the one with the dingy, nicotine-stained net curtains. Those, unfortunately, are questions you'll have to tackle on your own behalf and which the Fool is sadly unequipped to deal with. If you do find the answer, though, be sure to pop along to **www.fool.co.uk** and share it with the rest of us. There are one or two of us here – no names, no pack drill – who will be forever grateful.

---

[1]A week quaffing champagne at the Cannes film festival for all the Motley Fool UK staff would fit the bill nicely.

AND WHO ARE YOU ANYWAY?

Yes, now you've managed to give some kind of justification for being here (although frankly we don't favour those who only ticked option 'g'), we're going to figure out who you are. Who you really are. Before we get into the mechanics and nitty-gritty of investing, we, or rather you, need to find out what makes that bird brain of yours tick, whether you would bet it all on a single roll of the dice, or whether you're a more cautious character. You also need to know what you're prepared to commit to this entire enterprise and what kind of person you are.

There are many different ways to invest for your future, some better than others. Almost all of them, however, suit people of different temperaments and interests. It's no good choosing a terrific investment approach, but being the *wrong person* for it. That will only end in tears of frustration and anguish and a fair degree of penury. Above all in what comes, you must be honest with yourself. Particularly, try to think beyond the momentary inspiration this book has given you (it has, hasn't it?), and reflect on how much interest and energy you will have for all this business in three, six, or twelve months' time. Don't overstretch yourself and get involved in things which you're not prepared to follow through as a result of transient enthusiasm.

Also, we'll be looking at risk and your tolerance for it in what comes up. You may like to think of yourself as a risk-taker. Perhaps you enjoy reading the accounts of Everest mountaineers and all those assorted eccentrics who walk to the South Pole or across the Gobi desert, equipped with nothing but British pluck, a solar topee, an umbrella and a cheese and pickle sandwich. But are you truly one of those people? Only you can know.

Does this sound like a tall order? Are you not ready for this kind of self-analysis? Of course you are. It'll do you good. Let's start by posing a few reflective questions:

- How much risk are you willing to take?
- How much time can you really devote to investing?
- Do you enjoy taking the dog out for a walk in the evening or prefer dashing off to parties and raves?
- Does trying to become wealthy seem vulgar to you?
- Has your family taught you anything about investing?
- Do public companies inspire, frighten, bore or disgust you?
- Do you balance your chequebook or do your monthly bank statements always contain nasty little surprises?
- Are you a saver, a spender, or both?

Starting to mull over these questions may help point you in your own investing direction and you can begin to formulate your vision for yourself and your future by filling in the list below. This stuff may seem a bit corny, but if you think about it, it is incredible that many of us wander aimlessly through life without ever focusing down on what we really want out of it all. And even if we do take that trouble occasionally, it is always a good idea to keep updating our view of where we're going. In other words, Foolish reader, there is no way on Earth you can argue yourself out of filling in the following list. Stop wriggling and get out your pencil:

Ten things I would like to do, be or have

1. _____

2. _____

3. _____

4. _____

5. _____

6. _____

7. _____

8. _____

9. _____

10. _____

Skim through the list. At least some of those dreams are likely to require cash which you may not have at this moment. Bareback rider in a circus? Circus school isn't cheap, you know. Assemble a world-class reference library of late Victorian erotica? Now that stuff really is costly[2]! Maybe it's a home for retired greyhounds and whippets that you're wanting to start. Put a tick next to all those things which require lucre and you are getting more of the picture of why you're here, devoting an entire afternoon to reading a book about money. Refer back to this page frequently. It will help spur you on in your investing endeavours.

Now, we're not finished with the psychology. Not, I'm afraid, by a long shot. There's no way of avoiding it. You thought you'd sorted all this stuff out long ago, but you're now back on the subject of . . . your family!

_____

[2]We have a small collection at Fool HQ in London which discerning readers may peruse. Email FoolErotica@fool.co.uk to request a viewing.

FAMILY BACKGROUND AND BELIEFS

Some people had wonderful upbringings, others not so great and we're not here to point the finger. Once you're grown up you have to take on the mantle of responsibility for your own life and it doesn't do anyone any good to cry over spilt milk and perceived past injustices. But it can be very useful indeed to understand the roots of the thoughts and ideas we have today.

Some people's families are very positive about money and the process of making it grow. Others are not so positive and are fearful at every turn. One woman came up to me after she had read *The Motley Fool UK Investment Guide* and said, 'You know, my father was always a Fool and made sure we were brought up with a healthy attitude towards investing.' The gentleman in question, a former military man and actually quite a hero, had saved regularly from his service pay and invested in blue chip stocks throughout the 1940s, 50s, 60s and 70s. Starting without inherited wealth of any kind he was a millionaire by the time he retired. He had always made a point of encouraging his daughter not to believe at face value anything a broker or financial salesman told her. I did offer her a copy of the book for him, but she said he was getting a bit grumpy in his old age and might not appreciate it.

Other people, meanwhile, had very different family experiences of money. The father of a friend of mine bought some shares from a door-to-door salesman in the late 1960s. Unsurprisingly, the money he'd invested – £250, a substantial amount back then – was all lost within a short time and the whole thing turned out to be a fraud. You can imagine the effect that had on the family concerned, which was not well off at all. All members remain scarred by that experience today and have a deep fear and mistrust of any investment other than a bank account, especially any kind of stock market investment.

Below, try writing down three negative thoughts about money from either family or friends in the past. Give your mind free rein. Anything's allowed here because the only person who is going to give marks to the answers in this book is you.

1. _____

2. _____

3. _____

Now take another couple of minutes and write down a one line refutation of each of those negative thoughts.

1. _____

2. _____

3. _____

If this sounds like one of those naff exercises in positive thinking, well . . . it is. But it's a very valuable one. Look squarely at those three rebuttals and recognize that these may be the first steps on the path to remaking your attitude towards money. It may radically change your life. On the other hand, if you find this all old hat and something which doesn't touch you at all, never mind, for we're about to set our pulses racing in other ways and talk about . . .

RISK

Feel the fear. Yes, feel it and run a mile. Or feel it and want more. You are about to find out where you stand in the risk stakes. This is a vital thing to learn about yourself and influences not only the way you invest, but the way you run your life. You're only paying us here to help you learn about investing, but taking this quiz might throw some light on your general approach to life. Isn't this turning into such a terrific voyage of discovery?

Risk Tolerance Test

Respond to the questions below with the answer that most accurately reflects your point of view.

1. Your idea of an ace foreign holiday is
   a) the Isle of Wight.
   b) a walking tour of Southern France.
   c) bungee jumping and white-water rafting in New Zealand.
2. You back up your computer data
   a) at the end of every day, **without fail**.
   b) when I get round to it.
   c) back up? Can't be bothered, frankly.
3. The M4 out of London. Friday, 7 o'clock on a freezing, foggy January night. Do you
   a) sit 3 feet behind the car ahead in the fast lane, angrily flashing your lights at him?
   b) proceed nervously in the middle lane, wondering if this is your night to die?
   c) pull off as soon as you can?
4. £1000 from Great Aunt Kitty (aka 'The Old Trout') for your birthday. It goes
   a) straight into this year's Individual Savings Account (ISA) to invest in shares.
   b) straight on to Ginger Tom in the 3.30 at Kempton Park.
   c) straight under the mattress.
5. You are offered a flight to the Russian space station, Mir. Do you

a) accept the offer to be Grimsby's first astronaut?

b) politely tell them you wouldn't go in a Lada to the shops, let alone into space?

c) immediately retreat to bed at the very *thought* of it?

6. Your next meal is most likely to be

a) in that new, spicy Cuban eatery that's just opened up round the corner.

b) beefburger and chips in front of the telly.

c) something a bit interesting, but not too hot – a chicken korma, say.

Scoring:

1.	a) 0		b) 5		c) 10	
2.	a) 0		b) 5		c) 10	
3.	a) 10		b) 5		c) 0	
4.	a) 5		b) 10		c) 0	
5.	a) 10		b) 5		c) 0	
6.	a) 10		b) 0		c) 5	

Now write down your total score, followed by the celebrity you most resemble (listed below):

_____

Over 40 points – **John Noakes** of *Blue Peter*. The free-wheeling former children's TV presenter who spent the 1970s tumbling out of aeroplanes with his sheepdog Shep. This man lived to take risks. His lifeblood was danger. Get down, Shep!

16-40 points – **Captain James T. Kirk** of the Starship Enterprise. You are willing to take risks in a worthwhile cause, after having scrutinised the pros and cons and calculated which move is the most prudent. Beam us up, Mr. Scott[3].

15 points or less – **Private Godfrey** from Dad's Army. Unfortunately, you'll have to ask your sister, Dolly, whether you're allowed to read any more of this book. Oh dear.

_____

[3]He never actually said: "Beam me up, Scottie."

Well, Private Godfrey, assuming you get the OK from Dolly, this book may help you feel a little more able to go out and dabble, to make your mark on the world. Go on, live a little! Meanwhile, Captain Kirk will boldly go into the world of investing and make the best of the opportunities available there. As for you, John, just try and calm down a touch, otherwise you might do yourself and the rest of us a mischief.

Now that you've got a clearer idea of how much risk you can take, you need to figure out how much time you'll have to dedicate to all this.

HOW MUCH TIME DO I HAVE?

One thing which puts many people off investing for themselves is the perception that it will take a lot of time which they don't have. Answering the following questions will help us identify how much time you may have available:

Circle the response (true or false) which most applies to you.

1. Someone else is in charge of my diary and I can't get an appointment with myself.   T   F

2. I require a crib sheet to remember the names of my children.   T   F

3. I regularly turn off my mobile phone and pretend reception was bad to get a moment's peace.   T   F

4. Often I am so busy I forget to eat.   T   F

5. I am home so infrequently my spouse calls me by the dog's name.   T   F

If you answered True to any of these, you probably need a nap more than you need this book. Fold back the top corner of this page, draw the curtains and give yourself two hours. When you come back, you'll be returning to a book which proposes that you need spend no more than six hours a year keeping track of your budget, your savings money flowing into investments and those investments providing healthy long-term returns. Even better, you won't ever have to meet with a financial adviser to do so. *Schlaf gut!*

HOW MUCH TIME AM I WILLING TO SPEND?

Only you can decide how much time you wish to devote to all this, over and above your commitments in your overloaded professional and public life. How much time you wish to devote has a direct bearing on the types of investments you should be considering. The bottom rung on this Foolish ladder has you overseeing your budget and giving thought to your finances for six hours a year or 30 minutes a month. From there you can add hours to strengthen your financial position, but you will eventually arrive at a trade-off position. Some people spend hundreds of hours a month doing this stuff, but unless they're crushing the market by dozens of percentage points after all expenses have been deducted, it doesn't seem worth it.

Before you get out your pencil again and circle in grey lead how much time you are prepared to give to investing, we are talking here about *total* time in a month, which includes reading the financial pages of the newspaper, not switching over when the business news comes on and time spent in the bath contemplating your next investment. Depending on your outlook, that may make the following choice of time commitments look more or less onerous. Now,

Fool, let's twiddle those pencils:

1. Begrudgingly, I shall commit 30 minutes per month. No more!
2. I shall gladly and joyfully commit 30 minutes per month, but no more.
3. 1-5 hours per month
4. 5-10 hours per month
5. 10-30 hours per month
6. 30-100 hours per month
7. More than 100 hours per month
8. I cannot hear what you are saying as my head is buried up to the neck in sand and I don't really want to talk about this anymore. It's quite pleasant and cosy in here, by the way.

If you circled option 1, then you really shouldn't go much beyond the first chapter, chapter 5. You don't like this stuff much, but see it as a necessary evil. Who knows, though, if you do make it all the way through this book and visit the site once or twice – just for fun, mind – you may get the bug?

If you answered options 2 or 3, then plough through the following robot chapter, chapter 6, to see if that style of investing suits your temperament and you're prepared to take on the extra uncertainty of those strategies. You may also start to think about investing in some major, well-known companies in important industries and holding them for the long-term.

If your pencil hovered and then finally descended on any of the options from 4 to 6, then the whole of this book is for you. You should be thinking about investing in all kinds of companies, from solid, giant ones to smaller ones with the capacity for much higher rates of growth, especially if you're in the upper limit of this time range. You should also consider investing in the USA.

Option 7. Ah. OK. You're either that skeletal shadow of a human being known as a day trader, buying and selling shares many times a day, chained to your computer, curtains drawn, cheeks sunken, fuelled by caffeine and adrenalin, or you love this subject so much you should be applying for a job at the Fool.

Option 8. Please remember to clear an air hole.

UNDERSTANDING THE MIRACLE OF COMPOUNDING

In the summer of 1999, we started putting compound interest tables on the back of our business cards. **GOOD** idea! People, even very sophisticated, investing people, were mesmerised by what they saw. The power of compound interest to grow your wealth is truly extraordinary, if it is just given enough time to do so. What is even more extraordinary is the degree to which very few people seem to truly understand the nature of this phenomenon. If you don't already, then very shortly you will be one of a select bunch who do.

In *The Motley Fool UK Investment Guide*, we quoted the five Foolish Laws of Compounding and they're worth restating here:

The Five Foolish Laws of Compounding

1. Start early, Fool!
2. Small differences in investment return matter. A lot.
3. Don't squander your inheritance on sex, drugs and rock and roll. (Unless you want to, that is.)

4. Over time, regular saving of quite small amounts can build up an astonishing sum of money.
5. Time and patience are the friends of compounding and, therefore, of investing.

Stated baldly like that, in a list, they don't seem to have much flesh, do they? Not much vibrancy, bounce, life. About as much, in fact, as this writer's hair and beard after a ten-day camping trip. (*Ugh!*).

The information below, however, will change all that and if you've never seen them before may reshape the way you look at your life and how much you contribute to some kind of investing plan every month.

The first Foolish Law cannot be repeated too frequently: Start early, Fool! There's no better example than the one we used in *The Motley Fool UK Investment Guide* of a young woman, Fay and her ne'er-do-well partner/ husband Ferdinand. They're a couple of years older now, but still doing well, a pair of yuppy types, living in a house in Fulham, two children, Jamie and Jessica and a labrador, Ben. You can guess the rest. Anyway, the story is that Fay works diligently throughout her twenties, putting away £100 per month into an index tracker (we come on to these later). At the age of 30, she marries Ferdinand and stops working (for whatever reason, we're not judging here) and also stops contributing to the index tracker, but leaves the money to keep growing where it is. Ferdinand was a bit of a Hooray Henry in his twenties, smashing up quite a few cars, getting into a lot of trouble and a bit of debt and only now, at age 30, starts contributing to the same index tracker as his wife. He keeps doing so until age 60, however. The question: who will be worth more when they're both 60? Ferdinand, who contributed for 30 years, or Fay who contributed for a mere ten? The clock starts now.

Tick

. . .

Tock

. . .

Tick

. . .

Tock

. . .

Tick

. . .

DING!

The answer is: _____

You wrote 'Fay', didn't you? But you don't really believe it. That was just your tricky second-doubleguessing triple falco answer, because you thought we were being clever, so you had to be even cleverer to outwit the trick. No, go on, be honest, be straightforward for once in your life, who do you really think is going to be worth more? The fella who contributed for three times as long, or the lass who started earlier, but contributed for only ten years?

This is what I really think the answer is:

_____

You sticking with that? OK, no more badgering or harassment from this end. Here's the answer, presuming average growth of 14 per cent per year, which is somewhat under what the stock market has returned over the last twenty years:

	FAY	FERDINAND
	(£100/month age 20-30)	(£100/month age 30-60)
Age 20	0	0
Age 30	£26,453	0
Age 40	£98,069	£26,453
Age 50	£363,562	£124,522
Age 60	£1,347,806	£488,084

Fay, it is, who is worth three times as much as her unfortunate partner. There's no trickery here. Start early, Fool!

Now the second law. Small differences in investment return really do matter. A lot. They matter so much it hurts. One of the major things which hits investment returns is charges levied by financial services companies for the investment products they sell. Take a look at the graph on the next page, which shows how quickly your money grows at different levels of investment return. Squeezing in just a few more per cent on your investments brings a disproportionate increase in growth and the way that just a few per cent commonly get knocked off your investments is through charges levied by financial services companies for the investments they have sold you. Factor in major underperformance from those investments on top of that (which we'll look at later) and you're looking at a significant fall in your potential investment earnings. Minimising the cost of investment is one of our major aims here at the Fool.

The last three laws follow on naturally from the incredible numbers above and are engraved on the heart of any Foolish investor:

3. Don't squander your inheritance on sex, drugs and rock and roll. (Unless you want to, that is.)

4. Over time, regular saving of quite small amounts can build up an astonishing sum of money.
5. Time and patience are the friends of compounding and, therefore, of investing.

Maybe these three could be summarised as 'Be (a bit) sensible, be steady and give it time.' Talking of which, the box on page 25 contains an intriguing tale of someone who did just that. Maybe she was just a bit *too* sensible, though, maybe in her position you or I would have

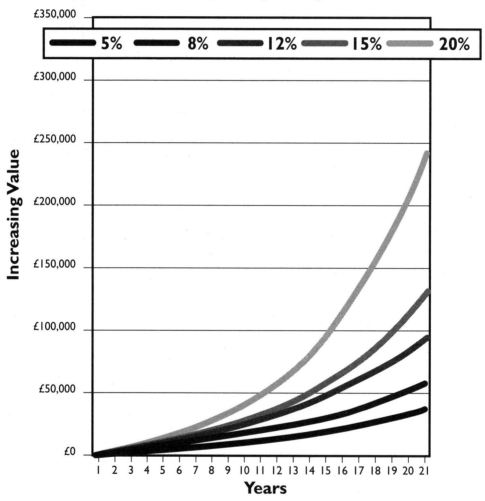

£100 per month for 20 years, growing at different rates

£100 per month for twenty years

	Value
5%	£40,580
8%	£56,900
12%	£91,121
15%	£131,171
20%	£243,886

splashed out on a gold lamé cage for Billie the Budgie, or a new teapot perhaps. Maybe we would have, but let's not knock Mrs Hargreaves who provides an extraordinary tale of compounding inspiration, if not exuberant *joie de vivre*, and at this point is in severe danger of becoming a Motley Fool folk hero. (I have no doubt that if she were alive such a thing would make her shudder, as it would her son, so we'll spare them that.)

An Everyday Foolish Tale

Gleaned from the Daily Telegraph, 10 July 1999:

A WIDOW who grew up in poverty and lived a modest life with her pet budgerigar has left a £6.3 million legacy to her bachelor son.

Rosa Elizabeth Hargreaves, 89, amassed the fortune from investments started by her husband John, a grocer, before his death 47 years ago. He is believed to have received windfalls through shares in the pharmaceutical company Glaxo. Any profits were intended to provide them with financial security in later life, but when the stock market price rocketed, so did their wealth.

After her husband's death, Mrs Hargreaves, a former factory worker, continued to live in an end-of-terrace house with her son John and pet bird Billie. Friends and neighbours in Ravensthorpe, near Dewsbury, West Yorks, had no idea that Mrs Hargreaves was a millionaire several times over.

Her son 51, a research chemist, said his inheritance would not change his life and he would continue to work for a local chemical company and stay living in the community where he grew up. He said: 'This money has never made any difference to mother's life and it won't make any difference to mine.

'I will control the money. It certainly won't control me. There will be no fancy cars or holidays abroad.' He is content with his three-year-old Vauxhall Astra and described himself and his mother as typical Yorkshire people who knew the value of money.

Mr Hargreaves said: 'I have never gone mad with money and I don't intend to start now. I have been fortunate to receive this and I will not let it ruin my life.' He was four and his mother was 42 when her husband, who ran a grocer's in the close-knit, working-class district, died.

Mrs Hargreaves was born in Armley, Leeds, and her family moved to Ravensthorpe when she was two. She left school at 13 to work in a factory before getting an office job, which she left to nurse her mother.

Mr Hargreaves said: 'Coming from a poor home made her careful with money. That is why she couldn't spend it when she had it. I knew all along how much my mother had and how much she would be leaving me. I had seen the money grow and we knew how much the shares were worth.

'My mother lived a simple life. She kept herself to herself and was content looking after her budgie Billie and tending her plants. She never took long holidays and never went abroad in her life. She preferred days out and would always return home to sleep in her own bed. The only time she went out was in my car.'

The money she left, however, has almost halved in the six months since her death. Robert Jordan, the family's solicitor, said £2.3 million had gone on inheritance tax and the value of the shares had fallen by £500,000.

He described Mrs Hargreaves as a delightful woman with a great sense of humour. He said: 'She was very shrewd and knew what she was doing. I remember telling her once that she was worth millions and all she did was giggle.'

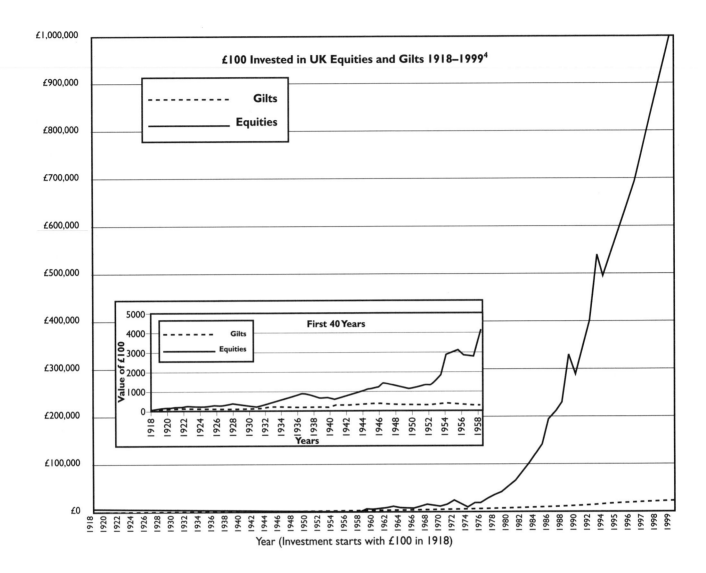

HOW TO TURN £100 INTO £1,000,000

It can be done. Within the likely lifespan of many people reading this book. Clap your eyes on the graph above, which shows what would have happened if you'd come back from the trenches in the World War I and invested £100 into the stock market. By the way, 'Equities' are shares and 'Gilts' are risk-free government bonds, which give a much lower return.

Yes, £100 invested into the stock market in 1918 would be worth £1,000,000 today. Of course, back then there was no way of investing generally in the stock market, which there is now and which we look at in the first 'Be a Robot Investor' chapter. But that growth from £100 to £1,000,000 remains a general reflection of the stock market's progress through the major events of this century: from the boom years of the 1920s,

---

[4]Data kindly supplied by Barclays Capital from the *1999 Barclays Capital Equity-Gilt Study* and reflect gross income reinvested at nominal terms (in other words, not taking into account tax or inflation).

past the crash of 1929, into the depression of the 1930s and the rise of Nazism, World War II, the Cold War, the Suez crisis, the Cuban missile crisis, the Beatles, the oil crisis and consequent economic recession and share price slump in the early 1970s, the high inflation of the 70s and 80s, the Bay City Rollers and Slade for heaven's sake, the property boom and bust cycle in the eighties and now the era of the Internet, the mobile phone and . . . hmm, what else is emblematic of our present era . . . Viagra!

Through all that time, your £100 (or rather grandad's) has just kept marching quietly along, in step with the stock market, growing at an average rate of 12.2 per cent per year. After 81 years, it reaches a million just as your own grandchildren tire of your endless accounts of the Normandy landings (viewed from behind the serving counter of a NAAFI canteen in Portsmouth, we hastily add) and slip another sleeping pill in your tea. Truly, this tells us again that slow and steady wins the race, but it tells us more than that, it tells us that the place for the long-term investor to be is in the stock market. In fact, that comparison with the return on gilts tells us that the place the long-term investor *has* to be is in the stock market.

'Too risky for me, this stock market lark,' say many people, to which the pat Motley Fool reply has now become, 'Look at Mrs Hargreaves and Billie the Budgie. It wasn't too risky for them.' (Oh dear, she is becoming a folk hero.)

And not only is there the example of Mrs Hargreaves, there are statistics to back her up. The stock market is *not* risky for the long-term investor. More risky is to leave your cash barely keeping pace with inflation in a deposit account (returning 5.6 per cent since 1918, as compared to 6.2 per cent for gilts) as the stock market

ploughs steadily on, bringing in year after year of outperformance. Oh, there are down years in the stock market, yes, very hefty down years, sometimes several in a row, but if you can take a long-term viewpoint and not panic, you will come out alright at the other end. In the *1998 Barclays Capital Gilt-Equity Study* (we read this avidly each year), they looked at all the four-year periods since 1918 (1918-22, 1919-23, 1920-24, etc.) and found that equities have outperformed cash in 82 per cent of them. For gilts, the number is 84 per cent. For consecutive ten-year periods, the numbers rise to 97 per cent and 96 per cent respectively. In other words, since 1918, money in equities stood a greater than 80 per cent chance of outperforming cash and gilts over *any* four-year period and a better than 95 per cent chance of outperforming them over *any* ten-year period. Commenting on these figures, Michael Hughes, Chief Economist at Barclays Capital, had this to say: 'The greatest risk for most investors would therefore be to have too much money in cash.'

Later on, when talking about investment planning and the types of holdings to have in an investment account, he says: "It is clear that *equities have higher real returns* than gilts over *all holding periods* and for holding periods up to 10 years also carry higher risk. However for longer holding periods, equities have lower risk characteristics than gilts. *For the long-term investor therefore, equities are a safer bet* [our italics]."

With those noble sentiments ringing in our ears, pride in Mrs Hargreave's achievements swelling our breasts and a slight unease as to the fate of Billie the Budgie, we close this chapter to move on and examine You Ltd. in the next.

CHAPTER 3

You are a Company (only you may not know it yet)

'My own business always bores me to death. I prefer other people's.'
Oscar Wilde

WHAT DO YOU MEAN, A COMPANY?

It's a pretty bland statement, isn't it? 'You are a company.' What on Earth does that mean? Well, let's look at what companies do and then draw some parallels with ourselves. In the last chapter you listed down ten things you would like to do, be or have. All companies should also do that on a regular basis. Of course, a large part of their *raison d'être* is to turn a profit (if they want to stay in business over the long term, that is), but any decent company will also make a regular re-statement of where they're heading and why. Usually, that takes the form of a mission state-ment and/or a set of core values. The Fool's mission statement, for instance, is:

- To educate, amuse and enrich the individual investor

Meanwhile, its core values are these:

- An uncompromising honesty in all our endeavours, great and small
- A cheerful, optimistic spirit, to be shared with customers, partners and colleagues alike
- A belief in social progress through cooperative endeavour, championing civil and open debate
- A relentless search for better solutions

It's probably fair to say that most of us have a personal mission statement and a set of core values. One of the most attractive ones I've yet come across was from a doctor in North Devon, a surfing nut, who'd come from Germany to indulge her life's passion. Her mission statement was simple, yet elegant. Her aim in life, stated over coffee one day, was: 'To surf an eight-foot barrel at Croyde.'

I'm not sure she's managed it, but perhaps that's one of the great things about mission statements.

Below is the opportunity to set down your personal mission statement and any core values you may have. If you decide not to fill them out, then that's fine, but it can be refreshing to think about these things once in a while and it definitely helps further the company analogy, which may make it a little easier to swallow some of the painful stuff we may be asking you to do a little later. Anyway, no-one's looking. Go on, we won't tell . . .

Mission Statement _____
Core Values
1. _____
2. _____
3. _____
4. _____
5. _____

Whatever your mission statement, then, you have to fund those aspirations through your operating activities, just as companies do. Instead of selling groceries, running an airline or putting up an Internet site, we call what we do as individuals 'earning a living'. Some of us are fortunate enough to love what we do for a living, even to have it as a core part of our mission statements, while for others it's just a chore which we put up with to allow us to get on with what we really want to do. And to get on with what we really want to do we probably have to turn a profit from our incomes, to have a bit of spare cash left over after the most basic bills are paid: food, water, shelter, light, heat, TV licence etc. That's absolutely true of companies too.

One of the things which can cripple a company is debt, especially short-term debt which carries high interest payments. That's also one of the things which can cripple the individual, as we'll see.

In fact, the similarities are so great that it's true to say that if you can run your own finances

effectively, you've already got a good handle on what it takes to run those of a business.

And now that we've suffered through all the wiffly-waffly stuff, raked over your character type, risk tolerance and uncovered some highly surprising life goals, mission statements, core values and assorted what-have-you, let's get on with it. OK, brother or sister Fool? Let's set about the actual business of growing our money, of *investing*. That's why we're here, isn't it?

Whoa! Hold your horses.

Unfortunately, despite all the ground we've covered, we're not yet ready to talk about investing in any kind of specific way at all. First, we have to find out if you even have any spare cash to invest. It may be that we discover you shouldn't *start* investing at all for several years. You signed up when you bought this book to take it one step at a time[1], so let's not run ahead of ourselves just when it was all looking so-o-o good.

Before we even start talking about spare cash, let's get one thing straight: it's you who sets the tune around here. That's a reminder too few of us ever receive. Even if we give our money over to someone else to manage, then that's still a decision for which we bear responsibility. Recognising this fact is a quantum leap in terms of becoming Foolish about money, and what we're going to do below is all about getting squared up for that quantum leap. It may not be pleasant, it may not be what you want to do at this moment, when you'd rather get on to the nitty-gritty of making some cash, but it has to be done. Yes, we're going to ask you to

Show us the money!

_____

[1] We know you didn't actually do that, but it sounds the right sort of thing to say at this point and, dammit, you *should* have!

You're about to bare all. Financially speaking, anyway (although if you do send us a colour snapshot of you reading this book in the altogether we'll reward it with a sumptuous gift from our Fool stores). What we want to know is how much you're worth. In other words, whether we'd be prepared to lend you a fiver out of the petty cash here at Motley Fool European HQ in London, or whether you're so rotten with debt that you might slip the country with it. We also want to know what your expenses are and how much profit you make every month. All those things, of course, are the kinds of things we'll be wanting to know about companies later on in this book.

One of the things we look at when investigating companies we might like to invest in is their future growth prospects. Now, that's important for you too – if you're about to lose your job, then you'd best be putting money into a deposit account so you can draw on it soon, rather than investing in the stock market – but as we do when looking at company accounts, we're going to start with the state of your balance sheet, a term we'll be explaining in more detail in a short while. Are you carrying any debt? Think back to the LTCM hedge fund we talked about in Chapter 2 for the potentially devastating effects of debt.

Why, Fool, methinks another little quiz is coming up and this one will tell us whether you run your money, or it runs you . . .

Who's the Boss?

Pick whichever of these most closely applies to you. And no fibbing . . .

1. What percentage of your take home pay goes to cover your mortgage or rent each month?
    a) 95 per cent.
    b) I don't know. I just know it's too much.
    c) 25 per cent or less.
2. How many credit cards do you use on a regular basis?
    a) None.
    b) Less than two.
    c) Two or more.
3. How many of those credit cards have balances on them that you don't pay off in full at the end of each month?
    a) All.
    b) Half.
    c) None.
4. Have you ever gone to pay and been told you're over your limit?
    a) Oh, all the time. I pull out another card.
    b) It used to happen a lot, but not any more.
    c) Never.
5. Do you have any savings already?
    a) Yes, a little.
    b) Yes, a reasonable amount.
    c) Zero. Nothing. A dead duck.
6. Do you pay into a pension of any kind?
    a) Yes, an occupational pension.
    b) Yes, a personal pension plan.
    c) Nope.
7. Do you eat out a lot? How much of your monthly income do you spend on eating out every month?
    a) 40 per cent.
    b) 20 per cent.
    c) 5 per cent.
    d) I have no idea, but if I didn't eat out I would die. Have you ever tasted my cooking?
8. At the end of the month, after everything has been paid, how much of your income is left in your bank account?

a) Is this a joke? If so, it's a pretty sick one. You people should know better.

b) 5 per cent.

c) 15 per cent.

d) Over 25 per cent.

There's no score on this test, no roll of shame, but it's pretty obvious which are the 'better', more comfortable answers to have made. If you're not running the tightest ship in the house, don't worry, because by knowing that fact you're well ahead of 90 per cent of the population already. Anyway, the reason you're here is that you've made an honest decision to sort things out. Which, by a funny coincidence, is what comes next.

A Foolish Tip – The Salaries Futures Market

At the Fool we try to steer clear of any kinds of financial games (aka 'Investments') which involve betting on the level of a price sometime in the future. These include things like options and futures, and if you think back to Chapter 2 you'll immediately see why: that first vaporous quote came from a piece written about options. The trap many of us fall into, though, is to start playing the *salaries* futures market. We start spending today on the basis of how much our salary is scheduled or likely to rise over the next few years. While those may be reasonable expectations, they're unlikely to be certain and to overstretch today in the hope of future increases can be a Very Bad Move. If things go wrong, you can end up with no bolthole and some very ugly men with very flat noses knocking on your door asking for your stereo. This leads us the Foolish conclusion that, 'When playing the salaries futures market . . . don't!' Taking this philosophy one step further, one of the most popular message boards we have at the Motley Fool UK web site is entitled 'Living *Below* Your Means.'

COOKING THE BOOKS – 1. YOUR BALANCE SHEET

This is a snapshot of you, not quite as titillating as that snapshot of you reading this book in the altogether, but definitely more informative. It looks at what you're worth today, not where you'll be after next week's salary payments or if that legacy from Uncle Edward finally rolls in.

Filling in your balance sheet may require a little field work, rummaging through files, drawers and the back pocket of your jeans in the washing basket. You'll be looking for bank statements, credit card statements and what-have-you and you may even have to make a phone call or two. You won't like it, but it will be worth it. Believe us.

Assets and Liabilities

You'll need a pencil, a calculator and a vivid imagination which pictures a sheet of paper with a line down the middle of it and 'assets' labelled on the left side and 'liabilities' on the right side. We'll go item by item and do the maths as we go along.

First, though, what are assets? We tried, but couldn't do better than the definition from the *Concise Oxford Dictionary*, Ninth Edition: "2 a property and possessions, esp. regarded as having value in meeting debts, commitments etc. b any possession[s] having value. . . . via Anglo-French *asetz* from Old French *asez* enough."

And liabilities? The *Concise Oxford*

Dictionary again: '3 what a person is liable for, esp. . . . debts or pecuniary obligations.'

The best and most logical place to start is with your short-term assets.

Short-Term Assets

We're going to call these cash or anything you plan to convert to cash to pay expenses in the next twelve months or . . . anything which you could convert to cash easily if you had to. Are we starting to sound like accountants yet? We are? Great!

The reason for including that last category – 'anything which you could convert to cash easily if you had to' – is that we're going to pencil down any share investments you own under your short-term assets. Now, the aim of holding shares, of course, is that they should be long-term assets. But if you had to, if the sky was about to fall on your head, you could convert them into cash at the click of a mouse, the lifting up of a telephone receiver or the licking of a stamp on a letter to your stockbroker. That's why, for accounting purposes, they are considered short-term.

Anyway, you may not even have any shares yet, so let's not waste too much breath on that.

Rummage in your pocket, shake out your wallet, count up the pennies in the glass jar on the mantlepiece and retrieve the stash from under the mattress – we want to know what you have in cash, real, ready cash. (Actually, a rough estimate to the nearest £50 or so will be fine.)

But before we actually get you to write this number down, we have a suggestion to help make this whole thing easier to understand. We've asked Julian and his 'friend', Sandy, those irrepressible, out-of-work actors from the classic 1960s radio series with Kenneth Williams and Kenneth Horne, *Round the Horne*, if they'd mind going through their balance sheet with us as well

and adding it up as they go along. You'll remember they were quite a pair of exhibitionists, so we didn't have much trouble persuading them. 'Oooh no, Mr Fool, we *always* like to lay our assets bare.' (And between you and us, they were glad of the PR: they've had enough of hairdressing and want to break back into acting.)

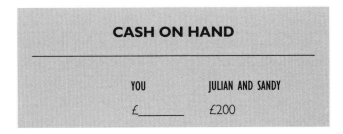

Next, write down how much money you have in both your current and savings accounts. If you're the type who keeps their cheque book stubs up to date and keeps track of their debit card receipts, then you'll be able to do this fairly quickly. Otherwise you'll be reduced to your last monthly statement and a rough guess of where you stand now. If you bank on the Internet or by telephone, you'll be able to get closer to where you stand now, but still be aware that there may be a large purchase in the last week or so which may not have come through to your account. Julian and Sandy like to live on the edge and have nothing in the way of short-term savings:

SHORT-TERM ASSETS		
	YOU	JULIAN AND SANDY
Current account	£_____	£500
Savings account	£_____	£0

Next, what about investments which you

could get your grubby hands on if you had to? Essentially, this means shares, unit trusts or investment trusts, whether held in an ISA or PEP or not (don't worry, we explain what all these are later), bonds and gilts (these are government bonds). It doesn't include any type of pension or endowment policy because you can't get your hands on these with any degree of ease. All those will come in the long-term assets list a bit later on.

INVESTMENTS

	YOU	JULIAN AND SANDY
Shares	£_____	0
Unit trusts	£_____	£0
Investment Trusts	£_____	£30,000
Bonds	£_____	£0
Gilts	£_____	£0
TOTAL INVESTMENTS	£_____	£30,000

Julian and Sandy had a bumper year in the late 1960s when they set up a hairdresser's shop near Carnaby Street. That was the year green beehives were in ('Oh, green beehives, weren't they just *wonderful*, Sandy?') and they put away £1700 into an investment trust. They haven't touched it since and it's grown to £30,000, a growth rate of around 10 per cent per year. Very nice.

Here is what your and Julian and Sandy's short-term asset list is looking like:

SHORT-TERM ASSETS

	YOU	JULIAN AND SANDY
Cash on hand	£_____	£200
Current account	£_____	£500
Savings account	£_____	£0
Investments	£_____	£30,000
TOTAL SHORT-TERM ASSETS	£_____	£30,700

Long-Term Assets

The difference between short-term and long-term assets is that the latter are not readily convertible into cash. Long-term assets are things like houses, cars, pensions (occupational or private pensions), endowment policies, that valuable set of British Rail keyrings you put together over many years, any jewellery and what-not. When you list these items you need to list them at their 'fair market value' – not what you paid for them. As an example, if you bought a new car, it's likely that it's currently worth at least 30 to 60 per cent less than what you paid for it. It does unfortunately get a bit worse than this, however.

You see, most of the long-term assets you hold, which are not your house (which will almost certainly appreciate) or things like pensions or endowments (which will hopefully do the same), are going to depreciate significantly in value over the next five years. In many cases, such as with your television or stereo, they may depreciate down to zero. And it's that estimated five-year value for your depreciating long-term assets which you are going to have to put down on your balance sheet. (By the way, re-read that last sentence and marvel that you not only understand it, but are nodding with furrowed brow in earnest agreement as you do so.)

It's easy to get a bit obsessed with putting a precise value on all this stuff, but all we're after here is reasonable estimates and it's surprising how accurate those often turn out to be. It's easy to get a feel for what your house is worth by looking in a few estate agents' windows or perusing the local property paper. Now, let's start filling in some numbers.

LONG-TERM ASSETS

	YOU	JULIAN AND SANDY
Home	£_____	£250,000
Other	£_____	£12,000

Julian and Sandy bought their house for a small sum in 1973, just before the oil crisis. It's a small terraced house in Putney and, as you can see, it's worth the incredible sum of £250,000 today. It's crammed full of their assorted possessions, but between you and us, they're all mostly junk and not worth very much. We had a hard time persuading them of that, though.

Now, that isn't all they've got. Mindful of their upcoming retirement in 2000 or so and with the hairdressing business ticking along, they also started paying into a personal pension plan in 1987, shortly after PPPs were founded. They have a total of £52,000 in the pension fund. Unfortunately, due to current government rules, they will only be able to convert 25 per cent of that amount to cash when they retire and the other 75 per cent will have to be put into buying an annuity before their 75th birthdays. Despite

this, we'll count the lot as cash for the purpose of filling in the long-term assets table: although it can never actually be cash, that 75 per cent still represents a store of long-term value.

And we're still not quite finished. Julian and Sandy took out an endowment policy eight years ago as a savings vehicle. They have contributed £100 per month since then and the worth of the policy today is £9400, just marginally less than the amount they have paid in. If this seems incredible, then step right up and join the rest of us Fools, blown away in the psychedelic Land of Disbelief, Incredulity and Frank Agog-ness. The charging structure for endowment policies involves taking 80 per cent, or sometimes more, of the initial contributions in charges, so taking 8 to 10 years to break even is not untypical. We wax lyrically, and none too admiringly, on endowments in the companion *Motley Fool UK Investment Guide*.

Here's the list of final assets for Julian and Sandy:

FINAL BALANCE SHEET
JULIAN AND SANDY (ASSETS)

SHORT-TERM ASSETS

	JULIAN AND SANDY
Cash on hand	£200
Current account	£500
Savings account	£0
Investments	£30,000
TOTAL SHORT-TERM ASSETS	£30,700

LONG-TERM ASSETS

	JULIAN AND SANDY
Home	£250,000
Other	£12,000
PPP	£52,000
Endowment	£9,400
TOTAL LONG-TERM ASSETS	£_____
TOTAL ASSETS	£_____

MY FINAL BALANCE SHEET (ASSETS)

Your name:_____

Date:_____

Favourite 60s, 70s or 80s comedy series (one only allowed):_____

SHORT-TERM ASSETS

Cash on hand	£_____
Current account	£_____
Savings account	£_____
Investments	£_____
TOTAL SHORT-TERM ASSETS	£_____

LONG-TERM ASSETS

Home	£_____
Other	£_____
Pension plans	£_____
Endowment	£_____
TOTAL LONG-TERM ASSETS	£_____
TOTAL ASSETS	£_____

Fire up your calculator, Foolish reader, or even scribble down the working on a piece of paper and then tell us if we're right. We say Julian and Sandy have total assets of £354,100. Not bad. Not bad at all. Or at least it wouldn't be bad if that was the end of the story.

For the moment, though, let's knuckle down and see what *you* have on the plus side. *Courage, mon brave, courage*:

Not bad, hey? It's a bit more than you thought, isn't it? Oh. It isn't? It's much *worse* than you thought? No, look, please don't cry like that. It really isn't that bad. Here, why not take a short break and consult your cerebral equilibrium and stability maintenance organisation? When you've fully recovered from your electric shock therapy, we'll take a look at Julian and Sandy's and your liabilities.

See you shortly. You'll feel so much better soon.

Bzzzzzt!

Liabilities

Welcome back. The tingling in your head should stop in a short while.

Now, liabilities. Here's the Concise Oxford Dictionary again: '2 a person or thing that is troublesome as an unwelcome responsibility; a handicap. 3 what a person is liable for, esp. . . . debts or pecuniary obligations.'

We've all got our fair share of liabilities under definition '2'. You won't find much help here, unfortunately, with them. Are you thinking of your pet terrapins, Alex and Donald, bought when they were an inch long and so terribly sweet? Why is it that now they're each a foot long, have a favourite diet of human digits and stink like a Calcutta fish market, no-one seems to want to take them off your hands? Nope, you're on your own with Alex and Donald. But if we're talking about definition 3 and totting up all those things which are going to count against that smaller-than-you-thought sum you had on the assets side, then we're *on your side*.

As with the assets, we're going to divide liabilities into short and long-term. The reason for doing that, though, is slightly different. With assets we were looking at which assets were easily convertible into cash as we attempted to define which would count as long and which as short-term. With debt, it's a question of price. As a rule, short-term debt is very costly and hence unFoolish, while long-term debt is generally much cheaper and can be a very Foolish proposition indeed (see the box coming up on interest-only mortgages).

Short-Term Liabilities (aka "Debt")

Let's make a start by including any bill that is paid on a monthly basis or is now current. Credit cards, high-interest, unsecured personal loans and paying for things on the 'Never-never' come to mind immediately. These are some of the most pernicious destroyers of long-term wealth and thus personal opportunity in our modern world. Many, many people fall prey to their clutches and the results can be gruesome. Let's start with credit cards.

Firstly, let's make this clear: being a credit card organization is a terrific business to be in. The basic premiss is that the company lends you money free for a month up to your credit limit. If you pay it off in full at the end of the month, then the story stops. If not, then you start paying interest on the outstanding balance at rates as high as 25 per cent per year. That's a stack of money and far more than most people will ever make out of investing. In fact, Julian and Sandy have a little secret they'd like to share with you, don't you chaps?

'Errm, oooh, er . . .'

And here it is (sorry, you two, it had to come out, you know it's better this way):

Julian and Sandy are carrying £8000 of credit card debt on a selection of cards. And the one with the worst rate of interest happens to be the affinity card from the Association for Retired and Past-It Sixties Hairdressers (ARPISH) which started with a special offer discount rate. Unfortunately, Julian and Sandy didn't read the ARPISH smallprint, because, after all, if you can't trust your own trade association, who can you trust? Sadly, this meant they failed to notice that the interest rate on any outstanding balance more than doubled after the introductory six months.

But it gets worse. Julian and Sandy wanted

to go off on the holiday of a lifetime – a cruise on the *Queen Elizabeth II* to the West Indies with Julian's mum. They didn't have the cash and the credit cards were up to their limit, so they looked in the back of one of the tabloids for a personal loan. The back pages of the tabloids seem to be crammed with these ads which offer loans at punitively high rates of interests. Whoosh! Two weeks in the Caribbean and scratch another £6000 in loans.

How are we doing so far? When pencilling in your own situation, include any personal loans you may have, even if they're only from your bank.

SHORT-TERM LIABILITIES

	YOU	JULIAN AND SANDY
Credit cards	£_____	£8,000
Personal Loans	£_____	£6,000

The next category is the 'Never-never'. This means hire purchase credit agreements and 'Never-never' is an apt name for this kind of credit arrangment, because if you're not careful you may 'never-never' get free of it. These days you can buy many things – white goods, TVs, cars even – with an interest-free credit agreement. Usually the interest-free period is limited to a year or less and if you have to continue the payments after that, then watch out – you're likely to be paying similar rates of interest to credit cards. Unfortunately, Julian and Sandy have quite a lot of these kinds of loans. They just had to have the latest model Ford Mondeo with all the trimmings, a new bathroom incorporating Jacuzzi and mirror extravaganza and are still paying off their new Scandinavian kitchen.

Chaps, we know life is for living and you can't take it with you, but honestly:

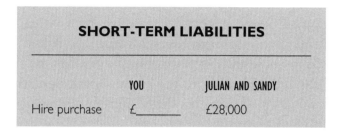

SHORT-TERM LIABILITIES

	YOU	JULIAN AND SANDY
Hire purchase	£_____	£28,000

Ouch. If we tot all this up, we find that Julian and Sandy have £42,000 of high-interest short-term debt. Just to pay the interest on all this debt, Julian and Sandy are having to pay over £800 per month. The calculation is, of course, a simple one, assuming you know the interest rate for each part of the debt you're carrying. Unfortunately, it's off to the filing cabinet or sock drawer again to ferret out all those most recent loan statements:

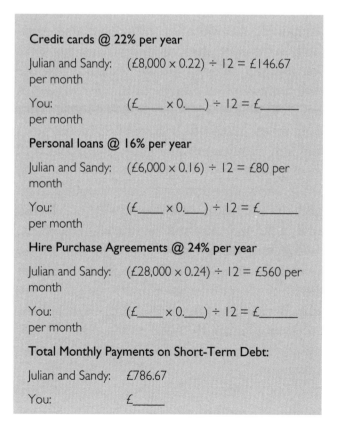

Credit cards @ 22% per year

Julian and Sandy: (£8,000 × 0.22) ÷ 12 = £146.67 per month

You: (£____ × 0.___) ÷ 12 = £_____ per month

Personal loans @ 16% per year

Julian and Sandy: (£6,000 × 0.16) ÷ 12 = £80 per month

You: (£____ × 0.___) ÷ 12 = £_____ per month

Hire Purchase Agreements @ 24% per year

Julian and Sandy: (£28,000 × 0.24) ÷ 12 = £560 per month

You: (£____ × 0.___) ÷ 12 = £_____ per month

Total Monthly Payments on Short-Term Debt:

Julian and Sandy: £786.67

You: £_____

If you've had to beep over that last section because you're not carrying any short-term debt at all, then congratulations. You're well on the way to becoming a Foolish investor. If you've had to beep over that last section because if you didn't you'd worry about what you might do, then take heart, go back, fill it in. The journey of a thousand miles truly starts with a single step, and by facing up to what you do owe and how much it is costing you, you'll actually be knocking a good 250 miles off that journey in one stroke.

Back to Julian and Sandy. Almost £800 per month in short-term debt payments is enough to cripple any but the most wealthy. OK, well, with a slightly heavy heart, let's go on to take a look at their *long*-term liabilities.

Long-Term Liabilities

Large companies often finance their long-term growth through various forms of long-term debt. As individuals, when we talk about long-term debt, we're most often referring to just one item – a mortgage. Here, then, we want to know the total amount of all mortgages on any properties you own. What you're going to need here is your most recent mortgage statement. If you've got a standard repayment mortgage, then that will show how much of the actual loan you have paid off and how much you still owe. If you have an interest-only mortgage, then you will have the full amount of the loan still to pay off. Hopefully, though, you will have some kind of investment set up to cover the cost of the house. This often takes the form of an endowment policy, but in recent years people have been using PEPs and now ISAs for this very purpose.

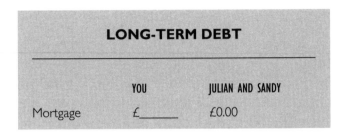

LONG-TERM DEBT

	YOU	JULIAN AND SANDY
Mortgage	£_____	£0.00

Pretty good on the long-term debt front – they haven't got any. They took out a simple, 25 year repayment mortgage when they first bought the house and have now paid it off entirely. The house is theirs.

The problem is that currently long-term debt in the form of a mortgage stands at around 6 per cent, while they are carrying a solid block of short-term debt at well over 20 per cent. They'd do much better if they could have a mortgage for £42,000 instead of paying off all that money every month on their punitive short-term debts. But we're getting ahead of ourselves. Let's start thinking about net worth: yours and Julian and Sandy's.

Net Worth

If you can add and subtract, you can calculate your net worth. Think back to Julian and Sandy's assets:

BALANCE SHEET FOR JULIAN AND SANDY

ASSETS

Short-Term Assets

Cash on hand	£200
Current account	£500
Savings account	£0
Investments	£30,000

Long-Term Assets

Home	£250,000
Other	£12,000
PPP	£52,000
Endowment	£9,400
TOTAL ASSETS	£354,100

Now, what was the total of their liabilities?

LIABILITIES

Short-Term Liabilities

Credit Cards	£8,000
Personal Loans	£6,000
Hire Purchase	£28,000

Long-Term Liabilities

Mortgage	£0
TOTAL LIABILITIES	£42,000

So what's the difference?

Total Assets	£354,100
Total Liabilities	£42,000
NET WORTH	£312,100

Julian and Sandy invested well when they bought their house back in the early 1970s. In fact, property has been an uncommonly good investment over that period. They have also been well served by making regular investments in the last ten years or so which have built up into a tidy sum. What lets them down, though, is their attachment to shiny trinkets they simply can't afford and which causes them to rack up levels of unsustainable debt.

Before we go on and look at what they can do about this crippling problem of their short-term debt repayments, we'll send Julian and Sandy off to learn a trick or two at that useful message board at the Motley Fool site which we've already mentioned: 'Living *Below* Your Means'. Meanwhile, we're going to fill out your balance sheet.

Gird your loins, reader, we're going in . . .

What does all this mean? It means that

MY BALANCE SHEET

Name:_____

Date:_____

How I plan to recover from this experience:

_____

_____

_____

ASSETS

Short-Term Assets

Cash on hand   £_____

Current account   £_____

Savings account   £_____

Investments   £_____

Long-Term Assets

Home   £_____

Other   £_____

PPP   £_____

Endowment   £_____

TOTAL ASSETS   £_____

LIABILITIES

Short-Term Liabilities

Credit Cards   £_____

Personal Loans   £_____

Hire Purchase   £_____

Long-Term Liabilities

Mortgage   £_____

TOTAL
LIABILITIES   £_____

Total Assets   £_____

Total Liabilities   £_____

NET WORTH   £_____

Now you know your net worth. Was it as bad an experience as you thought? OK, maybe it was, but there is at least something satisfying in knowing the answer. In the next section, we'll look in more detail at what it all means and what you can do about it.

COOKING THE BOOKS – 2. THINGS TO LOOK FOR IN YOUR BALANCE SHEET

Positivity versus Negativity

Is your net worth positive or negative? If it's positive, then accept a big slap on the back and a hearty 'Huzzah!' You may still have some problems to sort out, however, and that knotty question of high interest rate debt is the most likely of those to figure highly. It certainly does with Julian and Sandy.

And what if your net worth is negative? Is that always going to be a long-term, unmitigated disaster? Not necessarily. It depends whether it's negative through an excess of short-term, expensive debt or not. If it is, well, that is bad and the answer for you is clear: you need to stop shopping at Versace and start to patronize British Home Stores. You also need to do something about consolidating all your different types of high-rate debt into one lower-rate debt. And that's what comes shortly.

However, many people in the early 1990s found themselves with a negative net worth almost through no fault of their own. They had bought property on a maximum – 95% or even 100% – mortgage, only to watch the value of their property fall as prices tumbled. This left them with a debt (the mortgage) larger than the value of their property, in other words it left them in negative equity. In that situation, where your debt is funded at a low long-term level, all you can do is plod on and wait for property prices to rise, which they will eventually. In fact, as long as you don't actually need to sell your house, the whole issue is somewhat theoretical.

A Foolish Tip – Interest-Only Mortgages

Since the late 1940s, the average mortgage interest rate in the UK has been around 8.65 per cent. Currently, it rests around 6 per cent, or lower. The returns from the stock market since 1918 run at around 12.2 per cent and if you invest in an index tracker, you could expect to make – at a conservative estimate – a *long-term* return of at least 11.4 per cent after all charges are taken into account (more on index trackers later in the book). If you take out a repayment mortgage, then a small part of your monthly payment goes to pay off the amount you have actually borrowed and most of it goes to pay the interest on the loan. On the other hand, an interest-only mortgage just covers the interest on the loan, leaving you free to invest the difference to grow a lump sum. At the end of the mortgage term you'll use that lump sum to pay off the amount you first borrowed and make the house yours. You with us so far? Now, wrap up your tracker fund in an ISA, which shelters it from tax (more on these later too) and off you go:

Mortgage interest rate	£100,000 Repayment monthly payment	£100,000 Interest-only monthly payment	Difference	Net profit from tracker ISA @ 11.4% on 25-year mortgage
11%	£980	£889	£91	£19,367.00
8.65%	£815	£699	£116	£39,412.88
7%	£706	£565	£141	£79,458.76

That last column shows how much profit you can expect to make out of your tracker fund *after* you've paid off the purchase price of your house and, as you can see, it won't cost you any more each month than a repayment mortgage. The lower mortgage rates are, and the higher stock market returns, the more you make. There's much more on this in our Foolish Homeowning series at **www.fool.co.uk** but please don't rush out and do this until you've read more of this book and got things sorted in your own mind. In particular, read our section 'Are You Ready To Invest?'

Good Debt/Bad Debt, Long-Term/Short-Term

In considering debt, it really is best to divide it up according to the rate of interest you have to pay on it. In some ways, whether it's long-term or short-term is irrelevant and the only reason we divide them like that is that long-term tends to be much cheaper than short-term. If you reckon that you may be paying 6 per cent on your mortgage, and that long term you can earn 12 per cent or more in the stock market, it can make sense to have that kind of debt (see our upcoming Foolish Tip). If you're paying 10 per cent or more for your debt, as you most definitely will be with a credit card, then forget it – you need to get shot of it as soon as possible.

Paying Down Debt

Whether your balance sheet is positive or negative, the big thing is to organize to pay down any higher rate debt you have. As we've seen, that's mostly credit card debt, personal loans and hire purchase credit agreements.

Let's look at four of the options facing Julian and Sandy, two of which revolve in some way around the value of their house, which they of course own outright:

1. They've long been thinking of selling up and moving down to the South Devon coast. Seaton, in fact. They fancy the salt air and the more easy-going pace. Also, they can pick up a more than adequate cottage for under £120,000. That leaves them more than enough to pay off the high rate debt (their current house is worth £250,000, remember) and still have a fair bit left over to invest. Of course, it means they'll be waving goodbye to any hopes at all of a showbiz comeback, but if you catch them at a quiet moment over a Campari and soda (Sandy prefers a Buck's Fizz) they'll admit they're really not all that bothered about it; it's a dog's life on the boards and the competition from those new drag acts is terrible. This is a very easy and obvious solution for them and we heartily commend Seaton's excellent environment, but suppose they didn't want to move, what could they do then?

2. The next option would be to actually take out a mortgage on their home for £42,000 and use that money to pay off the other debts. If they were technically minded, Julian and Sandy would call this 'realising some of the equity' on their home. ('We most definitely are *not* technically minded, Mr Fool, we'll have you know, are we, Jules?!' 'Oh no, not technically minded, no!') At a rate of 6 per cent per year, that would leave them paying interest at £210 per month, instead of almost £800.

3. The third option is to try to merge all that debt into a personal loan from a bank or building society, at a higher rate than a mortgage, but a lower one than they are currently paying.

4. Sandy has a book advance coming in the next month or so for the monumental sum of £50,000. (Since you ask, the book's called *Oooh! What a Carry On: A Survey of British Slapstick Comedy at its Rib-Splitting, Hilarious Best*.) They had planned to spend most of the money on another world cruise on the QEII with Julian's mum, but maybe they ought to bite the bullet and use it to pay off the debt.

And those are the options. They would be

well advised to choose one of them. What if you're in a similar position *vis-à-vis* debt, but have no assets like a house against which to borrow? Then option (3) is still open to you and will probably be the way you should head. If you do have a mortgage you may be able to persuade the mortgage company to advance you somewhat more than the value of your property in the form of a loan. There is one company, at least, to our knowledge which does this. Alternatively, there may be a kindly relative who can help you out for an interest rate similar to that of a mortgage, or maybe slightly more. Be sure to pay them back, though – we don't want to be held responsible for any family break-ups!

Of all the things that filling in your personal balance sheet will tell you, the most important is the amount of short-term debt you're carrying and potential ways of getting rid of it. This is the balance sheet mantra:

Pay down highest rate debt first.

Where's the Money?

This is another thing which your balance sheet will tell you. Assuming the debt problem is under control, where are your savings sitting? Do you have large sums, which you may nevertheless not need to use for a good long while, sitting in underperforming deposit accounts? If you do, then flag them up as potentials for some of the other, higher-performing, but longer-term investment vehicles we'll be talking about further on in the book.

And that's it. Your balance sheet has been filled out. You know where you are and who you are. Easy, hey?

COOKING THE BOOKS – 3. YOUR INCOME STATEMENT

In this section, we'll be asking, 'Where does my money come from and where does it go?'

The income statement is all about ebb and flow, while the balance sheet was a snapshot. The income statement reveals the fluxes which occur in your bank account over the month as your pay staggers breathlessly over the lip of your bank account on one day and your expenses slip away, effortlessly and seemingly without halt, for the next thirty. Truly, it is an awesome sight to behold.

Changes in your income statement will show up eventually in your balance sheet. While the balance sheet was excellent for showing where all your assets were deposited, the income statement can fire off warning flares and alarms when your expenses are too high for your income. It will also help suggest ways for you to slim down your spending and yield more money for investment.

Starting the Paper Chase

To start with, just choose one month for analysis. You're going to need all your chequebook stubs for that month, Switch or debit card receipts, credit card receipts, cash dispenser receipts, receipts for all purchases and more. Now, if you're the type of person who has all those to hand, you probably don't need this book and can definitely teach us a thing or two, so please apply for a job as our financial controller at the Motley Fool. If you don't have those to hand, well, sorry, you're going to have to wait a month out in the wild world before turning to the next page. In the meantime, save all your receipts, phone your mother at least once a week, don't wear burgundy shirts with white collars and . . . Fool, be careful out there.

Whichever month you do choose, disregard all one-off costs or gains like buying a house or the back pay from your one-off stint as a performance poet on the Northern nightclub circuit. Let's hope, especially in the case of that performance poet gig, these are unusual benefits or costs, not to be repeated on a regular basis and which will only skew what's happening week-in and week-out with your money. We're here to evaluate the *regular* flow of your income.

Below is a list of what you actually need to get hold of to fill out your income statement. Each item has a natty little space nestling just to the right of it, designed specifically for the insertion of a tidy tick when you have ferreted it out. Don't we just think of everything?

Here's the information you have to gather to hand:

Chequebook stubs and bank
statements   _____

Cashpoint deposit and withdrawal
slips   _____

Payslip(s)   _____

Receipts for any other income you
received during the month   _____

Credit card statement(s) for the
month   _____

Debit card statement(s) for the
month   _____

Receipts for all purchases – groceries,
books, meals out, clothes, magazines,
season ticket, etc.   _____

Loan or hire purchase statements   _____

Life insurance statement   _____

Mortgage statement   _____

Monthly rent payment   _____

Other regular monthly outgoings   _____

What You Get

This is really quite simple. We just want to know how much you and/or your spouse are making. Julian and Sandy have kindly agreed to let us use their finances as an example again. Both our chaps are working as hairdressers at quite an upmarket salon in Chelsea. A cut and blow dry is £85, but their after-tax salaries don't quite reflect those prices. They each earn £1300 per month after tax and National Insurance contributions have been deducted. Unfortunately, they didn't have a very good agent when they were in showbiz in the 1960s and so they don't get much in the way of royalties now for all the hard work they put in back then.

MONTHLY INCOME		
	YOU	JULIAN AND SANDY
Salary	£_____	£2,600
Other Sources	£_____	£0.00
TOTAL	£_____	£2,600

If you're self-employed, then simply tot up roughly what you think you make each month after tax and National Insurance have been taken into consideration. Similarly, in the other sources of income may go rents from property you own and let out, dividends on shares, interest from money on deposit or payment for that regular article you submit to *Traffic Warden Monthly*.

That, unfortunately, was the easy bit.

Where It All Goes

Where *does* it all go?! For verily it seemeth to flow away with miraculous ease and facility . . .

We're not going to lament the high levels of consumer spending which seem to be the oxygen of modern life and which lead so many of us into debt. We are capitalists at the Fool, believers in the market as the driving force for society and opting for choice in our lives as opposed to control. So don't look for any tub-thumping condemnation for your spending habits here, just a gentle suggestion that for the select group of Fools reading this, a wee bit of trimming may do no harm at all.

Below is a nice clean worksheet for us to be going on with, where we can compare our outgoings to Julian and Sandy's:

MONTHLY EXPENSES

	YOU	JULIAN AND SANDY
Mortgage / Rent payment	£_____	£0.00
Utilities	£_____	£175.00
Telephone	£_____	£83.65
Groceries	£_____	£504.91
Eating Out	£_____	£628.38
Car Insurance	£_____	£0.00
Life Insurance	£_____	£0.00
Other Insurance	£_____	£26.42
Loans and Hire Purchase	£_____	£640
Credit Card Payments	£_____	£146.67
Clothes	£_____	£302.45
Travel	£_____	£168.75
Other Stuff	£_____	£180.25
TOTAL MONTHLY EXPENSES	£_____	£2856.48

If you're as sharp as we think you are, then you'll already have figured out that Julian and Sandy's expenses are more than their income of £2600 per month. That is, of course, **B-A-D**.

But let's take a look at the details of their expenses before we jump to any conclusions.

Mortgage / Rent payment. This is zero and, as we remember, Julian and Sandy's greatest asset is their house which they now own outright. Nice start on the income statement, not having to pay any mortgage. It's hard to come down firmly with a general rule, but if your monthly mortgage or rent payments are nudging up over about 30 per cent of your income after tax, then that's looking a bit hefty and in the case of a mortgage leaves you very exposed in the case of a mortgage interest rate increase.

Utilities. £175. Well, you've got to live, haven't you? Electricity, gas, water. And Julian and Sandy love old British comedy which means they have to subscribe to a satellite TV service so they can watch reruns of *Dad's Army* and *On the Buses* all weekend. If they turned off a few lights when they went out and perhaps took out the bulbs from just half of the twenty-five bulbs they have around their bathroom mirror it might help too.

Telephone. £83.65. And these days, it isn't just the regular telephone, it's the mobile too, of which they have one each. Really, though, for this pair who yakkety-yak-yak all day, they're not doing too badly. Thank Heaven Julian's mum only lives in Hackney and it's a local call. Lord knows what their bills will be like if they move to Devon. (They'll have to take her with them!)

Groceries. £504.91. Julian and Sandy like their delicacies and ever since that new Italian deli opened up round the corner they've been in clover. Really, though, this wouldn't be such a bad bill if it weren't for what came next . . .

Eating Out. £628.38. Well, they do enjoy eating out and you can't really get a decent evening meal these days in London for less than £50 for two. Sometimes you have to splurge on a good bottle of wine and then it comes to over £100. If you eat out like that two or three times a week, pretty soon it all adds up. Let's flag up eating out as a potential area to be trimmed back, but we don't want to cramp their lifestyle if we can help it. They've always eaten out often and it means a lot to them.

Car Insurance. £0.00. None of that for Julian and Sandy. Who needs a car in London? It

may be a potential source of savings for you, though. Try shopping around; it's amazing how few people do.

Life Insurance. £0.00. They don't have this either. It's not because they don't want it, mind, but because they both had an AIDS test in the late 1980s. Some of their friends were having them, so they did too. There was no particular reason for Julian and Sandy to get tested, however, and it's unfortunate they didn't think through the possible consequences, because now they can only get life insurance at disgracefully high rates. Be warned.

Other Insurance. £26.42. Their annual house insurance. So far they've never had to make a claim. Fingers crossed . . .

Loans and Hire Purchase. £640. Now we're getting to the nitty-gritty and now that we can see how much they earn each month, we're able to put this amount in perspective. It adds up to *one quarter* of their total net income. And that's only paying off the interest, not the capital sum they owe. This really is bad.

Credit Card Payments. £146.67. Oh dear. Add this to the previous section and they are paying almost one third of their total net income to service their short-term debt. With heavy heart and leaden feet, let us move onwards.

Clothes. £302.45. Well-dressed isn't the word for this pair: they are *style*!

Travel. £168.75. Shanks' pony only gets you so far, even in London. Eventually, you have to hop on a bus or the tube or hail a cab. A bicycle can save a fair amount in travel costs, but Julian or Sandy on a bike? A tandem maybe, a bike never.

Other Stuff. £180.25. There's always a bigger pile of other stuff than you can ever believe.

Before we get into the details of what your

income statement can tell you we're going to do a ridiculously simple calculation which we like to endow with the Foolish name 'Over/Under':

MONTHLY OVER/UNDER		
	YOU	JULIAN AND SANDY
Net Monthly Income	£_____	£2,600.00
Net Monthly Expenses	£_____	£2856.48
MONTHLY OVER/UNDER	£_____	-£256.48

Oh yes, we knew it as soon as we started reading their expenses list and saw how much they were spending on eating out. Julian and Sandy are living beyond their means. Every month they go more and more into debt, put more and more on their credit cards, pay more and more in interest and wonder where it will all end up.

Are you in the same boat as Julian and Sandy? We can't see what you've written, so we're relying on you to be honest with yourself.

And in that spirit of honesty, it's time to be looking at . . .

COOKING THE BOOKS – 4. WHAT YOUR INCOME STATEMENT CAN TELL YOU

What we're really after from our income statement are ways to reduce our costs and use our cash flow in the most effective manner possible. Looking at poor old Julian and Sandy's statement again (we are putting them through

the mill, aren't we?), it's fairly clear where the problems lie. There's nothing earth-shattering about those problems, they don't take much to figure out and are all too prevalent. They revolve around:

Too much debt
Too much monthly expenditure

The irony is that if they can get out of the vicious debt cycle, they wouldn't even have to cut back on their expenditure all that much. If they could refinance their debt of £42,000 at an average rate of even 15 per cent per year, they would save £300 per month on their debt repayments, which would just about keep their heads above water. But they can do better than that. As we saw, they have a number of options with their debt and can probably refinance it at an even lower rate than 15 per cent, if not wipe it out entirely.

At the same time, if Julian would actually get into the kitchen and cook some more of those absolutely fabulous meals he cooks for his mum and Sandy at Christmas and on their birthdays, they could cut down a lot on their eating out bill. Come to that, Sandy is a bit of a dab hand at the feta cheese and spinach roulade as well. He just needs a bit of coaxing.

Combine refinanced/absent debt with only half the number of evenings at Costa's, their favourite Greek place on the King's Road and a general attention to expenditure elsewhere in their budget and they could be looking at having as much as £1000 in spare cash to play with every month. If they were to start investing that, it would develop into a very handsome pile indeed over time.

Certainly, it does mean a refocusing on their goals and outlook, but sadly from where we're sitting it looks as if they don't have much choice if they want to avoid long-term disaster. They may be pushing 60, but they've both been taking very good care of themselves and may well be looking at another 20 or 30 years, or more, before the heavenly chorus starts to sing.

Enough about Julian and Sandy ('Yes, Mr Fool, I think that *is* quite enough, thank you very much. Honestly, we weren't prepared for all this, you know. Not everything hanging out like this, were we, Jules? Honestly!') and back over to you. Whip out your pencil and fill in the three best ways you could save money without ruining your quality of life:

1. _____

2. _____

3. _____

And if striking from your budget private flights to Deauville to see the racing has demanded more mental and emotional energy than you'd normally like to expend on money matters, you're in good company. Errol Flynn was feeling just the same way when he groaned: 'My problem is reconciling my gross habits with my net income.'

See the box on Living Below Your Means for a few ideas about dealing with your gross habits.

Living *Below* Your Means

Culled from our message board of the same name at the Motley Fool UK online area, these Foolish ideas will get you thinking about saving. The first thoughts were extracted from a message posted by 'Petrea' and were in response to a series of previous messages about the merits or otherwise of penny jars:

Petrea's Penny Jar Principles

1. Even if you think you have nothing, you have more than you think you have.
2. Saving little and often is a good habit to cultivate.
3. A little soon adds up to a lot.
4. Money kept in a jar is just a pile of useless metal.
5. Money is a tool to that can be used for growth.
6. Look after the pennies and the pounds will take care of themselves. (Never underestimate the truth of this statement).

Somebody mentioned that the habit of saving frugally was sad. I certainly didn't think I was a sad person last Christmas when I was learning how to scuba dive in the Maldives and I was swimming with sharks and turtles. And to think, it all started with my little penny jar . . .

By stretching my saving muscles I found that I began to use my brain (finally) and the creativity I employed to save more opened my eyes to other and different money making opportunities. Sometimes I traded my time for money (i.e. I had a job) and sometimes things came my way via which I could make a profit. By this time I had mentally turned myself into a business. This business came into reality eventually.

My penny jar was put on display for anyone who was reading these boards and thinking, 'It's all right for them – they've got money to invest.'

Congratulations to all who use the penny jars and the concepts behind them. I know you've "got it" and it's a wonderful feeling to know that I am not alone . . .

Now just where should I go on holiday next?

The next couple of tips are extracted from a message by 'JKew', another regular poster on the Living Below Your Means message board:

1) Tracking and budgeting.

I've talked about this before, but this is where the really big savings come in; until you **know** what you're spending, how can you stand a chance of reining it in? I use Microsoft Money, put almost all my spending through a credit card, and I'm rigorous about entering and categorising the receipts. The accumulated data leads to a realistic budget which helps me to plan ahead and points to areas in which I'm not getting value from the money I'm spending.

An example we've used before is newspapers: is it worth buying a paper or having one delivered every day? For me it's not; I rarely have enough time to read it in any detail and I can get the subset of news and information that I would read for free on the Web at coffee-break. Better to pocket that £5/week and invest it. I do enjoy reading the papers when I have time, so I often (but not always) buy a Saturday or Sunday paper.

For me, this exercise is about maximising bang-for-the-buck. Bang I can measure myself by how much I enjoy the activity or item; tracking spending gives me a way of measuring the buck.

(One final comment: I mentioned using a credit card above. I don't totally agree with the "credit-cards as instruments of the Devil" viewpoint; they're tools with a sharp edge that can work for or against you. I make mine work for . . . I take advantage of the interest-free period, and I **always** pay the entire balance. I also always know what the balance is.)

2) Paying yourself first.
Saving doesn't necessarily come automatically; I encourage it by making it effortless. I have a set of standing orders and direct debits that tuck away a proportion of each paycheque into (a) a tracker ISA, and (b) a number of savings accounts. That way I never really **see** that money before it gets saved and I don't get tempted to spend it.

Hopefully, this chapter will have lent a little more clarity to your personal financial affairs and, who knows, may even have planted the seed for Seaton in Devon as your retirement destination? Anyway, now that you've completed your financial profile, filled out your balance sheet and income statement and identified how you can pay down excess short-term debt and save money on a monthly basis, it's time to:

a) Whip out your credit card and book two weeks in the Caribbean to recover from the experience.
b) Get on with the rest of the book and learn about investing.
c) Devise a complex and brilliant Internet financial fraud to clear your debts.

(Only *one* of these answers is right.)

CHAPTER 4

Are You Ready To Start Investing?

'Are you, sir? Are you? Are you really, sir?'
The Fast Show, 1999

Now that you've defined some of your goals and established that you do have some money to put into investments, let's get on and make sure you are ready to do some investing. Probably the single greatest mistake that would-be investors make is jumping into the market too quickly.

Take Michael. He invested in Molybdenum Mining Magnates at 4p a share on a tip from a friend. MMM (Mike couldn't actually pronounce 'Molybdenum', always a bad sign) had apparently struck a rich seam of moldy-thingummy in Western Australia. Working in office supplies (expert field: paper clips and staples) in Surrey and never having been farther than Malaga, how much does Mike know about molybdenum mining in the parched wastes of Western Australia? How much does he know about molybdenum? How much do any of us know about molybdenum? Needless to say the shares collapsed, the directors fled and Mike was a sadder and wiser paper clip bloke, although quite a lot poorer. Hold on to this line, because it will probably save you more money than any other over your investment career:

No foreign languages.

If you find you're having to speak in tongues you don't understand when it comes to investing, don't. But it isn't all so hard that you need let the professionals convince you that you need their advice to help you. Learning to invest your money intelligently is less like learning to fly a Jumbo than learning to ride a bicycle.

And if you don't believe us, let's start with a short quiz:

Have you

_____ Eliminated your high-interest credit card debt?

_____ Obtained a postgraduate degree in economics?

_____ Stashed away £100,000 in a stock-broking account?

_____ Left your job so you can trade shares full time?

_____ Learned all about options and futures?

_____ Learned about candlestick charting, McClellan lines and moving averages?

_____ Paid £3000 for expensive software and a share-quoting pager?

_____ Smiled and emitted a bit of a chuckle just now?

Here's hoping you only ticked the first and the last questions (although if you do happen to have £100,000 tucked away, then we won't deny it is a fortuitous start). It is unfortunate that many people think they have to have very large amounts of cash, a dollop of expensive training behind them and a high level of technical knowledge to invest in shares. Nothing could be further from the truth.

How well you invest will depend on many factors and not one of them has anything to do with the amount of cash you are starting with or your ability to roll investing jargon off your tongue. Your success mostly relies on the degree to which you understand your own circumstances. If you have continued reading this far, you should have a pretty clear view of what your financial goals are. To get to this page you also have a regular stream of new money coming in, perhaps a bit of cash to invest and you've consigned your short-term debt to the dustbin of history. You're also fired, burning, absolutely itching to get on and conquer the Brave New World of investing. Onward, gallant crusader!

TIME HORIZON

After the stumbling block of debt, the most important question facing the new investor is what money they should happily invest in the stock market and what money they definitely shouldn't.

So often you hear people talking about the stock market, and even writing about it in the newspapers, using phrases like:

'Take a punt'
'Don't invest more than you can afford to lose'
'It's all a bit of a gamble'

Foolish reader, please rest assured we are not here to lose our money on a high-risk gamble in the stock market. We are here to grow long-term wealth. Generating winnings over a short time period is not one of our goals. The simple rule of thumb is not to invest any money in the stock market which you'll need for at least four, and preferably five, years. If you need it tomorrow, next month or next year, then stay out of the market. Over that period the value of your shares and the market as a whole could get hammered, decimated, crushed. You could lose 50 per cent of your 'bet' in a few weeks.

During the bear market of 1972-74 share prices disintegrated, before recovering in 1975. If you'd needed to pull out your money in 1973, you'd have been in severe *shtooch*[1]. What money should you be putting into shares? Well, this is a workbook, so you tell us . . .

_____

[1]Yiddish term. You'll have to imagine the combined nod, shrug and look of existential agony which goes with it.

Money You **Shouldn't** *Invest in Shares*

Below are ten investing scenarios and the challenge facing you is to number the choices from 1 (worst) to 10 (best) in terms of the attractiveness of the situation to Foolish investors. The question is:

What do you think of investing money in the stock market for the following goals *or* from the following sources?

a) _____ For your retirement

b) _____ For your two-year-old's university education

c) _____ For the down payment on a house in three months

d) _____ For the down payment on a house in two years

e) _____ From an inheritance, once all short-term debts are paid down

f) _____ For a holiday this autumn

g) _____ From a cash advance on your credit card

h) _____ For a top-of-the-line new sports car you'll buy next year

i) _____ For your grandma's private hip operation in 18 months, which you can pay for if shares just do averagely over that time

j) _____ From your redundancy payment

OK, this stuff really isn't complex, is it? It all follows logically from what we've just been saying about investing horizons. Let's go from what are in our opinion the worst to best of these answers, making a few apposite comments along the way.

First – (g). This is a disaster. Given what we've already said about debt and credit cards, we won't devote any more time to it, except to

say: 'Errgle!'

Second – (c). This is also likely to be a disaster. Investing over a time period of three months isn't investing, it's trading or gambling. Plus, your investment will be taxed five times (possibly six) in that short period. That's twice by the stockbroker who charges commission on the buy and the sell, twice by the marketmakers who make money off the difference between what a share can be bought for and what it can be sold for and once by the Inland Revenue who take 0.5 per cent of the cost of every share purchase (but not sale) in a charge known as stamp duty, aka 'tax'. Finally, add to that Capital Gains Tax if you were investing fairly sizeable amounts and were indeed lucky enough to make a large gain.

Third – (f). You would have thought we'd have put that second, given that 'this autumn' could be just a few weeks away. We didn't, because losing your holiday isn't as bad as losing the mortgage downpayment on your house and, you know, we've been watching you and your spending habits quite closely. *Three* Caribbean holidays in a year is quite enough for anyone.

Fourth – (h). Timing-wise, you know what we'll say – a year is much better than the three months from example (c), but it's still far too short a time period to invest in the stock market. That said, you'll probably do better by making a moderate loss in the market over that period than by buying the car, driving it off the garage forecourt and flushing 30 per cent of its value away in the process. Don't fritter away money on snazzy new wheels unless it's really important to you. If it is, be aware of just how much this privilege is costing you.

Fifth – (i). The only positive aspect to investing in the market for your grandmother's hip operation in 18 months' time is that if you're showing a 40 per cent loss by then, she'll probably have come to the top of the NHS waiting list and be able to have it done for free.

Sixth – (d). Nope. Still too short. OK, if the market did get pummelled in that time you could always put back your house-purchasing plans for another year. That wouldn't be an unmitigated disaster, but still one to avoid if at all possible. If you will categorically *need* the money in two years, the market is not the place to put it.

Seventh – (j). Fine things are starting to happen now. If you think that you may not have to live on any of your redundancy money in the next five years, then the market is a good home for it. If, on the other hand, you think your skills in the care and employment of narrowboat tug horses will not be at a premium in the early years of the 21st century, then you may want to keep some of it back to pay the bills.

Eighth – (e). Finer and finer all the time. You may want to make a modest donation to an organisation which sits well with your late benefactor's ideals. But beyond your donation to the Foundation for Retired Battleaxes and Distressed Gentlefolk, plough the money into the market and plough on with the book!

Ninth – (b). A fine and noble aspiration. The little fellow will toast your health when he reaches maturity and buys his first beer in Freshers' Week. With each subsequent glass, that memory will grow dimmer, but at least initially he'll have been thankful. By the way, why not start him with his own investment account when he reaches seven or eight?

Tenth – (a). Excellent. Nothing more to say.

Now that you've clearly identified which money you will be investing in the market, we're going to tackle a short section on some common financial stuff. At the end of it you'll be so *au fait* with strange financial terms that this will be tripping effortlessly off your tongue: 'Of course,

the gross yield rate on AVCs is nothing to the annual surrender rate of an ISA and as for PEPs, well . . . by the way that cylinder head gasket is looking like its tappets are knocking on the solenoid and frankly if you ask me that '76 Escort was the best of the lot . . . '

THE JARGON DEMYSTIFIED – POOF!

It can be done. By the end of this section you *will* understand what some of the most vital terms and abbreviations used in financial services mean, or we'll die trying. They're actually very simple concepts, but most of us have never taken the time to figure them out and sometimes the financial services industry doesn't seem to have a very great interest in explaining them. The fact is, though, that we are definitely with the government in principle on the incentives they are giving to people to save for their future. Essentially, these take the form of tax breaks, such as:

  ISAs
  PEPs
  PPPs
  AVCs / FSAVCs

**** *Foolish break in the text for a moment of history* ****

It was not uncommon during World War I for men in the trenches suddenly to fall asleep when the whistle, which signalled they had to mount a suicidal attack against heavily defended enemy positions, was blown. It was a kind of psychological defence, a mental withdrawal, in the face of an utterly horrific experience which no human being should have to suffer. Some people no doubt feel the same way about going into the details of the tax advantages of one kind of investment shelter against another and which one allows you to withdraw your money at will and which doesn't and what percentage tax rebate one of them gives on dividends and how much you're allowed to pay into another one and which offers the best value . . .

. . .

. . .

. . .

. . .

Zzzzz

. . .

. . .

. . .

. . .

. . .

Wake up! And knuckle under, brave heart, you've got a little studying to do, particularly as we've got a multiple choice *exam* taking place later in the chapter (remember, you bought a workbook and you want your money's worth). We'll start with perhaps the most important item on the list.

Individual Savings Accounts (ISAs)

These replaced PEPs (more on them below), as of 6 April 1999. The basic idea of the ISA is to help you save by giving you an envelope in which your savings can grow tax-free. Let's just take that sentence again:

> The basic idea of the ISA is to help you save by giving you an envelope in which your savings can grow tax-free.

And that's it, that's all it is. Just an envelope, a wrapper, a shelter. There's nothing else to the basic principle of it. What is important from the investment point of view is precisely what you put into that envelope to shelter from tax. The government lets you put cash, insurance-related investments (like endowment policies) and shares into an ISA. Because this is the Fool and shares represent the best form of long-term wealth creation, we are going to spend most of our time talking about shares. Of course, so that you don't get away without paying any tax at all, the government limits the amount of money you can put into an ISA. In the first year of their existence (i.e. from April 1999 to April 2000), each person can put up to £7000 into an ISA. After that, you'll only be able to put a total of £5000 in each year.

The people who sell you an ISA will often – read 'almost always' – be keen to sell you an ISA which contains one of their own investment products, often a unit trust, which is a pooled investment in shares. They like to sell you one of these because they earn more money by doing so. The problem for you is that it's likely the unit trust they wish to sell you, all neatly wrapped up in an ISA with a little pink bow on top, has a 90 per cent chance of being a poorly performing one. In other words, one which performs *worse* than the stock market average. We'll see why exactly that is a little later in the book. For the moment, though, just bear with us, trust us and believe this outrageous statement, OK? Right now, though, we're going to split ISAs into two:

'Empty' ISAs
'Full' ISAs

You won't see stock market ISAs classified like this anywhere else, or even by us like this again. It's totally non-standard, it's Foolish and you owe us 50p if you quote it anywhere in any forum whatsoever. 'Empty' ISAs are ones where you are allowed to buy and sell whatever shares you like. They are known out in the normal world as 'self-select' and as a concept they are Good. They allow you to buy and hold shares for the long-term and shelter the gains from tax. For the share-buying Fool they are manna from heaven.

Now, 'full' ISAs are what we were talking about just before when we were considering little pink bows (at this point you may justifiably be wondering if you've just wandered into somebody else's LSD trip). These are ISAs which already come with a natty little investment product – a unit trust – for your delectation, but which, despite the hard sell which often accompanies them, may not be the best thing for you. A little later, we'll talk about what we at the Fool consider the most Foolish type of 'full' ISAs. If you want an advance preview, they're called index-tracking ISAs, they mostly conform to the government's CAT standards (see box), mimic the average performance of the stock market over time, and investing in them requires absolutely minimal effort or expertise. Very Foolish.

Important word on ISAs: you can get your money out at any time, without paying a tax penalty.

ISAs: Maxis and Minis

No, not a discourse on great British cars (although no-one could accuse the Maxi of being great in any way, except perhaps a great waste of space). Basically, you have a choice every year when you select which bits of your ISA allowance you want to take up (remember: cash, stocks and shares, insurance). You can stick the lot with one manager

for the whole year or you can pick and mix from different companies and get a Cash ISA at Bloggs Bank and a Stocks and Shares ISA at Whizzy Fund Managers.

A Mini ISA: You can cut into three bits, like a cake. You can have a separate Mini ISA (remember? cash, shares and, if you must, insurance) with three different companies every year if you want. The snag is you lose £1000 worth of shares allowance if you pick one separate Mini ISA for cash (£3000 limit in 1999-2000 and £1000 per year after that) and one for shares (£3000 limit every year), instead of going for one Maxi Shares ISA (see below). All this can get confusing, so what the Wise are banking on is that lots of their wealthier customers will sign up for a big fat Maxi ISA.

A Maxi ISA: This simply means you are committed to one bank, building society, insurance company or whatever for all your ISA needs during a single financial year (April to April). A few companies, mainly the high-charging, old-fashioned mob offer all three bits (yawn: cash, stocks and shares, insurance) within their Maxi ISA. (Although even some of the insurance companies aren't bothering with offering insurance within an ISA. That's how grim insurance-based investments are.)

Or you can have a Maxi ISA that invests in shares plus the chance to save some cash.

Or you can have a Maxi ISA where all that's on the menu is shares. These don't let you keep any of your savings in cash within an ISA. So pick a Maxi ISA if you want to save the full whack in shares.

'Full' and 'empty' ISAs: So where does all the 'full' and 'empty' malarkey we mentioned in the main text come into all this? Remember, 'full' and 'empty' are our own, patented Foolish terms. They basically apply to any stocks and shares ISA, whether a Maxi or a Mini. 'Full' ones come with an investment product already in them. 'Empty' ones allow you to select your own share-based investments.

Got all that? Good.

The CAT Standards – The Government's Value Guidelines

All ISA providers can choose to comply with the CAT standards on value for the customer. Or not. We'll let you guess which of those two options gets the Foolish thumbs up. You'd have to have a pretty good reason to want to invest in a non-CAT ISA, because you'll likely end up paying higher charges for poorer performance.

Here are the CAT standards for ISAs which invest in shares:

Charges – annual charge of no more than 1 per cent of the value of the investment and no other charges

Access – minimum savings of no more than £50 per month or £500 per year

Terms – can invest in shares, or a variety of other pooled share investments

There was a lot of fuss over the charges on the shares ISA CAT mark. The Wise have boycotted the CAT mark scheme and are really hoping that customers won't notice they are being overcharged for their investments. Luckily, the 1999 Budget helped to stick a sock in their mouths. Gordon Brown announced that the City watchdog, the Financial Services Authority, will start to produce league tables of charges and performance on investments. Bravo!

Personal Equity Plans (PEPs)

This is going to be short. PEPs were the forerunners of ISAs and since 6 April 1999 you have no longer been able to open one. Before then, PEPs allowed you to save up to £9000 per year in share-based investments in a similar tax-sheltered state as do ISAs. Here's all you need to know about PEPs:

1. If you do already have any PEPs, they can continue to exist and grow in the same way as they did before; you just can't open any new ones.
2. If you don't have any PEPs, then simply forget they ever existed.

Personal Pension Plans (PPPs)

PPPs. We deal with these in a lot of detail in *The Motley Fool UK Investment Guide*. Here are the barest bones:

1. Savings into a PPP attract tax relief. In other words, the government gives you a tax concession on your contributions. If you're a top-rate taxpayer, paying tax at 40 per cent, that is quite a concession.
2. When you finally draw on it (at the earliest when you're 50), you can take 25 per cent as a tax-free lump sum, but the rest must ultimately (at the latest by your seventy-fifth birthday), go into purchasing an annuity to provide an income.
3. Annuities are poor long-term investments, with poor rates of return, particularly in the current era of low interest rates. The income from them is also taxed, unlike the proceeds of an ISA or a PEP.
4. You can't pass the sum invested in an annuity on to your children / grandchildren / pet poodle Fifi.
5. Many PPPs have poor rates of investment return, accompanied by horrendous charges.

In particular, 'front-end loading' charges can take 80 per cent of your first two years' contributions in charges. In fact, when compounded over your lifetime of contributions, it is not uncommon for PPP charges to consume around 25% of all the cash you invest.

6. It is much more difficult and expensive to manage your own investments within a PPP, in contrast to an ISA.
7. The most Foolish type of PPP contains an index tracker with low charges, as does the most Foolish type of 'full' ISA.
8. The great lack of flexibility puts many people off.
9. The upfront tax relief attracts many people.
10. Mostly, the Wise make a killing on sales of PPPs.

AVCs and FSAVCs

These are the last abbreviations you'll have to put up with for a while. They're a kind of 'PPP add-on' to an occupational pension scheme. If you have an occupational pension, i.e. a pension contributed to by your employer, you're not eligible to have a PPP. However, you can have one of these. 'AVC' stands for Additional Voluntary Contribution and 'FS' stands for Free Standing. One major difference is there is no tax-free lump sum, as compared to a PPP. FSAVCs, in particular, generally represent alarmingly poor value and are often given a very heavy sell by financial advisers because they stand to make so much in commissions. Many cases of pensions mis-selling – where advisers flog pensions which are not in the best interest of the customer – are being found amongst sales of FSAVCs.

For more on both AVCs and PPPs, see *The Motley Fool UK Investment Guide*.

How to Get More Help

At the Motley Fool UK's online area you will find message boards dedicated to ISAs, PEPs, pensions and the rest. Questions asked by you there – it's free – will likely be answered by other Fools such as yourself. These may be people who have had similar experiences to you or have specialist knowledge of the subject. Some may even be financial advisers. It's likely, but not guaranteed, that you will find some or all of the responses helpful; that is for you to judge. We encourage you to use the incredible resource of the Motley Fool message boards as a part of your decision-making process and in turn to give others the benefit of your experience.

For more jargon, we have an extensive section at the end of this book.

The Jargon Busting MCQ

'MCQ' stands for 'Multiple Choice Questionnaire' and they are a popular, remarkably effective way of testing knowledge. They are used widely in medicine and many other fields and, as good as they are at testing how much you know, they are also very good at helping reinforce what you already know and inserting new knowledge too.

Have a read through and tick the answer for each question which you think is most correct. There is only one right answer for each question. The answers are on the next page. Try not to cheat, but if you do, Fool, then you will, of course, have to answer to your own, personal

God for this pernicious transgression. You have been warned.

1. The Motley Fool was founded
    a) to confound, confuse and bamboozle the individual investor.
    b) by David and Tom Gardner in the USA in 1993.
    c) as a millennial cult, awaiting the arrival on Earth of the Great Fool on 1/1/00, whence we shall all sell our shares and rise up to Fooldom.

2. ISAs
    a) replace PEPs from April 2000.
    b) only allow you to invest in shares.
    c) have a maximum £7000 investment limit in the first year and £5000 per year thereafter.

3. ISA
    a) is the name of a river in Greek mythology, by the side of which Mythos himself sat down and was made wealthy.
    b) is the name of a remote mining town in Western Queensland.
    c) means 'wicked' in the Wuhai dialect of Mandarin Chinese.

4. A Maxi ISA
    a) will only ever allow you to invest in shares.
    b) means you can't open any other ISAs that year.
    c) does not allow you to remove your money for at least a year after opening.

5. Which of the following is true for Mini ISAs?
    a) all three types can be opened by one person each year, but must be with the same company.
    b) all three types can be opened by one person each year, but can be with different companies.
    c) you can invest the same total amount in shares and cash Mini ISAs as you can in one Maxi ISA.

6. A CAT mark is given to an ISA
    a) for superior investment performance.
    b) for good quality service and reasonable charges.
    c) by the financial services company which markets it.

7. PPPs
    a) are tax-free investments.
    b) often receive CAT marks.
    c) may carry high charges.

8. PEPs
    a) have now ceased to exist and all money invested in them has been paid out.
    b) allowed a less generous annual investment in shares than ISAs.
    c) were a lot simpler to understand than ISAs.

9. Annuities
    a) were popular and highly effective in the nineteenth century.
    b) are a useful means of growing your lump sum.
    c) are a compulsory purchase when your ISA matures.

10. Who said, in 1977, 'There is no reason for any individual to have a computer in their home'?
    a) Ken Olson, President of Digital Equipment.
    b) Bill Gates, President of Microsoft.
    c) Sir Clive Sinclair, he of the ZX 81.

Answers

1. No comment.
2. (c). ISAs replaced Peps from April 1999 and some types do allow you to invest in things other than shares. The investment limit in the first year (1999-2000) is indeed £7000 and

thereafter it goes down to £5000 per year. Incidentally, the government has committed to keeping ISAs going for at least ten years, with a review of the scheme after seven.

3. (b). It's Mt. Isa, cobber, in remote Western Queensland. Probably not the kind of place you want to spend your holidays. We made the other two up. (You mean, you could tell?!)

4. (b). If you have a Maxi ISA, you can't open another one that year. Some Maxi ISAs are indeed limited to shares only, while others also allow you to tuck away cash. That's why you have to be certain when opening a shares-only Maxi ISA that you don't want to tuck away any cash that year. If you will want to do that, then you have to open a Maxi ISA which does have the dual facility for cash and shares. You can, of course, take your money out of any ISA at any time without penalty. Got that?

5. (b). Not all three Mini ISAs of one financial year have to be with the same company. Unfortunately, you can only invest a smaller combined amount in the two Mini ISAs, as opposed to the single Maxi ISA which allows the two different types of investment.

6. (b). CAT marks have nothing to do with superior investment performance. They are awarded by the government if the ISA complies with the kinds of guidelines we outlined. They're not awarded by the financial services industry itself.

7. (c). PPPs are not tax-free investments, you get tax relief on them and they are tax-*deferred*. In other words, you pay tax when you finally come to draw the income from them. They also commonly have brutally high charges. CAT marks are only applied to ISAs.

8. (c). They were definitely simpler (see questions 4 and 5). They also allowed greater annual investment into them than do ISAs and those set up before 6 April 1999 continue to exist and grow in their tax-sheltered environment.

9. (a). Annuities were highly popular as a means of providing a lifetime's income in the nineteenth century. Partly, this was because there was almost no inflation and so the value of lump sums only eroded very slowly, if at all. Today, with longer lives and steady inflation, annuities are much less attractive as investments. Some annuities do increase in line with inflation, but you have to pay a large penalty for that. Annuity rates – in late 1999 – are very low indeed, with not much prospect of a rise in the near future. Unlike with PPPs or AVCs and FSAVCs, you don't have to buy an annuity with the money you get from your ISA. Also, since you can take the money out at any time, it's wrong to say ISAs 'mature'.

10. (a). Clearly, both Bill Gates and our own Sir Clive have always been champions of personal computer use. Anyone can make a mistake and here's hoping Mr Olson is enough of a Fool to have these erstwhile remarks of his displayed in a prominent gold frame on the wall in his office at the Digital Equipment Corporation's headquarters.

DO YOU NEED 'INDEPENDENT' FINANCIAL ADVICE?

'Independent' financial advice is touted everywhere on ads, in newspapers, in magazines: 'If in doubt contact an Independent Financial Adviser'. The word 'independent' has a fine, upstanding ring to it, no doubt, and is one of the nattiest pieces of branding we can think of at the

Fool. We're just not at all convinced that much of it is either a) independent, or b) worthwhile.

Here are a few questions which may help set the scene, tell us what kind of person you are, and define where financial advice should fit into your life. It's an illuminating quiz, as much about self-discovery as investing, so once more pencils at the ready and . . .

Tick whichever answer most applies to you.

1. Do you
    a) like to check out prices and haggle for all you're worth?
    b) wish the ground would swallow you up when your partner haggles and checks out prices for all he / she is worth?
    c) prefer to pay a bit more and not get involved in any hassle?
2. Do you
    a) absolutely trust a used car salesman to sell you the best car for you?
    b) not trust a used car salesman one nano-inch not to sell you a crock?
    c) feel outraged because you *are* a used car salesman?
3. Do you
    a) regularly tie your own shoelaces?
    b) employ someone to tie your shoelaces for you?
    c) wear shiny, grey slip-ons with white socks and therefore have no shoelaces?
4. Do you
    a) not invest and simply buy a lottery ticket every week?
    b) enjoy the challenge and cut and thrust of investing?
    c) have nightmares about the responsibility of providing for your financial future?
5. Do you
    a) reckon that investment is a very complex

area, requiring much training to begin to understand?
    b) feel a bit overwhelmed by investing and are about to put this book back on the shelf where it belongs?
    c) reckon that much of what is written about investing is a load of hype and drivel?

Scoring: This falls into three different categories. If you answered: 1a, 2b, 3a, 4b, 5c, then you should definitely avoid 'independent' advice and may even want to skip directly to the next section. If you answered anything else at all, even if you are a used car salesman, then read on through what comes next, because you may well be able to stand on your own two feet much more effectively than you think.

Sir Mark Weinberg, who designed key parts of the 1986 Financial Services Act, which governs the activities of Independent Financial Advisers (IFAs), gave a talk in London in November 1998 to the Linked Life Assurance Group. He made a number of damning comments, as quoted in *The Independent* on 11 November 1998. Because it was to an insurance group, he obviously made more reference to the insurance side of the business, which includes endowments, a particular bugbear of the Fool and a very poor investment proposition indeed, characterised by exorbitant charges. He said that the independence of financial advisers was compromised by the level of commission they received for selling an insurer's products. He said: 'I cannot think of a greater conflict of interest . . . An IFA would not recommend an Equitable Life term assurance policy even if its rates were the lowest of the market – nor would he recommend a Virgin tracker fund unit trust.'

He also accused networks of IFAs of using their marketing muscle to negotiate higher commissions from the life insurance companies whose products they sell. Of them he said: 'The people who run the networks will put their hands on their hearts and say that they choose the life companies purely on merit and without consideration of the commission rates offered . . . Their position can only be described as one of a conflict of interest and a pretty fundamental one at that.'

Sir Mark went on to call for a shake-up of regulations which would bar IFAs from calling themselves independent unless they refuse to take commission. It is hard to think of a more categorical indictment of an entire industry from the very person who constructed its framework.

Payment by commission for financial advice is clearly a sham, for which there is no sensible justification. If you must have financial advice, choose a fee-based adviser, who takes no commission for advice given, and thus has no interest in advising you to sign up to an investment policy which pays him or her a high commission and which may not be the best for you. Phoning this number, provided by *Money Management* magazine, will give you details of fee-based advisers in your area: 0117 976 9444.

What we hope is that with the help of this book and the resources of the Motley Fool online (especially its community of others just like yourself), you will find that as time goes on you don't need to take paid financial advice. In the meantime, don't enter any financial advice zone without taking your Motley Fool Emergency Financial Advice Survival Kit™ (see box).

Motley Fool Emergency Financial Advice Survival Kit™

At all times pack this survival kit with you, photocopied and stuck on a card. If you should ever find yourself on the receiving end of professional financial advice, whip it out and start firing the questions. We suggest measuring the speed at which you can draw the survival kit from a number of locations on your body / in your handbag and storing it in the fastest one. You should be able to understand all the answers you receive to questions 1 to 5 on the card without more than 3.8 seconds of reflection for each one. If at any time you feel a foreign language is being spoken, then bring the line of conversation back into crystal clear, simple English. If it becomes apparent that that is not possible, then terminate the encounter immediately.

Questions for the Financial Adviser:
1. How do you get paid? Commission or flat fee?
2. How much will you make from this deal when I sign?
3. How much will you make in the future?
4. How easy is it for me to get my money out of this scheme?
5. How well has the investment vehicle you are selling me performed as compared to the FTSE 100 index over the last five years? Ten years?

The final questions are for you and you alone can answer them:
6. Do I value this advice highly enough to want to pay this person the amounts in questions (2) and (3)?
7. Is this really what I want?

CHAPTER 5

First, Think Like A Robot

robot . . . 3 a person who works mechanically and efficiently but insensitively.
Concise Oxford Dictionary, Ninth Edition.

You are an intelligent, rather good-looking person, with, if we may make so bold, a goodly dollop of charm. Your star sign is Virgo, favourite meal tripe and onions (?!) and you have never gone further than a kiss on a first date. We can tell all this because, firstly, you are still reading this book, which marks you out as an uncommonly discerning individual and, secondly, because we have astonishing powers of clairvoyance. Whatever Foolish or unFoolish methods we might have used to gain this information, however, you are undoubtedly an individual, standing far apart from the crowd. We should like to take this opportunity to affirm that difference and rejoice in the diversity of the human race and the human spirit.

Huzzah!

Good. Now we've got that off our chests, why might you want to throw it all away and become a robot?

Well, there's a lot to be said for being a robot, a voluntary robot anyway. In a world where the taking of decisions so often seems to fox us and lead us astray, not having to think about which road to follow can make life very simple indeed. Decisions also add an element of stress to our lives which we can often do without. A robot, glorying in its mindlessness, has no decisions to take over anything. The robot runs along pre-defined rails. It has no free will, it runs efficiently through its allotted tasks and does not complain of brain ache at the end of the day as it slips off its shoes to watch the *Nine O'Clock News*. It has no brain. Or at least no thinking brain.

Coming up is a set of questions which will tell us whether you are of the personality type and character to be a robot investor.

Do you have what it takes to be a robot? Tick the relevant box if any of these statements apply to you.

☐ I've had a secret crush on R2D2 ever since the first *Star Wars* film.

☐ I thought the Tin Man in the *Wizard of Oz*

was a pathetic shadow of what a true robot should be.

☐ My pin-up is a saucy, slate grey, car-body-painting robot at the Nissan plant.

☐ I gave my children numbers instead of names.

☐ I think you have clearly lost the plot. Get on with the book.

A tick in any one of these boxes qualifies you to continue.

One of the most compelling accounts of the power of our subjective minds to deceive is to be found in *What Works on Wall Street*, by James O'Shaughnessy. This book runs through the performance of a variety of mechanical investment strategies on the US markets over the last 45 years and could almost be called zealous in its assertion that the emotional, intuitive side of the human mind is most likely to lead you astray in investing. One example which O'Shaughnessy quotes is of a psychology experiment which clearly demonstrates the unthinking respect we all have for complexity over simplicity. Here's the experiment in brief:

• Two subjects, Smith and Jones, cannot see or communicate with each other and each face individual projection screens.

• Pictures of human cells are flashed up and each has to guess whether the cell is healthy or sick. They are tasked to learn the characteristics of each by trial and error.

• Here's the hitch: Smith gets true feedback on whether he's right or wrong, but Jones gets *Smith's* feedback, believing it to be his own feedback. In other words, whether Jones is right or wrong on a particular cell is irrelevant. He simply gets told Smith's answer as if it were his own.

• Very soon, Smith is getting 80 per cent right.

Jones, of course, is nowhere near that level. Neither are told the results.

• When asked to express the rules they have learned about the different appearances of healthy and sick cells, Smith comes up with a simple, concrete and to-the-point set of rules. Jones, on the other hand, uses rules that are complex, subtle and highly elaborate in an attempt to rationalise a totally irrational situation.

• Amazingly, Smith, rather than preferring his own, simple, coherent set of rules, prefers the 'brilliance' of Jones's rules and the more complicated, crazy and absurd those rules are, the more likely they are to convince Smith.

• Before the next set of slides, all Joneses and most Smiths predict that Jones will do better the next time round.

• In fact, Jones shows no difference, but Smith does significantly worse as he tries to guess on the basis of Jones's complicated rules.

This love of the complex in the face of the simple, and in the face of the available evidence, is to be found throughout investing, as we shall see shortly in the case of active versus passive fund management. Shedding this irrational prejudice is one of the main benefits of becoming a robot investor. The principle of keeping things simple was first and most eloquently stated by William of Occam (1285-1349), who said

Non sunt multiplicanda entia praeter necessitatem.

No? You were flicking ink balls all the way through Mr Slade's Latin lessons back in Class IIIb? Alright, this means 'entities are not to be multiplied beyond necessity'. Ockham's preference for the simple to the complex was stated by him so often and so powerfully that it came to be known as 'Ockham's Razor'. It is also known as the 'Principle of Parsimony' and forms some of the basis of modern scientific theory, in which a simpler explanation for a phenomenon is generally to be preferred over a more complex one.

Not only do robots always opt for the simple, they don't have feelings either. They are totally unemotional. They sweep blithely through life, looking neither left nor right, caring not a jot what is happening around them and, presumably, in some strange, metallic, unemotional way, this gives them a sense of fulfilment or satisfaction, or at least completion. We can only speculate as to what drives a robot.

No matter, but look at what emotion, specifically 'fear', might have done to you in October 1998. In the summer months of that year, share prices were falling, culminating, in the first week of October, in the fifth worst week for shares since way back in 1980. Shares screamed down 5.7 per cent in those dark, dark days leading up to 9 October. Youch! Would you be tempted to sell? Who wouldn't? I mean, it could just keep going down and down and down . . . and . . . it's the Crash of 1929 again, oh my Gahd! Run for the hi-i-i-ills!

Well, a robot wouldn't have sold. A robot would have contained within its data circuits the knowledge that shares have been by far the best investment in the UK since 1918, returning 12.2 per cent on average every year, that shares have never delivered negative returns over any ten-year period in that time, that in only four ten-year periods have they been beaten by gilts (government bonds) and in only two ten-year periods by cash in a deposit account. The robot would also have been aware that while missing the ten worst weeks for the stock market since 1980 would have just over doubled returns, missing the ten best

weeks would have almost *halved* them[1]. Finally, it would have been well aware that the key to investing is staying in the market long term and that timing the market is pretty well impossible to do with any degree of accuracy.

No, the robot was solid. The robot held. It wasn't even as if that week was any more of a trauma for it than any other. There was never any doubt in its printed circuit boards. It was just following its program. Lucky it did so, for in the following week, the week ending 16 October 1998, shares had their fifth *best* week since 1980, rising a monster 6.4 per cent. You know what this author bets? He bets that those poor old emotional souls who sold on the way down the previous week probably didn't get back into the market in time the following week (they were clapping themselves on the back for avoiding the coming stock market catastrophe and global recession, right?). Instead, they would have found themselves nursing a big loss, while the market had regained its ground. You can bet that after that experience they were even more emotional.

Whatever investment strategy you follow, you should adopt the attitude of a robot investor when it comes to market timing of the sort we've just been talking about. Don't do it, stay away, DANGER!

As we'll see now, though, being a full-on robot investor means a lot more than just holding your shares when all about you are losing their heads. As a true robot, too, you will always opt for the simple over the complex and will not allow emotion to feed into *any* of the specific investment decisions you take. It's quite a tall

---

[1] All this information is from the *Credit Suisse First Boston Equity-Gilt Study*, January 1999, a cracking good read and well written. No, really!

order, but once mastered pays dividends and by the end of this chapter you'll know whether it's for you and if any of these strategies are for you.

Oil your joints, crank up your gaskets and whirr along with us in the rest of the chapter as we look at the most basic type of robot investing:

The Index Tracker

THE INDEX TRACKER

Now, here's another short quiz. If one thing is better than another thing, for which thing would you expect to pay more? Circle your answer:

The better thing   The not-as-good thing

OK, no tricky little double-guesses because you know which one we want you to circle and therefore you go and circle the other one. Honestly, some people just have to be awkward.

You circled 'The better thing', didn't you? That's what you were supposed to circle. You would normally expect to pay more for the better thing. That's the way capitalism works, no? And this whole book is about capitalism. It's about the laws of the market which govern the world we live in and how best to make a profit from them, because that is also part and parcel of this whole capitalist adventure. Yes, this book is indeed about all those things, but it's also about more. It's about Folly and Wisdom and where the twain do meet.

The twain are meeting here, Foolish reader. Just, right about now. Here they come . . . THUNK!

In the case of index trackers, you pay less for the better thing, for the much better thing. It's

amazing but true. Index trackers are a type of pooled investment in shares called a unit trust. What an index tracker does is to mimic the performance of the stock market index (see Box). It does this by simply spreading the pool of investors' money across all of the shares that make up the index, investing more in companies that make up a greater percentage of the index and less in companies that make up a lesser percentage. For larger indices, such as the FTSE-All Share index, which contains around 800 companies, it may not be cost effective to actually buy shares in every company, so a representative sample of companies is bought instead.

Because very little in our world is perfect, index trackers get it wrong some of the time and, of course, they also have to pay stockbroking charges for the trades they have to make. This means they have to live with an inevitable degree of error, a tracking error. Good trackers can get this down to a fairly consistent 0.3 per cent or so over time, which isn't bad.

Hang on. What's an Index?

An index of shares is a list of important shares used to gauge which way the general trend of the market is going. As the values of the share prices in the index change, so the value of the index moves accordingly. Different indices are created to show how different sections of the market are moving. The major indices in Britain are the FTSE 100, the FTSE-ASI and the FTSE 250. The FT 30 is important to us as Fools, but almost no-one else, as we shall see. In the USA, the major indices are the Dow Jones Industrial Average and the S&P 500. Here's a thumbnail summary of some of the major indices:

UK
FTSE 100: The 100 largest companies on the

London Stock Exchange. Probably the most important UK index and what is meant when people refer to the 'Footsie'.

FTSE 250: The next 250 companies by size after the FTSE 100 group.

FTSE-ASI: The top 800 or so companies on the London Stock Exchange. Referred to commonly as the 'All Share Index'.

FT 30: Thirty of the major UK industrial leaders. By far the oldest of all the UK indices and very little quoted now.

US

DJIA: An old, old index, stuctured like the FT 30, but still very important and quoted *all* the time.

S&P 500: 500 of the top US companies. Also a very important index.

Incredibly, even just by being average and even taking into account the tracking error, index trackers consistently and resoundingly beat actively managed unit trusts. Actively managed unit trusts are unit trusts where the manager is trying to actively *beat* the market. The irony is that because these actively managed unit trusts require so much managing – trading costs, offices, research staff, six-figure bonuses etc. – and because they spend such huge amounts on marketing, they have much higher charges.

Repeated studies have proven this under-performance of actively managed unit trusts as compared to the index, which, remember, is just the *average* of how shares are doing. We quoted one such in *The Motley Fool UK Investment Guide*, which showed that more than 90 per cent failed to outperform the index over five years.

Here's another one:

According to Lipper, the research organisation, only 16 out of 280 actively managed funds, or 5.7

per cent, beat the All Share Index over the 5 years to the end of February 1999 when you take into account management charges. In other words over 94 per cent *failed to beat the index*.

And here's another one:

A very extensive study, performed by the WM company, is displayed on the web in its entirety at **http://www.index-tracking.co.uk/**. The gems from this study are that -

- Over five years, 106 out of 114 unit trusts studied (93 per cent) failed to beat the index between 1994 and 1998, when you take into account charges and the inevitable cost of buying and selling shares, known as the bid-offer spread.
- Actively managed unit trusts were more volatile (i.e. their value swung more extremely), but the more volatile they were, the lower the returns. In other words, taking on extra risk and a more volatile strategy didn't pay off.
- The cost of undertaking active management is around *five times* that of passive management.
- Over the entire period of the study the probability of selecting a unit trust in the top quarter of performance based on historic top performance was no better than would be expected by chance. In other words, simply picking the actively managed unit trusts which have done well in the past doesn't work. You have to find the top performing managers *before* they have started to do well. Hmm.

What all these studies confirm again and again is that just by being a robot, with not an ounce of original or creative thought in your slowly oxidising body, you can do better than over 90 per cent of professional investors. You, yes you, little old you! Maybe you had no idea what a unit trust was at the beginning of this chapter, but now you're a stellar investment outperformer. All you have to do is put a regular amount of money into an index-tracking unit trust, which can live inside an ISA to shelter it from tax, as we learned in the last chapter, and you will be an investor, beating all but the tiniest proportion of the world's professional investors.

How long will this take you to do? Well, you have to decide which index tracker to invest in (see Box), fill in the application form and direct debit form, send it off and, er, that's it. After that, you should probably devote at least 15 minutes a year to seeing how you're doing and asking yourself whether you couldn't be contributing a little more of your monthly paycheck into it.

Which index tracker?

This is an oft-asked question at the Motley Fool online area and the Index Trackers message board is a useful resource. Overall, it's very simple and this is what you're looking for:

Good past performance history. In other words, low tracking error (less than 0.3 per cent) for at least three and preferably five years. Tracking error is the inevitable amount by which trackers fail to match the index.

Low charges. Maximum 1 per cent per year, preferably 0.5 per cent or less. No initial charge.

CAT Standards. If you're buying your index tracker within an ISA, which many of us are, then you want it to conform to the government's CAT standards, which we discussed in the previous chapter.

What you shouldn't do is spend much time worrying about what the market is doing in between. If you read the financial pages of the weekend papers, you'll probably come across an article every two weeks or so on index trackers which takes the tack that trackers are fine in rising markets, but investors may get burned when the market starts to fall, because after all trackers will simply track the market down. The article usually finishes by leaving the reader hanging, with a hint of menace in the air about trackers: 'What if? What if the market does go down? Oh me, oh my. What to do?'

Here's a reassuring thing to say to yourself as you read one of these articles which worries about trackers tracking the market down:

That's the idea, stupido!

It is oft repeated in investing circles that you should buy on the dips, sell on the highs. As we saw with the way the market behaved in October 1998, it is pretty well impossible to time the market accurately in that way. However, by being a robot, investing in an index tracker, you can do just that.

It's time for a little bit of maths and a thought experiment. . .

You are contributing £100 a month into an index tracker. All is rosy, it is the month of June and it looks like maybe there *will* be a decent summer this year. You're a happy camper. The index has had a bit of a boring month, up a bit, down a bit and not really gone anywhere at all. For the sake of argument, each unit in your index tracking unit trust (now you see where the 'units' come in?) is currently costing you £1.50. First question:

a) In June, your £100 buys you _____ units.

Are you happy with your answer? That was easy. (You'll actually find the answers a little further on.) Now, something bad happens. Tummy-ulofa, a very fat man from the isles of Tonga in the South-West Pacific, is returning from a fishing trip. He swings round to exclaim to his friend, 'I could murder half a coconut and a dollop of boiled fish!' and this unbalancing action – Who-o-o-a! – turns over his dugout canoe. Splash! He enters the water and loses his fishing tackle and the day's catch in the chaos. This is a catastrophe for poor old Tummy-ulofa, but he also startles and scatters a large shoal of colourful fish which had been quietly cruising the upper regions of the coral reef scavenging for food. The effect of this unwelcome disturbance in the local marine environment in Tonga ripples outwards, one small thing affecting another and another and another, eventually changing the course of salty events for marine creatures throughout the seven seas.

Three months later, the unsuspecting head of the Japanese stock exchange is pitting himself against the mysterious forces of karma by dining on fugu fish[2] with a large group of Japanese and Asian business leaders. Unfortunately, the effect of Tummy-ulofa's ducking has reached the coast of Japan by this time. One effect is that a fugu fish with only a small amount of toxin is *ju-ust* nudged out of the fisherman's net by this extraordinary and yet so commonplace chain of events. In its place, by chance, a fish is caught with 100 times the usual level of toxin and delivered to the fugu chef to be prepared. You can guess the rest: by the time the Saki was served, they were all dead. A horrible death. Awful. The effect on the world's stock markets was, predictably, sheer panic. The long-awaited 'Asian recovery' was feared to be in ruins and shares everywhere tumbled and tumbled and tumbled. The Nikkei, the Hang Seng, the Dow, the Footsie . . . It was carnage! By the time the dust has started to settle in early July,

the Footsie is down 33 per cent, a truly massive drop.

If you weren't a robot, if you had normal human thoughts and fears and emotions, these kinds of market shenanigans could make you come over all queer. As it is, though, they don't. You're still in the market, still investing £100 a month. You are cool as a cucumber, have a sound understanding of the chaos theory underpinning this bizarre chain of events, and are ready for another question:

Each unit that you now buy in July costs you 33 per cent less than it did in June. That means that instead of £1.50, each unit now costs £1.00. Answer this:

b) In July, your £100 buys you _____ units.

Simple, hey? You did so well at that one that we're going to spring another one on you. This one's multiple choice:

c) At what average price did you buy the units in the index tracker in June and July? Tick the correct answer.
☐ £1.25
☐ £1.20
☐ £1.33
☐ £1.43
☐ This is a trick question and I refuse to commit myself.

If you ticked the second or the fifth options, dear Fool, you were right. Before we explain why, let's just make sure we got the answers to questions a) and b) correct:

a) In June, your £100 buys you **66.667** units. (£100 ÷ £1.50 per unit = 66.667 units).
b) In July, your £100 buys you **100** units. (£100 ÷ £1.00 per unit = 100 units).

---

[2] A fish of divine taste (allegedly), but whose liver contains a fatal neurotoxin. It must be prepared by specially trained chefs and even then is still firmly for risk-takers only.

Now, the average cost of the units in June and July is the total amount of money you spent (£200) divided by the total number of units you bought (166.667):

£200 ÷ 166.667 = £1.20 average cost of unit in June and July

You might have thought the average cost would be the average of £1.50 and £1.00, which, of course, is £1.25. It isn't, though, because you are buying *more* units at the cheaper price. That's why you don't worry when the tracker tracks the market down, because you're doing something called pound cost averaging. It's a very effective way of investing and all it requires is regular contributions of equal pound amounts. This allows you to buy *below* the average cost of the market and is one of those things which the thinking brain can have trouble getting its head around. It's the kind of thing which doesn't seem as if it should be true, but it is.

By being a robot, by avoiding the peaks and troughs of emotion and with absolutely no effort, you are outperforming almost everyone. It's incredible, but true. You outperform over 90 per cent of the professionals simply by investing in an index tracker; then by regularly contributing you maximize the long-term profit to be made from the stock market through the enchanting phenomenon of pound cost averaging.

As a first step on anyone's investing career, the index tracker can't be beat. For many, with neither the interest nor the time to go any further, it is a suitable place to stop. We'll repeat that: a goodly proportion of people never need go any further than right where they are now. It's enough. You'll do well. The effort is minimal and the returns far better than the professionals will make. The risk, too, is small as long as you are in the market for a long period (over five years, remember?) and as we've seen, the stock market's volatility is the regular investor's friend. So stop now. Don't go any further.

Unless . . .

of course . . .

you want to.

And if you do want to, then there's a good wodge of this book still to go, and we are convinced that some of the other mechanical strategies we're going to talk about, along with ways to pick and look at individual shares, have the potential to beat the market consistently over years. They also require minimal effort. For the moment, though, so you don't rush headlong into the rest of the book and neglect the opportunity which index trackers offer, here are some calculations of what they may provide. We have used two levels of index tracker return: the first and more conservative is 12.2 per cent per year, which is what the market has on average returned since 1918 and the second is 15 per cent per year, which is what the market has returned on average over the last ten years, according to the WM Company report we talked about earlier (it has returned 17.3 per cent annually on average over the last twenty years). With both, to make it realistic, we have deducted an annual charge of 0.5 per cent and also an average tracking error of 0.3 per cent:

£100 per month over 30 years @ 11.4% (i.e. 12.2% – 0.5% – 0.3%) = £271,117
£100 per month over 30 years @ 14.2% (i.e. 15% – 0.5% – 0.3%) = £473,652
£10,000 lump sum invested now over 30 years @ 11.4% = £255,009
£10,000 lump sum invested now over 30 years @ 14.2% = £537,010

Impressive numbers, no?

CHAPTER 6

Robot Investing II – Beating the Footsie

Always carry a flagon of whiskey in case of snakebite and furthermore always carry a small snake.
W. C. Fields

We're supposing now that you've been bitten by the bug, that you're curious to see what else may be lurking in this book of ours. Maybe, you're feeling a little Foolish. Well, what comes up, Foolish friend, is very Foolish indeed.

As for the index tracker, what you're going to read about in this chapter demands an almost total robotic approach to investing. While the index tracker takes around fifteen minutes of input per year, this will take at least 30, possibly even 45, minutes every year to follow and manage. Most people find they have that amount of time to devote to investing. Some people love mechanical strategies, some people can't understand the attraction at all. What they do provide is a sensible rationale for buying and holding a particular group of shares and a disciplinary framework in which to do it. Discipline, dear Fool, discipline, that's what we're talking about here.

At the Fool UK online, we're currently tracking the performance of a variety of different mechanical strategies. These are strategies with very clearly defined rules as to how to follow them. That is their very strength, and to go ahead and break those rules is to miss the point entirely.

These are the strategies we've been looking into at the Fool:

Beating the Footsie
The Pyad 26
RS 26 FTSE 100

The one we'll devote most time to here is Beating the Footsie, but we will touch on the other two. While Beating the Footsie can be followed without ever visiting the Fool UK web site, the other two cannot, for reasons which will become apparent.

But perhaps, Fool, it already sounds as if we're talking a foreign language? Never fear. All this stuff is very, very simple.

BEATING THE FOOTSIE

Here's an advanced jargon warning. You are going to hear the phrase "dividend yield" soon. Be of stout heart and fear not, for it is a simple thing, and a very useful thing at that. Beating the Footsie is a "dividend yield" strategy, you see. We will explain shortly, but first, a few words about cycles (and no, not the kind you sit on and pedal).

Ever noticed how things go in cycles? Flares and platform shoes, for instance. Somewhere, hidden in the biscuit tin where all the family photos are kept, is a picture of you in the early 1970s, assuming of course you'd been born by then. If you're a fella, you had sideburns, a moustache perhaps, and a chocolate-coloured shirt with collars sticking out past your shoulder tips. Girls in those days may have been sporting a splash of Bay City Rollers tartan along with some spangled four-inch platforms. Even kids got sucked into the ongoing fashion atrocity of that strange era. There is a picture like that of you, isn't there? Admit it.

Incredibly, extraordinarily, unbelievably, *flares and platforms are back*. We have an entire sociological research team at the Motley Fool dedicated to investigating how this could be so, but in the meantime reflect on how it would have been inconceivable just several years ago that these fashion icons – which we thought we were well rid of – could claw their way back into the national psyche. 'Flares,' we used to snort in a superior, rather world-weary manner, sipping our café lattes, 'platforms, they were *so* 70s.'

And now they're back. Well, these dividend yield strategies rely on just that cyclical capacity for very naff, out-of-favour things to shed their naffness and come back into style. We've given you flares and platforms, so let's see if you can think of a few other notable people or

organisations or trends which were once written off but whose star has risen again to new glory. We'll start you off once more with:

1. Barbara Windsor
2. _____
3. _____
4. _____
5. _____

Who did you come up with? Bill Clinton, perhaps? The Labour Party?

Fortunes also wax and wane in the business world. Take a look at the list of companies which follow. They constitute the FT 30 index, as of August 1999, which we mentioned in the last chapter. It's likely you recognise the majority of them because they're among the leading companies in Britain today.

Allied Domecq
BOC Group
Blue Circle Industries
Boots
British Airways
BG (British Gas)
BP Amoco
British Aerospace
British Telecom
Cadbury Schweppes
Diageo (Formerly Guinness and Grand Metropolitan)
EMI Group PLC
General Electric
GKN
Glaxo Wellcome
Granada
Imperial Chemical Industries (ICI)
Invensys (Formerly BTR and Siebe)
Lloyds TSB

Marks & Spencer
National Westminster Bank
P & O Steam Navigation
Prudential Corporation PLC
Reuters
Royal & Sun Insurance
Scottish Power
Smith Kline Beecham
Tate & Lyle
Tesco
Vodafone Group

Imagine if all these companies were wiped off the face of the Earth tomorrow, how would Britain fare? Not Very Well At All is the obvious answer. These companies are at the heart of modern Britain. The thing is, though, they are still all subject to the short-term whims and fancies of investors. Very few investors, particularly those investment professionals who invest for large banks, pension funds and actively managed unit trusts, have a long-term perspective, even with companies like these. They can't afford to. They are judged on a very short-term basis, often of three to six months. The media, too, tends to be short-term and often alarmist. That means that everyone loves a pretty face and no-one likes an ugly sister. When a company has some less positive news to report, WHOOSH goes the share price! Often the share price goes down before the news is very publicly known, but that's another issue and one related to the cosy relationship between City brokers and analysts and the companies they follow. (Don't get us started on it, or we may not stop.)

You, however, have something the City professionals do not have: time. There's no-one – except possibly your spouse – looking over your shoulder asking, 'Where's the money?! I gave you some money three months ago, idiot! What have

you done with it?!' That's a real benefit in all kinds of ways in investing, especially in this case.

Imagine if you were able to tell what the market didn't like, if you had some kind of pointer as to why that were so, and were able to buy that share, holding on to it until the market decided it liked it again, the price duly rose and then you sold it, clearing a neat profit. Wouldn't that be amazing? Well, that's the basis of the Beating the Footsie strategy. The problem is how do you tell whether the market likes the share or not? One way to do this is by looking at the dividend yield. At this point it is only human to want to say: 'This looks like it's getting complicated. I've had enough, I'm off down the pub.' Instead, we ask you to say: 'Dear Fool, pray finally enlighten my good self as to the nature of the aforementioned "dividend yield" jobbie.'

If you put it like that, why, yes we will! OK. The dividend yield. Hmm. Yes, it's an indirect indicator of whether the market 'likes' a share or not . . . But first, what's a dividend?

If you're a part owner of a company making lots of money, you want to receive some of it, *non*? You want some of the action. It's my right, dammit! (Calm down, calm down.) The share of the profits you receive is called the dividend and it is paid out on a per share basis. This means the amount of money you receive is related to the number of shares you hold, which is only fair.

Some companies don't pay dividends at all and the software mammolith[1], Microsoft, is one such, despite being *highly* profitable. The reason for this is that it feels it gives shareholders a better return by investing money it would have paid in dividends back into the business.

No matter, most companies do pay dividends and if they have a bad year, when profits

---

[1] The only word big enough to describe it.

are not so plentiful, they are under great pressure not to cut their dividend. To do so would be an admission that things are not going so well and is seen very negatively by the Wise establishment. Thus, dividends tend to change much less than share price.

On to the dividend yield. This is the percentage ratio between the dividend and the share price. Got that? Right, whip out your calculator, we're going in:

Eagle's Exotic Golfing Holidays plc has a share price of 200p and dividend per share 5p.

That means Eagle's dividend yield is _____ ÷ _____ x 100% = 2.5%

We've given you the answer and also the numbers which you have to plug into the equation, so all you have to do is decide which way they go. Easy. Come on, bet you can do it in no more than two attempts!

Now, Eagle's is struck by disaster. Several of their exotic golfing destinations around the world are riven by civil war. The year looks to be a bad one, the company warns that its profits are going to be down on last year. All of a sudden, no-one wants to own Eagle's anymore and the price drops to 125p. Eagle's, though, is a proud company, a solid company, the kind of old, established company you would want your son or daughter to marry into (getting the idea?), so despite the fact that profits are poor, it doesn't cut its dividend. That would be too ignominious. No, Eagle will struggle on regardless and anyway they're pretty sure things are going to be better next year, what with Paraguay, Ascension Island and Greenland coming into their brochure. Here's what their dividend yield is looking like now:

Eagle's dividend yield is now 5 ÷ 125 x100% = ____%

You got that right, hey? Yes, the answer is 4 per cent. The dividend yield has gone up. One way of looking at this is that the share price is relatively 'cheaper'. In other words, to receive the same dividend income of 5p per share, you have to pay much less for a share. Exactly the same thing happens with all the fine, upstanding, 'pillar of the British economy' companies in the FT 30 list we looked at just now. Poor results or problematic trading conditions worry the regular army of share buyers, who punish the share, by sending its price south. Often, however, because the market behaves a bit like a skittish mare, taking fright at a shaft of sunlight glinting on a tin can, this is an over-reaction, a short-term over-reaction. Long term, most FT 30 companies are solid – as we've seen, Britain would sink into the briny without them – and there is a tendency for the share price of high yielding shares to come back over periods of a year or more, after being unfairly 'punished' by the market for short-term underperformance. You, being a Foolish investor, have a longer-term perspective which allows you to profit, where others are afraid of short-term losses.

Note that we said there is a 'tendency' for this to occur. It doesn't always occur. It just occurs enough of the time to make it worthwhile. An excellent book, which any devotee of this field should think about reading is *What Works on Wall Street* by James O'Shaughnessy, already quoted in the previous chapter. In it he backtested a number of investment strategies in the United States over a period of 43 years and came up with the high dividend yield as being the best of the lot: 65 per cent of the time, or in 28 out of 43 years, high yielding shares beat large stocks in general (i.e. the equivalent of the index or market average), but over every rolling five-year period in the 43 years, they won 85 per cent of the time and over every ten-year rolling period they won all but once.

Less lengthy and less complete information is available for British shares, but Johnson Fry, a unit trust company, looked at historical information back to 1970 in a 1996 study. This involved a strategy of ranking the FT 30 by dividend yield, highest to lowest, then taking the ten highest yielders and selecting the five *cheapest* in share price of those. These shares were then bought in equal pound amounts and held for a year and the ranking re-done in exactly the same way. If the rankings had changed, as often they do, the share holdings were re-balanced to the new selection. All dividends paid were used to buy more shares at the end of each year. No account was taken of charges or taxes, but the numbers looked like this:

YEARLY AVERAGE

FTSE-All Share Index	15.6%
Footsie 5	20.5%

Pretty impressive numbers for a strategy which requires no thought and no skill to implement. An investment of £10,000 in the Footsie Five back in 1970 would have been worth £1,275,449 by 1996.

At the Fool UK in 1998, we ran some numbers of our own and found that the best results were obtained by using the simplest strategy available: buying the five highest yielders in the FT 30 and holding them for a year, forgetting all about the share price.

THE FIVE AND TEN HIGHEST YIELDERS

	FIVE	TEN
1983	67.88	60.75
1984	30.30	28.48
1985	36.43	27.30
1986	40.65	29.65
1987	14.49	17.45
1988	23.44	22.91
1989	27.64	23.41
1990	(0.06)	(6.57)
1991	29.09	25.89
1992	51.239	39.84
1993	47.99	42.27
1994	(12.57)	(8.28)
1995	(0.88)	10.96
1996	3.01	(1.05)
1997	29.49	19.34
1998	14.53	6.14
Avg.	23.41%	19.96%

(Numbers in brackets are negative.)

In other words, simply taking the five highest yielders does best of all, better than selecting the five cheapest of the ten highest yielders. The ten highest yielders, plain and simple, do pretty well, too.

These numbers contain several inconsistencies that we know about. They probably contain far more that we don't know about. *All* backtested numbers contain inconsistencies, wherever they are from. However, we think they are good enough to provide a pointer. They also agree with other published sources of numbers.

From early October 1997, we have been tracking our own imaginary Beating the Footsie portfolio at the Fool UK. For the first year, we used a method similar to that used by Johnson Fry, but since October 1998, we have been tracking simply the five highest yielders. Currently (August 1999), we are showing a paper gain of 38.4 per cent, as opposed to the FTSE 100 index gain of 17.2 per cent and the FT 30[2] index gain of 18.5 per cent. BUT, a big BUT, for a prolonged period, almost from the start, right through to early 1999, we were losing to both of the indices. Badly. At times, even we were dispirited, and had to keep pinching ourselves to remind us that this was a *long-term* strategy and could only be judged over the long term.

There's a big difference between a balmy July afternoon in Britain, with the prospect of a wonderful summer ahead and a grim, November morning, freezing rain coming down in sheets and months of the same to look forward to. Overall, most of us probably enjoy living here and are prepared to muddle on and take the rough with the smooth. We know the score, we're all old veterans at the British weather. Imagine, though, you are from the tropics, visiting Britain in July for the first time. You decide you quite fancy the climate and move here. Imagine the horror of that first November. Imagine the look on your spouse and children's faces as they say: 'You brought us to *this*? Are you insane?'

What follows goes for all of investing, and especially for mechanical strategies: be sure you can live with the worst that may happen, before you get seduced by the best. It is no good if you can only live with the best. Any investment strategy, from an index tracker to a mechanical

strategy such as this, or a selection of shares you've picked yourself, will have down times. At those times, you have to be a robot, unemotional and yet with sufficient programming (faith, if you will) to press on relentlessly with the course you decided upon at a more rational, less fraught, time.

Suppose you decide you want to get on and invest in the Beating the Footsie strategy. Well, the best advice we can give you is to visit the Fool UK web site, where you'll find the current rankings listed, regular articles on the topic, and an active message board where your questions will be answered and where you will find support. If you're not online, then you can still follow the strategy, except it is harder to find the current listing of FT 30 shares. The only places we know where it's openly published are at the FTSE International web site (**www.ftse.com**) and at the Motley Fool (**www.fool.co.uk**). It does change once or twice a year, so it is worth getting the current list. (If you're not online, you'll have to ask a friend who is to nip along and get it for you.) OK, let's presume you have got hold of the list of FT 30 constituents, the next thing to do is buy the Monday *Financial Times*, which has the yields listed next to the company name and share price (it says 'Yld grs' in the title line) on the prices pages. With all this spread out in front of you, simply list the companies in order of yield, from highest to lowest and, because we're just so-o-o obliging, we've given you the space to do that below:

---

[2]The only place you'll find the value of the FT 30 listed is in the Saturday edition of the *Financial Times*.

COMPANY	YIELD
1._____	_____ %
2._____	_____ %
3._____	_____ %
4._____	_____ %
5._____	_____ %
6._____	_____ %
7._____	_____ %
8._____	_____ %
9._____	_____ %
10._____	_____ %
11._____	_____ %
12._____	_____ %
13._____	_____ %
14._____	_____ %
15._____	_____ %
16._____	_____ %
17._____	_____ %
18._____	_____ %
19._____	_____ %
20._____	_____ %
21._____	_____ %
22._____	_____ %
23._____	_____ %
24._____	_____ %
25._____	_____ %
26._____	_____ %
27._____	_____ %
28._____	_____ %
29._____	_____ %
30._____	_____ %

All you then have to do is take the top five (or ten if you have substantially more money and are aiming for a more diverse, hence less volatile, holding of shares), buy them in equal pound amounts and hold them for a year.

For the purposes of showing how to follow the strategy, let's use some **imaginary** company names for our five picks and presume the amount you put into them is £1000 each. For this example, we're going to ignore stockbroking charges and all taxes to make it simpler:

COMPANY	YIELD	VALUE OF HOLDING
1. Mainliners	6.4 %	£1000
2. Essex Group	5.8 %	£1000
3. Cartel Unlimited	5.4 %	£1000
4. Wise Investments	5.3 %	£1000
5. Swindel Group	4.6 %	£1000
Total value of holdings:		£5000
Cash:		£0

It's a pretty reasonable year, a couple of the companies go down in price, but overall the strategy returns just over 18 per cent in total, including dividends, and your holdings at the end of a year look like this:

COMPANY	VALUE OF HOLDING
1. Mainliners	£745
2. Essex Group	£1460
3. Cartel Unlimited	£1360
4. Wise Investments	£1075
5. Swindel Group	£985
Total value of holdings:	£5625
Cash (from dividends):	£275
Total Value:	£5900

So far, so good. Sitting pretty. A gain! It's working! Jehovah! When you've calmed down, you re-do the ranking of all the shares in the index (or else pull them off the Fool UK web site) and find the following ones are now the top five high yielders in the index:

COMPANY	YIELD
1. Mainliners	8.6 %
2. Surefire	6.2 %
3. Mania Group	5.4 %
4. Antipasti	5.4 %
5. United Scareways	4.9 %

The only one that is still there is Mainliners, a real dog, showing a major loss for you. Therefore, your new selections are:

1. _____
2. _____
3. _____
4. _____
5. _____

Simple, hey? Your new selections are simply

the five highest yielders, which were listed in the previous box. Since Mainliners is the only company to stay in this year, you're going to have to sell four of your current holdings, which are:

1. _____
2. _____
3. _____
4. _____

Yep, also simple and the answers for that are at the bottom of the page too.[2] Next, knowing that in an ideal world you will aim to own the new five highest yielding shares in equal pound amounts, list below how you aim to have your portfolio looking after you have phoned your stockbroker, or else keyed in the trades you wish to make with your online broker:

COMPANY	VALUE OF HOLDING
1. Mainliners	£_____
2. Surefire	£_____
3. Mania Group	£_____
4. Antipasti	£_____
5. United Scareways	£_____
Total value of holdings:	£_____
Cash:	£_____

The answer is, of course, that in your ideal world you would like the total amount of £5900 reinvested equally into the five shares, leaving no cash at all. That means you have to figure out what £5900 divided by 5 is. In your head: '5 into

---

[2]The four to sell from your current holdings are: Essex Group, Cartel Unlimited, Wise Investments and Swindel Group.

5 goes once; 5 into 9 goes once, carry 4; 5 into 40 goes 8; 5 into 0 goes 0, so that makes, erm, 1180, £1180 for each share!'

OK, but why do we say 'in an ideal world'? That's because, depending on the charges your broker makes, it may not be worth getting too particular about making the amounts tally exactly. For instance, in the case of Mainliners, if you were to bring the £745 up to £1,180, that involves buying only an extra £435 worth of the share. There are some brokers with a charging structure which makes that worthwhile, but for most, say ones with a flat rate charge of £15, it is much less so – 3.5 per cent commission in this case. That means that:

1. You have to use common sense about how close to make the value of each investment when you reallocate.
2. Given the sums most of us are likely to be putting into this, choose a broker with a charging structure which doesn't penalise you for buying and selling relatively small amounts.

At the 'Getting a Broker' area at the Fool UK online, we keep a table constantly updated with the charges of all the major brokers for different amounts, so you can directly compare them. There's also a brokers' message board where you can discuss directly with other Fools the merits of particular brokers.

Backtesting and Data Mining

If you look hard enough and long enough at sets of old data, you will find that you can tease out associations which are, frankly, spurious. In 1998, a character called Leinweber[3] mined the United Nations database and found that butter production in Bangladesh was able to predict 75 per cent of the variation in the S&P 500 index. Clearly, that is ludicrous. Equally idiotic would be a stock selection protocol which gave market-beating returns, but which required you to buy on a Monday and sell on a Tuesday, except in August 1994, when you had to buy on a Tuesday and sell on a Wednesday, except, that is, for shares whose name begins with a vowel.

Does that mean all backtesting is ridiculous and can never suggest what is likely to happen in the future? No. Of course, you can never be absolutely certain about what is to happen in the future, but if the stock market has returned on average 12.2 per cent over 80 years and beaten gilts and cash over that entire period, why should the next 10 or 20 years be substantially different? Naturally, they might be, but they're more likely than not to follow the historical pattern. Similarly, if high-yielding shares have always outperformed, why should that suddenly change? There is risk inherent in all human undertakings, from getting up in the morning to using the phone (the house may get hit by lightning) to surfing the Internet fifteen hours a day (your brain may turn to jelly). The key is to decide which risk you prefer to take. For instance, given the historical outperformance of shares, is it riskier to leave your cash in the bank, where it is 'safe' and forgo the highly likely gains from shares over the next 20 years, or should you be putting your money in the stock market and risking a first-time-ever catastrophic underperformance? Only you can ultimately decide what kind of risk you're comfortable with. We hope the Fool is here to help with that decision and not to tell you what to do.

Harking back to Occam's razor, let's try and keep things simple and opt for the following

[3]Leinweber, D. 1998. *Stupid Data Miner Tricks: Overfitting the S&P 500*, Annotated slide excerpts. First Quadrant Corporation.

guidelines in assessing historical claims of out-performance for a particular strategy. You should:

1. Ask yourself whether there is a sound basis for the strategy; that it does not depend on doubtful explanations to substantiate its approach.
2. Ask yourself whether it is simple. Given the choice between a simpler strategy with good returns and a more elaborate, involved one with slightly better returns, have a good reason for choosing to follow the more elaborate one.

Applying these guidelines to strategies you read about and, perhaps, strategies which you yourself go on to devise (many people are proposing strategies all the time on our message boards), will help make things a lot clearer.

OTHER MECHANICAL STRATEGIES

At the Fool UK online, you will also find a number of other strategies under consideration. These include the Pyad 26 and the RS26 FTSE 100.

The first of these, the Pyad 26, is an attempt by one of the Motley Fool's writers to create his own index of shares on which to carry out a high dividend yield strategy. The argument against the FT 30 as an index on which to base such a strategy is that it is unloved, unremembered and frankly unwanted. It has been superseded by the FTSE 100 and that means it is only updated relatively rarely. The high yielding strategy involves buying those companies which seem to be performing poorly, but which have sound fundamentals. If the index is only updated rarely, you may get stuck with companies which really are doing very poorly indeed. These companies will keep appearing in the Beating the Footsie selections and will drag the returns down. The cable company BICC was a case in point for several years until it was finally booted out of the index.

The Pyad 26, by contrast, uses a positive five-year history of dividend growth, a market capitalization of over £2 billion and position as the largest company in its sector, to create a universe of shares (usually around 26) from which to pick high yielders. Due to its nature, there is only limited backtesting history available, but what there is seems promising. If you're interested, the selections and performance history are reguarly updated and discussed at the Fool UK online area.

The RS 26 FTSE 100 is an entirely different kettle of fish. Its basis involves buying shares with a high relative strength over the previous six months. In other words, you are buying the top performers in the FTSE 100 on the basis that they are more likely than not to continue in the same vein. Over the last several years this has been a fairly volatile strategy, but one which has brought excellent returns.

If you're interested in mechanical strategies, the Fool's StrategyMeisters await your queries, comments and thoughts at the Foolish Workshop.

TYING IT ALL TOGETHER

Which one should you choose of all these strategies, if any? There is no simple answer, except one: an excellent place for most beginning investors and many more experienced investors to put some or all of their investment money is into an index tracker. Of all the mechanical, no-brain, robot-like strategies – whatever you like to call them – this one is the most basic, has the least amount of risk, and will deliver spectacular returns over long periods. If in doubt about whether to start investing and how, your first action should be to do nothing at all. Simply watch, assess, learn, get a feel for the way the market works, the way it ebbs and flows. Do nothing until you feel confident, particularly in your ability to truly be a robot and keep your head when all about you are losing theirs.

When you are confident you understand what you're signing up to and why, then an index tracker remains an outstanding first port of call. There's no shame in it. You're no less worthy an investor, no less worthy a Fool if you're only invested in an index tracker. For heaven's sake, you're beating 90 per cent of the professionals already!

If you think you may be a mechanical strategies aficionado, however, then move on to investigate some of the other mechanical strategies we've been talking about in this chapter. Already, a world of options is open to you, none of them requiring more than an hour a year to follow and we haven't even got to the bit on individual shares yet.

Are you cooking, or what?

CHAPTER 7

How Do I Start Looking For Individual Shares?

'Never invest your money in anything that eats or needs painting.'
Billy Rose

If you've put together a portfolio based around the Beating The Footsie, RS26 or any other mechanical investment strategy, you are a part-owner of a public company. Sounds pretty powerful, doesn't it? Does it make you feel good about yourself? You can vote at Annual General Meetings, you receive the company's annual and interim reports and, in the form of a dividend, part of the company's profits are paid to you each year. Most private investors will only ever own a very, very small percentage of any individual company, but to you it will seem like a reasonably significant amount.

Once you've discovered the power of public ownership, and seen those dividend cheques roll in, the chances are that you're going to want to know more about this lark. You'll find yourself looking at companies in a different light. Is the publisher of your favourite magazine a quoted company? What about your mobile phone operator? Or your favourite bookshop? In your job, you will probably come across many different companies, whether that be as a teacher, doctor, accountant, lawyer, army lieutenant or professional footballer. The bigger the company, and the brand name, the more likely they are to be quoted on a public stock exchange, somewhere in the world.

And right about now it's time for another mind-expanding exercise, all about brands and the power they have to influence what we do and how we shop . . .

Name the following companies

_____ Sporting brand, best known for their trainers, and the 'swoosh'.

_____ Dominant UK High Street electrical goods retailer.

_____ The biggest brand in the world? Makes a syrup-based fizzy soft drink.

_____ The company which powers your computer.

_____ Biggest news agency in the world.

_____ Fast food restaurant, known for its hamburgers.

How did you do? Probably pretty well. These are the answers: (1) Nike, (2) Dixons (also owner of PC World, Currys and The Link), (3) Coca-Cola, (4) Intel. Some Fools may have answered Microsoft for this question, another huge brand name, but, though Microsoft probably provides the *operating system* for your computer, we were really talking about the processor. Interestingly, there is a reasonable chance that Intel does *not* power your computer, because it does have competitors in the computer processor field. However, courtesy of its enormous brand name, most people *think* Intel powers their computer. (And before indignant Macintosh users start calling us to complain, it's OK, we know *you* would never make such a mistake). (5) Reuters, (6) McDonalds.

The above six companies, seven if you include Microsoft, are all publicly quoted. Apart from Dixons and Reuters, all are US-based. It's a plain fact that when it comes to recognisable brand names, the US dominates. That doesn't mean that UK investors have to miss out on all the brand and consumer franchise action. You can buy shares in US companies far easier than you probably thought was possible, something we talk about in Chapter 12, 'America'!

Having completed that little exercise, you're ready to start looking for more great companies, and great brands. They are out there – we all need to just open our eyes and minds to them. Next time you're out shopping or walking home from the train station after a stressful day at work, instead of staring blankly ahead, look for great businesses and great brands. However, before we dive into the ins and outs of identifying these companies, it's worth looking at some of the great

investors of the past and present. They are living proof that it is possible to make significant sums of money through investing in the stock market.

SOME GREAT INVESTORS

Warren Buffett. Known as the world's greatest investor. His first 'business' was as a newspaper delivery boy, and in 1945 at age 14, he invested US$1200 into 40 acres of Nebraska farmland. Not long after that, a used pinball machine business proved to be a nice little earner. Now, as Chairman of Berkshire Hathaway, his wealth is estimated at over US$20 billion, and his company owns 10 per cent of Coca-Cola. He is the ultimate example of the advantages of long-term investing.

Anne Scheiber. A former IRS (the US equivalent of the Inland Revenue) employee, she invested an initial US$5000 into shares in the 1940s. When she died in 1995, her portfolio had blossomed to US$22 million, courtesy of time, compounding returns, and stock picking skill. Simple investment ideas, such as consumer giants Gillette and Coca-Cola, were two of her biggest winners.

John Maynard Keynes. Famed British economist and author. Was an early proponent of the focused portfolio, where a large portion of your wealth is invested in a very small number of individual companies, say less than five. Keynes emphasised learning one area really well, and not straying from it. It was as First Bursar at King's College Cambridge that he made his mark as a great investor. In the years from 1927 till his death in 1945, a period which included the Great Depression and World War II, he achieved an annual average return of 13.2 per cent versus the UK market's -0.5 per cent.

Josephine Public. Read *The Motley Fool UK Investment Workbook*, and at age 18, started investing in the stock market. Starting off with just £50 a month, as the years went by, she gradually saw her overall wealth increasing. Knowing she was on to a good thing, she vowed to save hard, and invest every spare penny into the market. By the age of 50 she had made her first million.

Whoa! That last one could be you! These are clearly remarkable people, but their investing feats are not inimitable. Most successful strategies surround the simple premise of buying and holding shares in great companies.

WHY BOTHER WITH INDIVIDUAL SHARES?

Having read about index tracking funds, Beating The Footsie, and other mechanical strategies, you may be thinking that's all you need to know about the world of stock market investing. Even if you stopped reading this book right here and now, you'd be more informed than a great many of your friends and colleagues. Ask them to name the best performing class of asset over the past 80 years and you'll probably be met with blank looks. But you know it has been shares. You're already one step ahead of the pack, and can proudly stand up in a packed train and pronounce – 'I'm a Fool'. If you get a few funny looks, don't worry, we've been getting them for years! And besides, you'll have the last laugh when it all comes together for you down the line.

Now, let's see if you're ready to go on reading about investing in individual company shares. Give yourself one point for each of the following reasons you want to invest in individual companies.

———— I want to try and earn even better returns than the index and Beating The Footsie.

———— I want to pit my skill against the investment experts, because I reckon my stock picking skill will be superior.

———— I've paid for this book, and damn it, I'm going to read it to the end!

———— I'm an accountant, and want to prove that I'm not boring. If I can tell my friends how to analyse individual companies, that should impress them.

———— I'm 11 years old, and am running twelve paper rounds a day, cutting hair in the evenings, and selling old computers on the weekends. I want to start investing my money at an early age. Buffett's got nothing on me.

———— I want to show my IFA how easily, and better, I can do this stuff myself. Then, with great pleasure, I'll tell the IFA his services are no longer required.

———— I want to retire early from my job.

———— I love the challenge of picking individual shares.

———— I'm a Fool.

———— I want to learn more about the stock market. If the so-called experts can do it, then so can I, but even better.

Scoring

0-2 points: Go back to Old Kent Road. Do not collect £200. Stick with index trackers or else start reading this book again, and this time concentrate, Fool!

3-5 points: You're getting the picture.

6-8 points: Excellent. You've grasped the basic concepts of this stuff, and are ready to move on to the next step.

9-10 points: You're a Fool!

Remember that identifying the companies you're interested in doesn't necessarily mean you should go out and buy some of them right this instant. Your knowledge of individual companies will not be built up in a matter of days. It takes time – time to learn about the company, its future prospects, its competitive environment and the integrity of its management. At the same time, you will be familiarizing yourself with the company's annual report, and watching its progress. Often it takes many years of learning about a company before you actually take the plunge and buy a part-ownership in that company.

The key to most things investment-related is time and patience. It can be frustrating watching the share price of a company you're following keep on going up and up, whilst you're sitting on the sidelines. However, you should never forget that with many of the great companies, given time, it doesn't really matter if you miss out on the first 75 per cent of its share price appreciation. There is almost always a buying opportunity, sometime, somewhere, somehow. You will undoubtedly miss a few great opportunities whilst you're learning and waiting, but you will win in the end – with time and patience.

WHERE DO I FIND INDIVIDUAL SHARES?

Peter Lynch, the successful former investment fund manager and best-selling author, advocates that investors should buy what they know. A trip down to the local High Street or shopping centre can give you a few clues. Keep your eyes peeled for all sorts of things. For example:

Did you see many people with mobile phones? Have you noticed more and more people with them? This may lead you to investigate the merits of Vodafone Airtouch, Orange,

and BT (owners of Cellnet). An investment made in the late 1990s in any one of those companies would have been a big winner for your portfolio.

Did you notice that Marks & Spencer's clothing range was recently lacking a little oomph? This may have led you to avoid buying shares in them at their peak in late 1997 and is something we should have paid more attention to when discussing them as an obviously great investment in *The Motley Fool UK Investment Guide*. Although in the long run there is a good chance M&S will recover, based on their past record, but you may have saved yourself a bit of money by waiting for the share price to fall.

Was Dixons busy? Did you see much in the way of competition to them on the High Street? If you decided to delve a little deeper into Dixons, you would also find out that they own Currys, PC World and part of The Link. You may also have seen a few Freeserve CD-ROMs floating about. A little further delving would have told you that Freeserve, the revolutionary free Internet access provider, was part-owned by Dixons.

Are people buying digital televisions, decoders, or dishes? Are you interested in signing up to this new service? Companies like BSkyB, Carlton Communications and Granada (joint owners of ONDigital) could be beneficiaries. Beware, however, of the spectre of the video cassette wars – VHS versus Betamax – where eventually one format came out on top. Sky and ONDigitial are currently embroiled in a price war and they both aim to build their customer bases as quickly as possible. The cable television companies are also looking for a piece of the action. This means that profitability, and market leadership for one of the services, could be some way off.

Which supermarket has the best range of goods, and cheapest prices? And was it busy? Of the local stores near Fool HQ, Safeway comes a poor last. Not surprisingly, this fact has been reflected in their share price over the past four years. Tesco are now the market leaders, having left J. Sainsbury behind a long time ago. An observant Fool may have picked up this trend long before it was confirmed by the official numbers.

Are people eating out? Have you been particularly impressed by one restaurant outlet? A household named company like PizzaExpress has been one of the better performing shares over the last 5 years. If you liked the concept, or 'experience' as the company itself calls it, and have seen more and more of the restaurants opening up across the country, you could easily have bought into PizzaExpress.

Of course, not all stock ideas come from a visit to the local shops.

KEEP YOUR EYES PEELED

Some of the very best investors are avid readers, and we're not talking trashy beach novels here. (Go on, admit it, you devoured *A Sandy Love Match* on your last holiday to Ibiza, didn't you?) They read the broadsheet newspapers, trade magazines and anything else they need in order to inform them of possible investment opportunities. Things they want to be looking out for include industry trends, competitive threats, fast-growing companies, bargain basement companies and new discoveries. The television also can throw up investment ideas, especially when it's time for the advertisements. As a Foolish investor, you'll soon be dashing off to make that cup of tea whilst the main programme is on, making sure you are back in time to see the

ads! You'll also be urging the networks and cable companies to air more ads, rather than less. Being Foolish is about being contrary. When watching your next ad break, see how many recognisable brand names you spot. Not all of these will necessarily be great investment opportunities, but they will help point you in the right direction.

How do companies build up their brand name? The marketing department will come up with all sorts of ingenious ideas, from television, to radio, to newspaper, to billboards. There's a classic example of a company that came from nowhere to be a nationally recognised brand name in the space of just a few months. To test whether you've been cast under the spell of their marketing department, complete this slogan.

The future's bright . . . .the future's _____.[1]

Did you get it right? I bet nine readers out of ten recognized that slogan. Some may also have seen the huge PR coup engineered by Orange when news of a missing Orange mobile phone was splashed across the front page of one of the tabloids. The owner couldn't find her phone anywhere, so she rang the number (as you do) and, lo and behold . . . a ringing sound came from inside the dog. The dog had swallowed the phone. But the phone still worked. Well, fancy that! Blow me over with a feather. Fancy, too, that Orange had their logo on the front page, along with details of the cost of the phone and the service. Very nice. Very crafty.

Some of the great advertising campaigns have helped build brand names into household names. Watch this space as we attempt to build the Motley Fool into one of the most recognizable brand names in the world. We're going to

[1]Answer: Orange

spread this brand *everywhere*, as far as it will stretch. And further. Let's see, now:

> To educate, amuse and enrich . . . your dog
> A Fool's Guide to Buying a Budgie
> Running a circus the Motley Fool way
> Fool! The new soft drink by the Motley Fool
> **Fool** (deep husky female voice), the new fragrance by the Motley Fools

Do you think we're on the right track? Can we swing it? We're a bit behind the Oranges, Coca-Colas, Levis, Gaps, Intels and Microsofts of the world, but they've been around a lot longer than us.

Having read this, you will now either be adding your own Motley Fool slogan to the already burgeoning list:

> Your slogan goes here _____

or else be noting a memory jogger in your little notebook: 'Never, *ever* invest in this company if they dare to go public!' And then another memory jogger: 'Watch out for companies which try to spread their brand too thinly, too quickly. Respect and trust for brand are important.'

Brand is important, but it isn't always everything. Colt Telecom and Energis, a pair of companies which don't exactly leap out at you and shout 'buy', have been two of the very best performing shares of the 1990s. Both of them are 'new wave' telecommunication companies, and their share price has benefited from their exposure to the fast growing world of data transfer, courtesy of the Internet.

Information technology companies have been excellent performers in recent times. You may not have heard of RM. They supply integrated IT solutions to the educational market.

In the 1999 budget the Chancellor pledged to continue to support this initiative. The shares began 1998 at 158p, and in 1999 at one stage soared to over 700p, a stunning rise of 340 per cent in just fifteen months. This is the sort of share performance all individual shareholders are forever looking for, yet you should be warned that it is very rare. You may never find one of these acorns, and yet still have a very successful investing career, seeing your overall portfolio growing at an average of 15 per cent per year.

For every winner, there is also a loser. Examples such as Safeway and Marks & Spencer are littered throughout the stock market. It will be virtually impossible for private investors to always pick winners, and always avoid the losers. The trick is to find out a little more about the company before trusting management with your hard-earned cash. The annual report is a good place to start. These can be ordered directly from the companies themselves and we'll go into what exactly you're looking for in a company report a little later.

We've already named quite a few companies in this section. Now it's your turn. Once you've written down their names, go through them and decide which ones strike you as potentially interesting investments, based on their strong brand, superior products or excellent customer service. Just stretching your brain in this way (ask the family to help if you get stumped) represents a great start at collecting a pool of companies to consider for your investment portfolio. Pencils at the ready . . .

Five companies which advertise on the television

1. _____
2. _____

3. _____

4. _____

5. _____

Five High Street shop names

1. _____

2. _____

3. _____

4. _____

5. _____

Five companies which appear on your credit card bill

1. _____

2. _____

3. _____

4. _____

5. _____

WHAT DO YOU DO WITH THE GREAT IDEAS?

You've now written down the names of fifteen companies, possibly including Orange, Coca-Cola and Marks & Spencer. Some of the companies may be big, others small. Some may be traded publicly on a stock exchange, and others may be privately owned. Virgin is a privately owned company, controlled by Mr Branson. It was once publicly quoted, but Branson took it private again in the late 1980s. Levis and Mars are US examples of privately owned companies.

How do you go about determining which companies are publicly owned, and therefore traded on a stock exchange? There are a number of options available to you . . .

1. The easiest and quickest method is to fire up your computer and check in at the Motley Fool web site. There you can get the latest share price for the roughly 2000 publicly quoted UK companies, or you can ask other Fools on one of our message boards – someone is always keen to answer your query. Also, online you can get basic company information – either at the company's own web site (for example, you can find contact details and shareholder's information for Orange at www.orange.co.uk), or from various other sources, including the Motley Fool.

2. Check the share prices page in the *Financial Times*. Companies are listed by sector, so it sometimes can be a bit difficult to find a particular company. However, for many of the household names, the sectors are relatively self explanatory. BT, Vodafone and Orange are in the Telecommunications Services sector. Boots and Marks & Spencer reside in the General Retailers sector. BSkyB and Reuters live in the Media & Photography sector. You get the hang of it? Try this for size – the answers are all relatively obvious, and at the same time you'll learn a few more sector names.

COMPANY	SECTOR
(a) Barclays	_____
(b) Tesco	_____
(c) SmithKline Beecham	_____
(d) BP Amoco	_____

Answers
(a) Banks (b) Food & Drug Retailers (c) Pharmaceuticals (d) Oil & Gas

3. Ring up the company. You can obtain its phone number either from the phone book, Directory Enquiries, or off a product or label. Ask them whether they are a publicly quoted company, and whether their primary quotation is on the London Stock Exchange. You will find that many of the biggest and most recognisable brand names in the world belong to US quoted companies. However, that's not to say you can't invest in them – in Chapter 12 we see how Foolishly easy it is to Invest USA.

4. Instinct. You probably know that Marks & Spencer is a British company, and that Coca-Cola is US based. The same goes for BP Amoco and McDonalds. You can probably guess that all four of those giants are quoted on stock exchanges around the world.

5. Open up an account with an execution-only broker. It's free and easy. Some of them don't require a deposit, and there's no obligation to buy shares once the account is opened. (See Box.) Once you've done that, either log in for real-time updated share prices if you have opened an online account, or feel free to phone your broker and ask them for either a share price quote on a particular company, or in fact whether it trades at all on the London Stock Exchange.

Opening a Brokerage Account

If you want to buy or sell shares cheaply in the UK, then the Foolish way to do it is through a UK execution-only broker. Not for us Fools are expensive advisory brokers who, not surprisingly, advise you how and where to invest your money, then go ahead and do it for you, once you've agreed to the trade. For that privilege, they charge you very large commissions, and may encourage you to trade in and out of different shares at regular intervals.

Remember: Each time you trade, your broker makes money.

Now you know why brokers are likely to be saying, 'I think you should switch out of Saudi Arabia Gold PLC and into South African Oil PLC'. Of course, despite their so-called expertise, there is no guarantee that your advisory broker's recommendations will be successful. In fact, because they encourage you to trade on a regular basis, when the charges are taken into account, there's a very good chance your portfolio would under-perform the market.

Execution-only brokers are the exact opposite of the advisory broker. They are usually cheap and cheerful, and execute the deal for you based on your instructions. There's absolutely no advice whatsoever – if you ask them what they think of the company you're about to buy, they are not allowed to comment. In fact, there's a very good chance the person you're dealing with has never heard of Alizyme or Zotefoams. Believe it or not, both those companies do exist!

Execution-only brokers come in three different forms, and you'll obviously have to decide which type best suits your needs.

1. Postal
2. Telephone
3. Online (Internet)

Postal accounts, by their very nature, don't allow you the privilege of knowing the price at which you are buying or selling your shares. You have to take a bit of pot luck in that respect. Most telephone brokers will, on the other hand, execute the deal for you whilst you are on the phone. A typical conversation might be;

YOU: I'd like to buy some shares in Metal Onion.

TELEPHONE BROKER: Metal Onion are 230p to buy. How many would you like to buy?

YOU: I'll take a dozen onions and half a pound of . . . Oops. I'll buy 430 shares, please.

BROKER: Let me just put that through the system. (This will be followed by background noises of computer keys tapping away, other phones ringing, some swearing as the computer fails to respond . . .) OK. Just to confirm, I'm buying 430 shares of Metal Onion (slight snigger) at 230p. Would you like me to go ahead with that trade?

YOU: Yes, please. (You're thinking these Metal Onion shares are going to make you your fortune!)

BROKER: Confirmed. Anything else?

YOU: No thanks. Bye.

Easy-peasy, hey? As for the settlement of that trade, some brokers require funds to be deposited in their accounts in advance of trading, whilst others allow you to pay within a few days.

Online trading has taken the US by storm, and it has now arrived here in the UK. One of the reasons why this form of trading has been so successful across the Atlantic has been because of the incredibly low commissions on offer, with some deals being executed for as little as US$5! As of writing, the UK market is just getting going, and we Fools will be hoping to see the cost of trades rapidly reducing over here. Online trading is the ultimate execution-only experience – you absolutely make your own investment decisions, and don't speak to a soul about them. You just fire up the computer, check the current buy or sell price, and if you like it – whammo! A few clicks of the mouse and you're a part-owner of a large, publicly owned and traded corporation.

At **www.fool.co.uk**, we've got a 6-part series on how to choose a broker. In some depth it helps you identify your requirements in a broker, and then runs you through our Foolish 12 criteria points. For example, do you want a nominee account or a Crest-sponsored member account? Is price everything, or is service more important? Check it all out at **http://www.fool.co.uk/personalfinance/ discountbrokers/DiscountBrokers1.htm**.

Once you've ascertained whether the company in question is UK based, phone them up and ask to be sent a copy of their annual report. Who knows – by the time you read this all UK quoted companies may even have an Investor's Relations department, and have a ready-made investment information pack ready to send to you. It happens in the US, so there's no reason why it shouldn't happen here too. In the chapters ahead, we'll help you dig through the annual report. As a cautious word of warning, don't be too struck by all the pretty pictures and glossy design work in the annual report. Many companies use them as marketing tools, and so they are hardly going to paint the company in a bad light.

THE BIG PICTURE

Just how big are companies and how do we measure that? Place the following household name companies in order from biggest to smallest.

Brands Hatch Leisure, Marks & Spencer, National Express, Body Shop, Prudential, Barclays

1. _____

2. _____

3. _____

4. _____

5. _____

6. _____

Answers: (1) Barclays, (2) Prudential, (3) Marks & Spencer, (4) National Express, (5) Body Shop, (6) Brands Hatch Leisure.

How did you go, and what criteria did you use? Put your hand up if you put M&S above Prudential. Go on, own up . . . I'm making unFoolish presumptions here, but I'm thinking you ranked them on brand familiarity. There's nothing wrong with that, and in fact this little exercise helps show you the power of brands. There's more about that later, in Chapter 9. This wasn't about brand names – it was about the size of the company, and how that is calculated.

It's often a case of the larger a company, the lower the risk, and by risk we're generally talking about the risk of the company going bust. Barclays are a huge banking corporation with branches all around the world. Although Nick Leeson broke Barings Bank, he'd have had a much harder job of breaking Barclays Bank. Barclays are valued at about £29 billion. On the other hand, Brands Hatch Leisure is valued by the stock exchange at about £75 million, small by comparison to Barclays, but still the 785th biggest company out of the 2000-odd UK quoted companies. There's a lot of little – in comparison to Barclays and even Brands Hatch – companies out there!

A recent study by Foolish writer Christopher Spink found that the value of the top 18 UK quoted companies was equal to the value of the next 332!

Most of us have heard of The Body Shop, the worldwide chain selling natural skin and health care products. But how big are they? This is the sort of information you'll want to know before investing in any company. We sort of think they are big, because they seemingly have shops on most High Streets and in the shopping malls, but we're not quite sure.

There are a few ways to measure the size of a company, but we're going to stick to market capitalisation. No matter what anyone else says – 'Hey you, Mr Stock Exchange. Our company is worth more than that' – the plain truth is that on any given day investors place a value on a quoted company. The Body Shop has 194 million shares of ownership, and each one is trading on the stock exchange at 120p. What's the value of the company right now? This one's too easy – it's the number of shares multiplied by the price per share, meaning Body Shop is valued by the market at 194 million times 120p which equals £232.8 million. That's what is known as the company's market capitalisation.

In comparison, let's have a look at Barclays. We know they are bigger than Body Shop, but by just how much? There are 1505 million Barclays shares of ownership outstanding, and each of them is currently trading at a price of 1900p. Out comes the calculator: 1505 million shares times 1900p equals £28.6 *billion*. Divide £28.6 billion (or £28,600 million) by the Body Shop market capitalisation of £232.8 million and you find that Barclays are 123 times more valuable than the Body Shop.

The biggest company quoted on the London Stock Exchange is oil giant BP Amoco. They have 9709 million shares of ownership and each one is priced at 1150p. That makes their market capitalisation a massive £111.65 billion, or almost four times bigger than Barclays and an enormous 480 times bigger than little old Body Shop.

MARKET CAPITALIZATION

Try calculating the total value, or market capitalization, of the following public companies. While you're doing it, try and get a perception for the size of the company we're looking at. As we said above, there are some very big differentials between brands we consider to be household names.

Capitalization Terminology

In addition to precise capitalization values (or 'cap'), investors normally classify companies by size. There are no hard and fast rules on this, but we think the following guidelines are appropriate.

Large-Caps – above £3 billion
Mid-Caps – between £300 million and £3 billion
Small-Caps – between £50 million and £300 million
Micro-Caps – below £50 million

COMPANY	SHARES OUTSTANDING	SHARE PRICE	MARKET CAPITALIZATION
Psion	78 million	850p	_____
Ted Baker	41 million	200p	_____
Pilkington	1092 million	90p	_____
Granada Group	917 million	1150p	_____
Fitness First	35 million	680p	_____
Abbey National	1418 million	1240p	_____
ICI	728 million	620p	_____

Answers (in order from biggest to smallest)

Abbey National	£17.6 billion
Granada Group	£10.5 billion
ICI	£4.5 billion
Pilkington	£983 million
Psion	£663 million
Fitness First	£238 million
Ted Baker	£82 million

You should now be able to place the above seven companies neatly into their respective categories.

Abbey National   _____

Granada Group   _____

ICI   _____

Pilkington   _____

Psion   _____

Fitness First   _____

Ted Baker   _____

Although you've no doubt suspected it for years, it's good to have confirmation that Abbey National is in fact a Large Cap company. Ah, you'll sleep better tonight now! And as for Psion? You probably weren't too sure about them. If you have heard of them, it's probably due to their popular hand-held computers. According to our classifications, Psion fall in the Mid-Cap range.

What Psion does

In 1998, Psion signed an agreement with Nokia, Ericsson and Motorola, whereby the latter three companies paid Psion some money so they could have a shareholding in a joint venture company called Symbian. Its purpose in life is to attempt to develop an operating system for wireless communication devices. Psion, and its partners in Symbian, are hoping this will become the industry standard operating system. Microsoft has a virtual monopoly on computer operating systems, and it is arguably the most successful company in the world. Psion and Symbian are hoping to emulate Microsoft but in the wireless telecommunications field. Only time will tell whether they are successful, because there's lots of competition out there for this lucrative market, including Microsoft themselves.

Let's talk a little bit about the general qualities of each category of classification.

Large-Cap Shares
These are also known as Blue Chips. Large companies are considered relatively safe investments, mainly because of their pure size. There's much less chance of them failing or going out of business, but at the same time they usually aren't going to grow as fast as their smaller counterparts. However, that's hardly a reason not to invest in these companies, because even though they are very big, the good ones can still grow at a reasonable lick. Add on the steady dividends these companies usually pay, and you're looking at decent long term investment prospects.

Every company in the FTSE 100 index is a large-cap company, in keeping with our definition. You probably already know plenty of them. Here's a quick test;

1. Sells petrol, characterized by its green and yellow colours_____
2. High Street bank, just gone through a re-branding exercise. Look out for the red and white triangles _____
3. The man from the _____

Answers
(1)BP (Amoco) (2) HSBC Group (3) Pru (Prudential)

Mid-Cap Shares
These are potentially the large-caps of tomorrow. You often get a bit of a mis-match amongst the mid-caps. Some will be passing through this

category as they make their way to the top, whilst others will be fallen giants, having dropped out of the FTSE 100 index. Obviously you want to be hunting for the former companies.

The range we've defined for this category largely follows the FTSE 250 index, made up of companies valued in size between numbers 101 and 350 on the stock exchange. Some company names you may have heard of include Safeway (a fallen large-cap), National Express, Capital Radio, JD Wetherspoon and Manchester United.

Small-Cap Shares

These babies have got the ability to fly, falter or stay put. How's that for a wide range of possibilities? But us Fools are not fence-sitting – anything and everything genuinely can happen to smaller company shares. Courtesy of their size, they can take advantage of opportunities that perhaps larger companies can't see, or can't be bothered tackling, and carve out a nice little growing business for themselves. And, if they grow it quickly, it hopefully soon won't be a little business for too much longer.

Smaller companies reside largely in the FTSE Small-Cap index. These are usually altogether riskier investment prospects than our first two categories, as smaller companies just don't have the financial resources to ride out a bad patch, should it occur. Although not too many companies thankfully go completely to the wall, you can sometimes find today's small-cap share residing in the *micro*-cap index in two years' time.

There are no doubt some great acorns hidden amongst the small-caps of today, just waiting to turn into oak trees. The challenge for you is to find them. If and when you do, it will be a very satisfying experience.

Micro-Cap Shares

Beware any investor who travels into this universe. These companies are extremely small. Some of these companies have relatively short operating histories. Those with longer histories will often have very erratic earnings records. Some of them may have been small companies gone wrong, and hence have plummeted down the market capitalization pecking order. Many are purely speculative plays – oil, mining or tiny Internet companies – each with grandiose plans, but paper-thin business models. The chances of any of these companies making it to the top is relatively low. Competition is fierce – if a large company thought it was under threat from a micro-cap, it could just throw a load of money at 'the problem' and it would be bye-bye, micro-cap.

Have we put you off yet? Again, there are exceptions to the rules, but the safest, most sensible and Foolish route is to steer clear of these companies.

What's in a Price?

Which is cheaper? A share trading at 110p, or one trading at 650p? The answer is . . . it depends. A share price is pretty much meaningless when examined in a vacuum. People often mistakenly think the 110p share is cheaper than the 650p share. Verna's Shoe Emporium may be way overvalued at 110p per share, while shares in Keith's Garden Supplies might be a great bargain at 650p each.

Another misconception is that penny shares, those trading for less than about 50p per share, are great buys. People think that a 10p share is likely to double quickly. Well, penny shares are usually trading that low for a reason. They are more likely to zoom to zero than to double.

BEYOND THE TWILIGHT ZONE – INDUSTRIES

Before we close this chapter, it's worth having a word about entire industries. When looking for individual shares it is always worth considering the industry in which that company operates. Is it a growth industry? What about competitors? Are there a few companies which dominate the sector, and hence are the only ones you should consider? Or are today's industry leaders tomorrow's laggards, as nimbler companies take huge swathes of market share?

By looking at an entire industry, you get a much better feel for firstly whether that industry is one you want to invest in, and secondly whether one company dominates, or is set to dominate, that industry. For example, a company distributing third party computer parts will probably be in a very competitive industry, where customers only want the cheapest price, and don't care from which company they buy them. Has this industry got attractive economics? And what competitive advantage has your company got over the one in the next block?

Understanding individual companies in their larger industry context is an important step in making sense of the numbers, and figuring out whether your company is going to be a winner. Things like operating margin, stock turns, days sales outstanding . . . whoa! Not too fast. This stuff is coming soon, starting with the next chapter. Don't worry, it's painless, fun and educational. Honest.

CHAPTER 8

Show Me Ze Numbers

Multiplication is vexation,
Division is as bad,
The rule of three doth puzzle me,
And practice drives me mad.
Anon

But before we do that, let's just be clear that if you do eventually decide to buy a part of a business, to become a shareholder, you're obtaining a stake in a living entity, not a set of accounts. You'll be basing your decision on a whole range of factors, from the helpfulness or otherwise of the company's customer service operatives, to the vision of its chief executive, to the attractiveness of its brand and also to the health of its accounts. Adopt a global view, and buy the company, not the numbers.

That said, the numbers can be exceedingly helpful in telling you the story behind the glossy image the company may want to project. With accounting standards the way they are in the UK and US, barring gross fraud, companies can't hide from what is revealed to the practised eye in their regularly reported numbers.

A Case of Fraud

Sadly, the odd case of gross fraud still occurs.

Anyone remember Asil Nadir and Polly Peck? This company was once a darling of the stock market, and even made it briefly into the FTSE 100 index. Yet that didn't stop it going bust, nor did it stop Mr Nadir skipping bail and flying back to his native Cyprus, where the sun always shines. As for shareholders of the former company, they've had to settle for a picnic in the local park for their summer holidays. In recent times we've seen cases of 'accounting irregularities' at a few smaller companies, for example Powerscreen International, Regent Inns and Azlan. They've managed to survive, but not before a few directors lost their jobs, and lots of shareholders lost a lot of money. Thankfully, these cases are very much in the minority, and as we shall see later, there are often warning signs the astute Fool can spot to avoid investing in these types of companies.

We all studied mathematics at school. Think back to those days before calculators, before computers. Many of us were quite number literate. The twelve times table was easy, as was long division. Some of us went further, into the world of logarithms, algebra and calculus. Oh, those were the days!

Many of us, this Fool included, have long since forgotten the ancient art of the 'work it out in your head' technique. Calculators and pure laziness put paid to that one. Just to get you up to speed again, because a simple facility with mental arithmetic is useful in what's coming up, as it is in our everyday lives, here are a couple of exercises. No cheating and no calculators, you sly Fool.

1.   235 ÷ 16 = _____
2.   18 x 23 = _____
3.   1 x 1 = _____
4.   15% of 250 = _____

Answers: (1) 14 11/16 (2) 414 (3) 1 (4) 37.5

If you answered '2' for question 3, step into the bathroom and recite your one times table fifty times: "1 x 1 = 1, 2 x 1 = 2, 3 x 1 = 3 . . . "

Now you're back, the good news is that this chapter is not going to be taking you back to your school days and the delights of long division. We're just illustrating the point that as we grow older, we tend to conveniently forget or ignore numbers. Yet, some numbers have great importance to our lives, and financial future. Do you balance your current account when the bank statement arrives every month? Do you know what rate of interest you are paying on your mortgage? Do you know how much you've contributed to your pension scheme, and whether it will give you enough to live on when you retire?

These questions are important, yet too many of us ignore them. We're either fearful of the answer, or too lazy to do the numbers. This is not rocket science! You can do it. Make your second resolution this coming New Year's Eve – we should all reserve number one for quitting either food, smoking, drinking or pigeon-fancying – 'I will take control of my finances and even learn about company accounts.'

Easy, isn't it?

What Are Ratios and Why Use Them?

In this chapter, and for the rest of this workbook, we'll be looking at various 'ratios' that are widely used to help investors gauge the financial health of a company. Very simply, a ratio is *a comparison of two numbers, expressed as a percentage.* For example, if you bought shares in a company for 300p and they are now quoted at 360p, they're now worth 360p ÷ 300p = 1.2 = 120% of their original value. Your profit to date is 20 per cent. If, on the other hand, the shares were now trading at 210p – heaven forbid – your investment is now worth 210p ÷ 300p = 0.70 = 70 per cent of its original value, meaning you're down 30 per cent. Ouch.

Why use ratios to express performance instead of the real numbers? Because percentages iron out the different sizes of numbers being used across different companies.

For example, take two companies that each had £100 million of sales last year. If they both grew their sales by 20 per cent, did they grow by the same sterling amount? Yep – they both grew their sales by £20 million. Hey, that's good going! But, if one company, instead, had £500 million in sales last year while the other one achieved £100 million, and they both grew sales by £20 *million*, the latter grew by 20% but the former grew by only 4 per cent. Using ratios allows us to compare companies of radically different sizes and understand how their growth rates affect their value.

Practically speaking, we'll be using ratios to get a sense of whether a company is relatively weak or strong, or overvalued or undervalued, according to some standard benchmarks. While it's not super easy, it's not that difficult. Your first form teacher threw some trickier sums at you than these, and you got past them. Why should it be that much harder in our adult life?

Many of you probably haven't encountered some of the stuff that follows before, and therefore your head may be swimming with new terms, acronyms or numbers the first time you read this through. But, don't despair, and don't give up. On the second and third reading, it may finally start to make some sense. And, don't forget this is a workbook – the best way to learn, as my mother always used to tell me, is by writing things down, and not giving up. I think I can, I think I can . . .

Before we go any further, however, I must make a confession. Prior to becoming a Fool, I was an accountant. I still retain some of an accountant's typical qualities – whacky dress sense, partygoer, shining wit and lover of extreme sports and danger – as well as an understanding of balance sheets, cashflow statements, and profit and loss statements. I hope these may come in useful in what follows, but if they don't, if you get just the teensiest bit bored, here's an accountant joke to crack repeatedly at my expense:

We all know that there are three sorts of accountant in this world . . . Those that can count and those that can't.

Now that you've pledged to take control of your own money and you've dispatched from your head your dread of numbers, it's time to tackle a company's key financial statements and ratios. It's not that difficult, and with a little know-how, could make or save you a lot of money. So, let's crack open your favourite company's annual report (have you decided on one now, haven't you?). First stop is the glossy pages. But before you dive straight into the annual report, it is worth bearing in mind that the document is produced by the company themselves, and as well as giving it to shareholders, they often give it to potential customers. You get the drift? If they can at all help it, they will always try and paint the prettiest picture possible about themselves, and I'm not talking here about the photos of the directors! However, there is usually some useful information hidden between the pictures of the company's products, its employees, plant, or whatever else they see fit to include. The Chairman and Chief Executive give a run-down of the company's activities, progress and future prospects. These latter statements can actually affect the company's share price – you can be sure that any mention of a 'slowing of sales' will not be received well by the stock market – although by the time you read it in the annual report, the stock market will already have had its say. The Finance Director has his little section too, not just to prove that accountants can write as well as count (allegedly), but to add a little explanation to the numbers that are presented.

Flicking past all the glossy pages, you'll find yourself eventually getting to the cheap paper. That's where the numbers live, almost given pauper status, even though they are the most important part of the document. This is where the action is! Standby, we're heading – deep, deep underground.

We have an example company whose numbers we will be looking at. If you have a company annual report to hand, why not refer to that too throughout this chapter?

THE BALANCE SHEET

These things are simple. Really. Why, you created one for yourself back in Chapter 3. The balance sheet for a company follows the same logic – it's just that the numbers get a little bigger, and those pesky accountants throw in a few more headings, just to confuse us all. But, as we'll see, it's easy to see through all the smokescreens, and get to know your company much more intimately.

Publicly quoted UK companies are required to produce a set of accounts every six months. It is at that time that they reveal to the world the progress (or not!) they have made, as reflected in the financial statements. In contrast, in the US, companies are required to report results every three months. The level of accountability and openness that the stricter US reporting requirement brings is something we strongly believe should happen here in the UK. A 6-month period is a long time for a part owner in a business to go without knowing exactly how it is performing. You wouldn't run your own family business that way. Although there are some disadvantages involved, such as additional paperwork for the companies themselves, we believe a quarterly reporting requirement would be a positive step in favour of the shareholder and introduce our slogan to that effect here:

"More than twice a year!"

We'll be working on the "More than twice a year!" campaign in the years to come, but in the meantime back to the balance sheet. It shows assets – reflecting what the business *owns* – and liabilities – reflecting what it *owes*. It is a snapshot of a company's underlying financial situation, with everything reflected, including cash, motor vehicles, property, computers, the fax machine and that annoying little executive toy the boss has on his desk and won't stop playing with. Let's take a detailed look at what each of these categories means.

Assets

Assets are things a company owns, and on which a value can be placed. The second part of that sentence is important. An office goods supplier still stocking abacuses should know that they are now worthless, and therefore should not be carried as a company asset.

Assets are sub-divided into three categories – intangible, fixed and current assets. The first is the most vague, and we won't spend too much time on it. Intangible means 'not susceptible to touch'. An example of an intangible asset is a company's brand name. You know *The Times* newspaper brand name is worth some money to its owners, but you can't actually touch it. The same goes for Orange, the mobile phone company. That brand name is worth a lot of money to the company, but you can't actually touch it. In the case of Orange, you won't find any value assigned to that brand in its balance sheet, because it is an internally generated, as opposed to acquired, brand name.

The most common form of intangible asset is called goodwill. It arises when one company acquires another, and in doing so pays a price that exceeds its fair value as reflected by its assets minus liabilities. Mostly that represents the value of its brands, trade marks and often its customer base. Again, goodwill is something that can't be touched, is very subjective, and can't easily be identified and sold.

Confused? We won't delve any further into the seedy world of intangible assets, suffice to say that you should know they exist, and that they are a special type of asset which is sometimes found on the balance sheet when one company takes over another.

Fixed assets are held and used by the company in the ordinary course of business. They are typically bigger and more expensive items, with relatively long working lives. They are not easily and quickly converted into cash, should the need arise. Examples are land and buildings, plant and machinery, office furniture, motor vehicles and computer equipment. As you'll see later on in this workbook, we like companies with relatively few heavy, or fixed assets, since asset-heavy businesses usually require large investments for relatively low percentage profit returns. Companies with a lean business structure, and therefore fewer resources tied up in fixed assets, often have an operational advantage over their rivals. This is one of the reasons why the UK support services sector (companies like recruitment agencies, couriers and management consultancies) is more highly rated, and growing more quickly than its manufacturing sector counterpart.

A TYPICAL BALANCE SHEET

TANGIBLE FIXED ASSETS

Freehold land & buildings

Motor Vehicles

Plant & Equipment

Fixtures & Fittings

Current assets are those that can be turned into cash relatively quickly, usually within a year, but often much quicker. They include such things

as cash at the bank, other short term investments, stock awaiting sale and money owed by customers (debtors). They are the heart and soul of a company, for without current assets a company would be grovelling to its bank manager for funding. That said, it is not efficient to have *too* much money tied up in things like stock and debtors. Getting the correct balance is something that constantly vexes the minds of finance directors across the country and is something we'll be looking at a bit later.

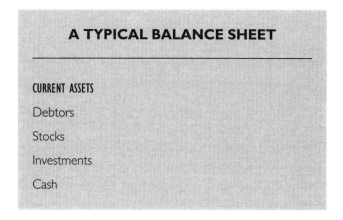

A TYPICAL BALANCE SHEET

CURRENT ASSETS

Debtors

Stocks

Investments

Cash

Liabilities

Liabilities are the opposite of assets. Instead of owning them, you owe them.

Current liabilities are those items that you have to pay within the next 12 months. If you purchase your raw materials on credit, you will have to pay your supplier within 30 days. This will be shown up as trade creditors, or accounts payable. Relating it to yourself, if you purchase goods on a credit card, you usually have at least 20 days before you have to pay that bill or else you get charged interest on it. These are goods you've received but not yet paid for. As you can imagine, a high creditor balance is not at all the end of the world, in fact it's a good thing because a company can generate profits by selling goods that they haven't yet paid for. Companies that buy on credit and sell for cash are often amongst the best out there.

Other current liabilities include bank overdraft, and deferred income. Most companies run bank overdrafts, because they can make higher returns on their money than it actually costs them to borrow. If you can borrow money for 8 per cent and get a return of 15 per cent, you're going to be quids-in to the tune of 7 per cent. People who buy investment properties hope to rent them out and cover the cost of the mortgage and other (not immaterial) items like upkeep. If they've got money left over at the end, and a property that is appreciating in price, they are on to a winner. (Warning – this is not a fail-safe method of making money. The property market is very fickle, depending a lot, as we know on location, location, location and you need to do a lot of research before taking your first steps towards becoming a property magnate.) Deferred income occurs when a customer pays you up front for goods and services which refer to a period in the future. Long term maintenance contracts are a good example.

A TYPICAL BALANCE SHEET

CURRENT LIABILITIES

Bank loans & overdraft

Trade creditors

Deferred income

Taxes owed

Proposed dividend

After current liabilities, not surprisingly you'll find that we've got *non-current liabilities*.

The bulk of this category is usually made up of long-term debt, which is essentially money you've borrowed but must pay back further down the track. A mortgage is a long-term debt.

The balance sheet is a snapshot on one particular day (the last day of the company's financial year) of the company's assets and liabilities. To sum up, in the top section we have assets – intangible, fixed and current – and beneath that we have short- and long-term liabilities, otherwise known as current and non-current liabilities. Got that? Now it's test time.

Circle each item's asset or liability class

1. Cash at bank
   a. current assets
   b. current liabilities
   c. fixed assets
   d. non-current liabilities
2. Accounts payable by you to your suppliers
   a. current assets
   b. current liabilities
   c. fixed assets
   d. non-current liabilities
3. Stocks awaiting sale
   a. current assets
   b. current liabilities
   c. fixed assets
   d. non-current liabilities
4. The company helicopter (The directors need to arrive at Goodwood in style. They have standards to keep up!)
   a. current assets
   b. current liabilities
   c. fixed assets
   d. non-current liabilities
5. £20 million owed to Bank of London over the next 12 years
   a. current assets

b. current liabilities

c. fixed assets

d. non-current liabilities

6. Outstanding bills owed to you within the next 30 days

   a. current assets

   b. current liabilities

   c. fixed assets

   d. non-current liabilities

7. The company's owned office block

   a. current assets

   b. current liabilities

   c. fixed assets

   d. non-current liabilities

Answers: 1, a. 2, b. 3, a. 4, c. 5, d. 6, a. 7, c.

Dead easy, hey? And just think that not so long ago you thought a balance sheet was something invented by accountants to confuse you and millions of others. Shame on you, Fool! Quite the contrary – it's all rather logical really.

BALANCE SHEET-OLOGY

Now that you understand the basics of the balance sheet, perhaps you want to know what to do with it? There are seemingly a million ratios that can be calculated, each telling you something, but frustratingly not everything, about a company. We're going to concentrate on a couple of important things which we think are key to your analysis of a balance sheet.

1. Comparing the entries from last year to this year

2. Studying the relationship between assets and liabilities

The first is relatively straightforward, but often ignored by the financial media, not to mention the odd company analyst or fifty. Knowing a number in isolation is no good if you have nothing to compare it to. Is a company growing its profits, but not collecting the cash promptly from its customers? Are stock levels rising, indicating that goods are not selling? Does the company need to borrow more and more money to keep growing? Is the company delaying paying its bills, using that extended credit period to its advantage? All these factors can point to a deteriorating, growing, or efficient business, therefore giving you a very good clue as to its progress from year to year.

On the second point, it can be relatively easy to see what sort of a business you're looking at by looking at the relationship between a company's assets and its liabilities. As we shall see, this doesn't just mean a company which has lots of assets compared to its liabilities is a good company. It's more an issue of how well a company is *managing* its assets and liabilities. In running a business, these things don't just happen by accident. Much planning goes into maximizing a company's resources, and that means knowing what you can and can't do with your balance sheet. The balance sheet also tells us how light or heavy a company's operating model is. In other words, if a company can create £100 of profit for every £500 of assets, that is surely better than £100 profit on £5000 of assets.

The best way to show this in action is to use a real life example, and there's nothing more real life than e-Meringue.com, the fast growing Internet company specializing in the home de-livery of meringues of all flavours and varieties.[1] Meringues, we're sure you agree, are set to be a

------

[1]Believe this and you'll believe anything.

key factor in the growth of our economy going forward.

Note: The numbers below look relatively small, especially given that e-Meringue is a major industry player in the cakes and confectionery sector. However, they are given in thousands, so you need to add three zeros to ascertain the proper figure. For example, "8000" stands for "8,000,000" because 8000 x 1000 = 8,000,000. Most larger companies use a similar protocol.

E-MERINGUE BALANCE SHEET AS AT 31 DECEMBER 2010 VERSUS 31 DECEMBER 2009

(In £,000)			
ASSETS	2009	2010	CHANGE
Fixed Assets			
Property & Equipment	8,000	11,000	+38%
Less accumulated depreciation	1,000	1,300	+30%
Total fixed assets	7,000	9,700	+39%
Current Assets			
Cash at bank and in hand	2,000	1,300	-35%
Stocks	5,000	9,000	+80%
Debtors	3,000	4,000	+33%
Total current assets	10,000	14,300	+43%
Total assets	17,000	24,000	+41%

Let's just pause there and take a look at a few things.

1. Cash at bank and in hand. Yikes. The company has seen its balances fall by 35 per cent. This surely can't be a good thing, although we can't be entirely sure until we look at the other side (liabilities) of the balance sheet. At the moment, this is a black mark against the company. It looks like e-Meringue is spending more cash than it is generating, and that can be a bad sign.

2. Stocks have shot up 80 per cent. Double yikes. Again, on the surface, this is not good news. The ideal scenario is for a company to have very little in the way of stocks. This is because finished goods cost a lot of money to make and then store, and whilst they are sitting in storage, they are not earning the company any money. In the case of meringues, we're also talking about a perishable asset, as they won't last too long in the company's refrigerators. Not good. However, before completely dismissing the company, we will have to find out a little bit more about them, things which aren't evident from the balance sheet and which may help explain why stock levels have built up so rapidly. The balance sheet is dated 31 December 2010, but what we didn't know is that on 2 January 2011, e-Meringue is scheduled to deliver £500,000 worth of goods to the Annual Meringue Lovers Conference in Brighton (it's quite an affair and it is amazing what some people do with meringues . . .). The balance sheet is only a snapshot in time, and is a constantly moving beast. Finally, stock growth should be compared to sales growth. A company which is growing its sales fast will often see a corresponding rise in its stock levels. However, falling sales and rising stock levels would not be a good sign.

3. Debtors, or accounts receivable – money owed to e-Meringue — have increased by a third. This is again not the best of news for our fledgling company. Rising debtors mean

that a company may be logging significant sales before receiving the cash for them. Although that is normal business practice, ideally you want your customers to be paying up front for their goods. This is especially so in the cut-throat meringue business, where you are selling fast-perishing goods. One possible explanation is that in order to sell the meringues, the company had to offer very generous credit terms. This is a poor use of the company's resources, because they've already incurred the costs of making the goods, yet haven't got any cash for them in return. What if e-Meringue had to sell their goods quickly, and did so to a customer with a less than impressive credit record? When a company has debtors, there's always a chance that those customers won't pay. It is much more desirable to have the cash in your bank account than to have to worry about collecting it at a later date. You will find that accounts receivable growth should generally increase in line with sales growth, so again you need to look at the balance sheet in conjunction with the profit and loss statement, which comes a little later.

On the surface, e-Meringue is potentially looking at three strikes on the asset side of their balance sheet. However, these numbers should never be taken in isolation. As you'll see later on, e-Meringue's sales grew by 20 per cent, and that puts some context on the movement of the company's assets. At the moment, our walk through e-Meringue's balance sheet is not looking too promising, but we'll give them the benefit of the doubt as we move forward to look at what the company owes, or its liabilities.

E-MERINGUE BALANCE SHEET AS AT 31 DECEMBER 2010 VERSUS 31 DECEMBER 2009

(In £,000)

LIABILITIES	2009	2010	CHANGE
Current Liabilities			
Trade creditors	3,000	3,500	+17%
Accrued expenses	1,000	2,100	+110%
Total Current Liabilities	4,000	5,600	+40%
Long-term debt	0	0	0%

Believe it or not, things are looking a little more promising on the liabilities side of the company's balance sheet. You may think that an increase in the amounts of money a company owes is a bad thing, but in fact it's the opposite, providing the company knows what it is doing.

Let's delve a little deeper.

1. Trade creditors represent the money that e-Meringue owes its suppliers, otherwise known as its accounts payables. Providing they have the resources to ultimately pay these suppliers, a 17 per cent increase can actually be seen as a positive sign. e-Meringue has £14.3m worth of current assets and just £5.6m of current liabilities, so in theory payment should be no problem at all. But, given the sales growth, which we already know was 20 per cent, the percentage increase in trade creditors could actually have been even higher if the company had actively and aggressively managed its accounts payable. If it had held off paying those customers, it could have kept hold of the cash

and used it for its own purposes. When you buy some goods on credit, you are essentially getting an interest-free loan. The longer you take to pay back that loan, the longer you have access to free money. If, in the meantime, you should also collect all your receivables in a timely manner, you're in very good shape. Let's put this whole paragraph and a couple of the ones before it very simply: 'The Fool who holds the cash is King.'

2. Meanwhile, accrued expenses have been having their own little party, rising *110 per cent* in the process. This category of liability refers to expenses a company has already incurred, but not yet paid out in cash. One example is where you pay your employees on the 5th of each month for their previous month's work. As at 31 December 2010, the company deducts that expense from its profits (it has already been incurred) despite not yet having paid for it. The liability, or amount owed, is shown in accrued expenses. When 5 January finally arrives, the cash is paid to the employees, but the amount is not deducted from the 2011 profits, because the work done referred to the previous year. Another example is the batch of eggs you received in mid-December, but for which your supplier, Eggs Galore, has yet to invoice you. You reflect that coming liability, or amount owed, in your balance sheet under accrued expenses. Like trade creditors, you'd rather see these rising than falling, because in most cases you are again putting off cash payment for expenses already incurred. Accrued expenses can be a bit of a black hole into which accountants can stuff all sorts of items, usually loosely called 'provisions'. Then, quite legitimately, they can manipulate the numbers in order to, for example, smooth out profit growth over the ensuing years. However, we won't get ourselves too worried about this now, because if some dodgy accounting is going on, we should find out about it later, when we look at the cash flow statement.

Top 5 Accounting Tricks.

1. Booking sales before they are actually sales – i.e. when a customer orders a product as opposed to when it is delivered. Sometimes orders don't materialize into sales.

2. Driving a lorry full of product out of your sales depot at 11.59 pm on 31 December and going for a 2-minute drive around the block, before returning to the depot with a fully laden lorry. The sale is booked in one financial year, artificially boosting that year's profits, but the return is booked in the next. No cash has changed hands.

3. Changing the company's depreciation policy, which has the effect of increasing profits in Year 1 at the expense of later years. Cash balances are not affected.

4. Transferring an item of expenditure to current assets from the profit and loss statement. The cost of a current asset is written off over a number of years, whilst an item in the profit and loss statements is written off in the year it is bought. Current year profits can therefore be boosted at the expense of later years. Cash balances are not affected.

5. Provision accounting, for example where a company announces a restructure. The full cost of that restructure will be accounted for in Year 1, but the cash spent will occur over a few years. The temptation is for companies to make big provisions in Year 1, so that they've got more than enough to cover the future costs of the

restructuring. As the years go by, a company can rather spuriously charge items against that provision, and therefore effectively manipulate future years' profits.

Balance Sheet Thoughts

Having looked at the comparison between the assets and liabilities of e-Meringue between 2009 and 2010, what are you thinking so far about the company's financial position? List your thoughts out under positive, negative and frankly baffled:

Positive points

_____

_____

_____

Negative points

_____

_____

_____

Frankly Baffled

_____

_____

_____

If your thoughts fell mostly into the 'frankly baffled' category, that's entirely understandable. At this point, take a break, kick yourself twice, dunk your head in a bowl of cold water and come back a little later feeling refreshed. If you're online, the investment workbook message board is also there for your questions and queries.

Even if you haven't written anything down, this simple exercise may have got you thinking about e-Meringue's business[2] and if you're like me, your gut feeling at this stage is that there are a few too many negative factors for your liking. Falling cash and rising stocks and debtors are the main areas of concern. These are warning lights, and they are flashing 'buyer beware' right into your eyes. You may think this is the best business idea in the world, but if management doesn't run a tight enough ship, eventually something will give. It could be that whilst you love their meringues, other customers have found them not to be up to scratch, and have been defecting to a competitor. That could explain the build-up of stocks. A little detective work can save you a lot of money further down the track. Why not pop down the shops and purchase an e-Meringue meringue now?

Before we move off the balance sheet, let's look at a couple of other items which can help you assess the health (or not) of a company.

Working Capital

This is another of those terms named so to confuse us. If you think literally about it, working capital could mean all sorts of things. What is capital, and how do you calculate it, and why is it working?

Let's scrap the term 'working capital' and Foolishly call it 'net liquid assets'. Before we go into the definition, let's look at how it is

---

[2]What, you say, when you're finished, you're going to pass this workbook on to the rest of your family and you don't want to give them a head start by filling in all the answers? Bravo! A noble aspiration. But may we gently suggest instead – and without an ounce of self-interest, mind – that you do fill in the gaps and purchase another 15 copies of this book for your kith and kin?

calculated. Start with current assets, then deduct current liabilities.

That's it. Dead simple.

The result is what's left over after you take all the current money you owe (current liabilities) from all the current money you're owed (current assets). If you were forced to pay all your bills right now, net liquid assets tells you firstly whether you'd be able to do it, and, if you are, how much cash you'd have left over. Net liquid assets is the same as the net worth (presuming you have no fixed assets or long-term debt) we calculated back when we did our own personal balance sheets in Chapter 3.

Let's work out how much working capital, or net liquid assets, e-Meringue has at the end of 2010.

WORKING CAPITAL

Current assets   _____

Less current liabilities   _____

Equals working capital   _____

Did you get £14,300,000 less £5,600,000 = £8,700,000? Of course you did.

Now, what to do with this thing called net liquid assets? It makes logical sense that the higher the net liquid assets number the better, and that is generally true. However, it is not always the case. Some companies run very effectively with negative net liquid assets. What the . . . ? How could that be, when by some counts they are effectively unable to pay all their bills? The answer is tied up in the fact that not all current assets are good current assets.

We saw previously that increasing debtor and stock levels are usually a bad sign. This is the case at e-Meringue. Neither of these are quite as liquid as one might hope. If customers aren't buying a company's stocks, they can't be easily and quickly turned into cash. No-one wants them, right? If your debtors either can't, or refuse, to pay you, you're also not going to be able to turn that into cash in a hurry. The same goes on the liabilities side, only this time the odds are stacked in your favour. If you want to delay paying somebody until the absolute last day your bill is due, you can do that. The bottom line is that cash is the only true liquid asset. Again, cash is King.

In the case of e-Meringue, the working capital figure is something to keep an eye on, although on the positive side it has increased from last year. Of more importance is the actual bank balance, which now makes up less than 10 per cent of the company's current assets. That doesn't leave much room for manoeuvre, and could easily see e-Meringue taking its begging bowl to the local bank manager. We all know how difficult and fraught that experience can be!

THE FOOLISH FLOW RATIO

We've had 'cash is King' a couple of times now. How about . . .

Stocks are super.

Doesn't have that same ring about it, does it? In fact, as we've seen above, high stock levels are distinctly un-super.

Stocks are stupid. That's more like it. As for debtors? Are they dandy or dangerous? This is too easy.

Here at Fool Balance Sheet Laboratories, a ratio has been devised to give you a fix on how well a company manages its non-cash resources, masterminded by Tom Gardner, co-founder of the Motley Fool. Its aim in life is to give you a measure as to how well a company is managing the pound notes that flow through its business. We're interested in non-cash items, because cash, yet again, is King. On the asset side, we're not worried too much about how companies manage the cash portion of their current assets, as long as they are not blowing it by speculating on the horses or penny shares. On the liabilities side, we deduct short-term debt from current liabilities, because companies have to pay interest on that debt, and therefore it is costing them money. We want to find out their *non-interest bearing current liabilities* – effectively the interest-free loans that suppliers and staff have made to the company.

We ultimately want to know how well, or not, a company is managing its non-cash liquid net assets. If that sounds daunting, rest assured that it's not that difficult a concept to firstly calculate, then understand. Like all things Foolish, it's plain common sense.

Enter the *Foolish Flow Ratio*, known to its groupies and devotees – and there are many – as the 'flowie'. It is calculated as:

> Current assets less cash ÷ current liabilities less short term debt.

Go ahead, try it. (The numbers you need, of course, are listed on previous pages.) You're about to calculate the flowie for e-Meringue and enjoy it, which makes you . . . a Fool:

(_____ – _____) ÷ (_____ – _____) = _____

You'll find the workings at the bottom of the page[3].

Now you want to know what that flow ratio actually means, don't you? Before we tell you, we're going to give you the chance to tell us. We'll make it easy.

Which is better? A higher or lower flow ratio?

a. High
b. Low

Hands up those who circled (b). Well done to all of you. I bet you were the ones at school who always volunteered to do the French translation, while slackers like me used to hide in the back corner, head bowed. How stupid I thought all teachers were. Now I know who was the stupid one!

Here's the logic behind liking low flow ratios:

Non-cash current assets are bad. Boo! Hiss! We hate 'em. Remember, that's because non-cash current assets consist mostly of:

_____

_____

Exactly right, stocks and debtors. Therefore, we want the top part of the equation, or the numerator, to be as low as possible. In the case of e-Meringue, suppose that instead of £4m worth of unpaid debtors these debts had already been collected and the money was sitting pretty in your bank account. Then, the flow ratio would have been:

---

[3]E-Meringue's flowie is: (£14.3m – £1.3m) ÷ (£5.6m – £0) = 2.32

(£14.3m – £5.3m) ÷ (£5.6m – £0) = 1.61

If this were the case, the company would clearly be managing its assets better, as reflected in a lower Flow ratio.

Now to the other side of the equation, the denominator. Is it better to have higher or lower current liabilities? You got it – providing a company is not in dire financial straits, the higher its current liabilities the better.

Which is the denominator?

Many many years ago, I still recall being taught by my primary school teacher how to remember which number, in fractional terms, is the numerator and which is the denominator. The 'd', being the letter the word denominator starts with, also is the first letter of the word 'down'. And, the denominator is always down, or below the numerator. Thanks, Mrs Charles, and may you rest in peace.

Taking our most recent example one step further, let's assume that e-Meringue was able to delay £2.5m of its accounts payables, to put off the hounds just a little longer. Their bank balance would increase by that amount, because that money hadn't been paid, and their accounts payable would also increase by that amount, as they would still represent an outstanding debt. This is an ideal scenario, which not surprisingly is reflected in an even lower flowie.

(£16.8m – £8.5m) ÷ (£8.1m – 0) = 1.02

As you can see, the lower the flow ratio, the better. In fact, the closer the flow ratio is to 1, or even less, the better. Truly great companies have low flow ratios, which succinctly sum up their competitive and financial strengths. Great companies can demand cash from their customers, whilst delaying paying their creditors. That means they have low levels of debtors. Ideally they will also have low stock levels, combined with high creditors. This scenario is the closest we'll see to a pure cash-generating machine. These companies really are the ones eating the spinach.

Summing up, the very best companies have:

1. Plenty of cash
2. Low debtor and stock levels – these are assets that are not working for the company, not earning them any interest, and potentially worth less than they appear to be on the balance sheet.
3. High accounts payables – this is money that is working for you, because it is essentially an interest free loan from your suppliers.

Let's take a look at the flow ratios of some selected UK companies – many of them household names – and do a little practising along the way. Before we dive in, remember that the flow ratio is not the be-all and end-all of balance sheet analysis. There's been many a company that has had a low flow ratio, yet has seen its growth flounder. However, it is often a good indication of a company that is doing the right things, and has its eye on the all-important balance sheet. Accounting profits are one thing, but if they are not cash profits, they are often illusory profits. Cash profits show up in the balance sheet, and ultimately in the flow ratio.

PRACTICE FLOW RATIOS

(in £000,000)

COMPANY	CASH	CURRENT ASSETS	CURRENT ASSETS LESS CASH	CURRENT LIABILITIES	S-TERM DEBT	CURRENT LIABILITIES LESS DEBT	FLOW RATIO
Glaxo Wellcome	1,857	5,509	3,652	4,145	1,317	2,828	1.29
BT	3,380	7,534	4,154	8,029	947	7,082	0.59
Unilever	7,329	15,435	8,106	12,688	1,641	11,047	0.73
Vodafone	6	792	786	1,530	377	1,153	0.68
Marks & Spencer	486	3,356	2,870	2,030	913	1,117	2.57
Misys	29	153	124	174	9	165	a._____
Sage	36	79	43	65	8	57	b._____
National Express	94	240	146	274	12	262	c._____
Orange	40	445	405	435	31	d._____	1.00
Rentokil Initial	180	817	637	906	132	e._____	f._____
PizzaExpress	5	16	11	40	16	24	g._____

Answers are at the foot of the page[4]

Based on the above, name one company that you'd be reluctant to invest in:

_____

I chose Marks & Spencer. How about you? This doesn't necessarily mean M&S are doomed, but it is something to keep an eye on. Glaxo Wellcome's flowie is also a little on the high side. In the coming years, you ideally want to see that falling.

_____

[4](a) 0.75, (b) 0.75, (c) 0.56, (d) £404 million, (e) £774 million, (f) 0.82, (g) 0.46

Shareholder's Equity

Have you noticed something missing from our balance sheet?
We've got:

Total Assets	£24,000,000
and	
Total Liabilities	(£5,600,000)

Our balance sheet doesn't balance! There's £18,400,000 unaccounted for.
Enter shareholder's equity, stage left.
As well as being the mysterious balancing item, it is also, as the name implies, the amount

that shareholders of the company have a claim upon. If e-Meringue was to be closed down right now, they would sell all their assets and pay all their debts, and the left-over money would be distributed to shareholders. This is also sometimes referred to as 'book value'. We'll come on to that when we look at some valuation techniques.

Shareholder's equity is also used to calculate ratios such as gearing (or debt-to-equity) and return on equity (ROE). Both are important and both of which we go on to look at later on. If a company has lots of debt in relation to its shareholder's equity, it's generally not in a financially strong position. In the case of e-Meringue, it is debt free, so this is not an issue. ROE is a favourite of Warren Buffett, the most successful stock market investor of all time, who places great emphasis on this ratio. In his 1996 letter to shareholders of Berkshire Hathaway, the company he chairs, he wrote, 'We did not consider the market to be overvalued *if* 1) interest rates remained where they were or fell, and 2) American business continued to earn the remarkable **returns on equity** that it had recently recorded.'[5]

Just before we leave ROE, be aware that that pesky mongrel known as 'purchased goodwill' can throw a spanner into the works of this number. It can mean a thriving company can have a balance sheet that shows negative shareholders' equity. It can also throw all sorts of spanners into gearing and ROE calculations. We'll tackle this little problem further down the book.

---

[5]You'll find all his recent letters to shareholders at the Berkshire Hathaway web site: **www.berkshire-hathaway.com**. They make excellent reading.

PROFIT AND LOSS STATEMENT

Unlike most City folks, we Foolishly began our walk through a company's financial statements by looking at the balance sheet. We believe it is too often ignored, and sometimes misunderstood, even by the pin-striped Wise, whose job it is to know these things. The balance sheet just isn't sexy for many people. We're not talking an evening with Tom Cruise or Elizabeth Hurley when we're talking balance sheet, we're talking tea with Ann Widdicombe or the Archbishop of Canterbury. Illuminating, yes, uplifting even, but definitely not sexy.

Twice every year, publicly quoted companies are required to report on their progress to the London Stock Exchange, and more importantly to their owners – the shareholders. The profit and loss statement is the thing that everyone usually focuses on, because that's where analysts can quickly and easily see how much the company has earned over the previous twelve months. They can also work out the company's growth rate by comparing last year's profits to this year's. The analysis of the profit and loss statement can take all of . . . er . . . would you believe five minutes?

City analysts spend much of their time trying to calculate how much money a company will make in a given period. In the short term, these earnings estimates are usually used as the basis for valuing companies, so therefore hold great importance for those people with relatively short-term investment horizons. By short term, we Fools mean anything less than three years, and maybe even five or more years. In the City, one year is often seen as being a long time. That's where we differ, and it's also the reason why the individual investor – that's you, Fool – has an advantage over the City Wise folks.

In the days leading up to a company's reporting date, the share price often jumps all over the place, as rumours of better than expected and worse than expected results circulate round the City wine bars. Then, when they are finally released, a huge flurry of trading usually occurs as analysts race each other to give the numbers the thumbs-up (or down). Quite simply, if the company beats earnings estimates, and is optimistic about future progress, the shares will rise, and vice versa. However, the longer-term investor, with their Foolish five-year time horizon, will take their time to assess the results, all the time thinking about where their company is headed over the next half decade, not the next five minutes. How very Foolish!

'Not all shareholders are created equal.' Oh yeah? Sez who?!

In theory, no-one is allowed to buy or sell a share on the stock market if they are in possession of information which might move the share price if it were widely known. That would give that person an unfair advantage, is known as insider dealing and is illegal. However, large companies regularly give private briefings to City analysts or brokers. The following is an extract from the Motley Fool's *Independent on Sunday* column from 8 April 1999 and shows what happened to the prices of three companies in the wake of such briefings:

'On Monday of this week, shares in Great Universal Stores fell 28p to close at 690p. This followed private meetings the company had with two brokers, CSFB and Cazenove, whom they saw fit to inform of a deterioration in the mail order side of the business. The two brokers cut their profit forecasts as a result.

'On Tuesday, shares in EMAP fell 62p to 1220p. Early on in the day, the shares had fallen as low as 1190p, a fall of over 7%. This followed private discussions the company had with a series of brokers, including BT Alex. Brown, Merrill Lynch, Morgan Stanley and SBC Warburg, which resulted in trimming of profit forecasts by the brokers.

'On Wednesday, Compass Group soared, closing up 19p at 717p after it was up as high as 740p earlier in the day. Again, this followed private meetings with brokers in which Compass Group was upbeat about its like-for-like sales and profits (a key indicator of financial health).'

In all these instances the brokers following the companies received price-sensitive information which might have allowed them to make trades to the benefit of their clients before that information was widely known. This means that the clients of these brokers – no doubt mostly large institutions – could have had the drop on the private investor, who by late Wednesday of that week had not had any of this news officially confirmed by the companies in question. Individual shareholders – that's you and us – are left wondering what is happening as the share prices of their companies move for no apparent reason.

This is wrong. Dead wrong. It has to change and the Motley Fool will help make that happen. In the US, a company, Xilinx, refused to allow the Motley Fool to participate in a brokers' conference call in which the company's situation was being discussed and then broadcast the transcript on the Web. This refusal, along with the company's fax number and email address was published on the Motley Fool web site and within a very short time the deluge of protests was such that they relented. One small reversal in a massive current, but the harbinger of a major shift in power in favour of the ordinary person.

Although I've seemingly binned it as a short

term measure of a company's progress, the profit and loss statement is far more important than that. You can learn a lot about a company from its income statement, even if you know nothing whatsoever about what it does. You can also use it to spot trends – not only whether the company is growing its profits, but *how* it is growing them.

Come in, e-Meringue . . .

E-MERINGUE PROFIT AND LOSS STATEMENT AS AT 31 DECEMBER 2010

(In £,000)

	2009	2010	CHANGE
Turnover	40,000	48,000	20%
Cost of sales	-24,000	-29,500	23%
Gross Profit	16,000	18,500	16%
Sales & Marketing	-6,000	-8,000	33%
Admin	-4,000	-4,500	13%
R&D	-1000	-200	-80%
Operating Profit	5,000	5,800	16%
Interest income	100	50	-50%
Profit Before Tax	5,100	5,850	15%
Taxes	-1,500	-1,800	20%
Net profit	3,600	4,050	13%
Shares outstanding	10,000	11,000	10%
EPS	0.36	0.37	2%

Let's have a look at what some of these terms and changes mean.

Turnover and Cost of Sales

Turnover is a fancy word for 'sales', and is sometimes also referred to as 'revenues'. It stands proud as punch at the top of the profit and loss account, and rightly so. That is why it is often referred to as the 'top line'. In most cases, a company with no sales won't be a company for too much longer.[6] Sales are what make a company tick. As your own company's sales force will often tell you, without them, no-one else has got a job. In fact, let the bloke from sales into the lift first: his work is more important than yours. And while you're at it, butter his toast and shine his shoes.

Now we've got that straight, let's see how e-Meringue is faring. In the year ended 31 December 2010, they generated £48m worth of sales, which was up 20 per cent over the previous year. That's not bad going, especially when you consider the economy is growing in the low single digit range. They must have something going for them if they can outgrow the economy. Smaller companies, such as e-Meringue, can often grow fast in their formative years. Hopefully they've latched on to a great new idea, and can grow very quickly, albeit from a small base. In other words, we'll give e-Meringue a big fat thumbs-up for sales growth. Now let's see how much their sales are costing them.

Cost of sales is the actual cost of producing the product for sale. It will include things like the cost of materials used, wages of staff employed in producing the product, depreciation of machinery used to make the product, and the cost of running the factory where the product is being made.

---

[6]Biotechnology companies with a huge cash pile to spend on research and development, and with no marketable products as yet, are an exception here. But, they ultimately still have to have sales to survive, because if not, the cash pile will eventually run out.

The £48 million sales that e-Meringue have made are just one part of the profit equation. Say that each product was retailing for £4.80. That means they've sold 10,000,000 of these juicy, fluffy meringues (I told you they were nice!). If I then said that each meringue cost the company just 20p to manufacture, what would that tell you about the company? I know what I'd be doing – I'd be logging straight on to the Internet and buying some shares in this wonder company. Well, not quite, because there are a few more things I'd need to know about them, but at the very least I'd suspect I *might* be looking at a wonderful company whose stellar growth was going to fund my retirement much earlier than I'd otherwise planned. On the other hand, if each meringue was selling for £2.00, but cost the company £2.60 to make, what would that tell you? Not pretty.

As we can see from their profit and loss statement, although sales rose by 20 per cent in 2010, e-Meringue's *cost* of sales rose by 23 per cent. It is costing them more to manufacture each meringue in 2010 than it did in 2009. There could be a very good reason for this, but usually this is not a positive sign.

BONG! . . . *Sound of single, slow church bell, signifying something melancholy may be about to happen in poor quality 1930s film . . .* BONG! . . .

Let's go on and see how bad it really is. We're going to look at some ways of assessing just how much profit the company is actually making, known, not surprisingly, as its profitability.

E-MERINGUE PROFIT AND LOSS STATEMENT AS AT 31 DECEMBER 2010

(in £,000)

	2009	2010	CHANGE
Turnover	40,000	48,000	20%
Cost of sales	-24,000	-29,500	23%
Gross Profit	16,000	18,500	16%

Gross Profit and Gross Margins

Gross profit refers to the amount of money a company has made from its sales after the costs of producing them have been deducted. In 2009, on sales of £40m, e-Meringue made a gross profit of £16m. Can you see a ratio coming? It's the gross margin, and is calculated as gross profit divided by turnover. You can do this. You're about to calculate another ratio.

GROSS PROFIT MARGIN

$$\frac{\text{Gross Profit} \quad £_____}{\text{Turnover (sales)} \quad £_____} = _____ = _____ \text{ or } _____\%[7]$$

OK, gross profit increased by 16 per cent from 2009 to 2010. This is quite a good performance and if you were judging a company by that measure alone, you might think you are on to a winner. However, when you look at the gross

---

[7] £16m ÷ £40m = 0.40 or 40%

margins for both the years, you might start to think a little differently. In 2010, the e-Meringue gross margin was:

£_____ ÷ £_____ = ____ or ____%[8]

Yep, that's right, 38.5 per cent, down from 40 per cent in 2009. That means they are making less profit on their sales in 2010 than they were in 2009 – generally not a good sign. The question is, why did it deteriorate? It could have been because a competitor started a price war and hence the company has had to cut the price it sells each meringue for. Perhaps it was because the price of raw materials has increased – a mysterious chicken virus has killed off half the nation's chickens and so the price of eggs has risen – or perhaps a new and expensive piece of machinery was required in order to ramp up the speed of manufacturing. An increase in the cost of manufacturing and/or raw materials, or a cut in the selling price will do it, but there can also be many other reasons too.

As with all financial ratios, there's no correct answer as to what is the best or optimum gross margin. It very much varies from industry to industry. Software companies traditionally have very high gross margins, because once you've developed the product, the cost of actually producing it is relatively small and if you distribute it over the Internet, that cost effectively becomes zero. On the other hand, manufacturing and engineering companies usually have lower gross margins, because of all the kit that is required to make the products. Think about it: a copy of Microsoft Word on a CD-ROM and a portable colour TV cost about the same to buy. However, discounting all development costs, which costs

more to produce? The telly, by miles.

Generally, the higher the gross margin, the better. Anything above 50 per cent is very good going. But always remember to compare it to other companies who operate in the same sector.

Operating Expenses & Operating Margins

E-MERINGUE PROFIT AND LOSS STATEMENT AS AT 31 DECEMBER 2010

(in £,000)

	2009	2010	CHANGE
Turnover	40,000	48,000	20%
Cost of sales	-24,000	-29,500	23%
Gross Profit	16,000	18,500	16%
Sales & marketing	-6,000	-8,000	33%
Admin	-4,000	-4,500	13%
R&D	-1000	-200	-80%
Operating Profit	5,000	5,800	16%

Moving on down the income statement, we get to what are known as the operating expenses. After the goods are manufactured (cost of sales), they need to be sold. Also, products don't just get manufactured. They have to be developed.

Let's lump *sales, marketing and administration* expenses into one category. It include things like salaries, stationery, office equipment, telephones, office rent, electricity, advertising and marketing. It also includes the cost of those overhead departments such as personnel, legal and finance. These are an essential part of any company. Basically these costs refer to anything that is not involved in actually making or preparing

----

[8] £18.5m ÷ £48m = 0.385 or 38.5%

a company's products for sale. As we can see for e-Meringue, sales and marketing costs have risen by a whopping 33 per cent from 2009 to 2010. When you compare that to sales growth of just 20 per cent, you can see that there are some potential worries here for our company. Ideally, you want to see sales and marketing costs falling as a proportion of sales. Of course, there could be a very good reason for this rise, such as a mega marketing campaign, for which the company hopes to see positive results in the early part of 2011, but this definitely merits further investigation.

Think of *research and development* expenses and you think of manic professors with wild hair, thick, tortoise shell glasses, and long white coats; a bit like David Berger, actually. They spend their day playing with test tubes and Bunsen burners, hoping like mad that they don't burn down the lab. After years of trying, when they finally discover a new concoction, you should see them hop around! Or was that just them setting fire to their coats?

Just about every company, if it wants to stay ahead of the game, and the competition, needs to spend some money on R&D. It's not just confined to pharmaceutical companies or software outfits. A different and innovative flavour meringue will first require formulating and in-house testing, then external testing. If three people out of ten turn purple with yellow spots, you know it's back to the drawing board. Some companies, in the face of declining growth, will be tempted to cut back on what many see as this discretionary expense. However, they will almost certainly be robbing Peter to pay Paul. The chances are that this decision will come back to haunt them in future years when they fall behind their competitors who are innovating as they stand still. Today's R&D expenditure is tomorrow's future. As we can see, e-Meringue

have actually chopped back their R&D spend in 2010. For the short term boost to profits it gives them, they may regret that decision, come 2015.

We're now getting a fair way down the income statement. (Was that a 'Thank Heaven!' coming from the back of the class? Out, Jenkins minor, **OUT!**) Starting with sales, we've deducted the cost of those sales, the overhead costs – sales, marketing and administration – and finally research and development costs. The resultant number is a company's operating profit – also known as profit before interest and taxes, shortened to PBIT, and from that we calculate its operating margin. No, that's wrong. *We* don't calculate it, *you* calculate it:

E-MERINGUE PROFIT AND LOSS STATEMENT AS AT 31 DECEMBER 2010

(in £,000)

	2009	2010	CHANGE
Turnover	40,000	48,000	20%
Operating Profit	5,000	5,800	16%

OPERATING MARGIN

Operating Profit
―――――――――
Turnover (sales)

2009: £_____ £_____ = ____ or ____%[9]
2010: £_____ £_____ = ____ or ____%[10]

―――――――――

[9]2009: £5m ÷ £40m = 0.125 or 12.5%
[10]2010: £5.8m ÷ £48m = 0.121 or 12.1%

This is too easy. Did you also calculate, on your own accord, that the operating margin fell by 3.3 per cent? You'll have this stuff licked in no time.

Just like the gross margin, e-Meringue's operating margin is falling, which means that for every pound of sales, the company is making less operating profit than it was in 2009. Good or bad? Presumably, bad. But while this is generally seen as a negative, the specific situation needs to be studied. If e-Meringue were building market share through sales discounts to customers, or increased advertising spend, the short-term impact on profits won't matter so much, providing they can benefit from these tactics in the future. Loss-making Internet and telecommunications companies are doing just this – forgoing current profitability as they continue to build their infrastructure and customer base.

What's a good operating margin? Again, it depends on the industry. Supermarkets run on operating margins of about 5.5 per cent, whilst pharmaceutical companies achieve operating margins of about 25 per cent and above. Companies with high operating margins usually have a high barrier to entry. In other words, if you or I wanted to start an international pharmaceutical company to challenge Glaxo Wellcome, we'd need a few hundred million quid, a database of information and a few thousand bright, talented, dedicated people. However, finding a company with high profit margins will not necessarily lead you to the Promised Land. Efficiently run companies – meaning they keep an eye on their balance sheet – can be very successful, even if they have razor-thin operating margins. Their pricing policy and efficiency are their barrier to entry. A low cost producer which sells its goods at the lowest price is very difficult to beat.

If Meringues Turn Sour

Have you spotted the main difference between cost of sales (part of the gross margin) and operating costs (part of the operating margin)? The first category is usually made up of relatively fixed costs. No matter if you are making one meringue or one million meringues, you still need a very large bakery to produce them. If things turn sour in the meringue market, these fixed costs are very difficult to pare back. On the other hand, operating costs are more variable. You can curtail your marketing or R&D programme tomorrow, at very little cost. When hard times befall a company, the less fixed costs (i.e. the higher the gross margin) the better.

Net Profit Margins

We're nearly at the bottom of the profit and loss statement. If you've got gross and operating margins mastered, this one's pretty easy.

E-MERINGUE PROFIT AND LOSS STATEMENT AS AT 31 DECEMBER 2010

(in £,000)	2009	2010	CHANGE
Turnover	40,000	48,000	20%
Operating Profit	5,000	5,800	16%
Interest income	100	50	-50%
Profit Before Tax	5,100	5,850	15%
Taxes	-1,500	-1,800	20%
Net profit	3,600	4,050	13%

Let's run through what we've got. *Interest income* is the amount of money the company has earned from the cash balance sitting in their bank account. Any company that runs on a bank overdraft will have an interest expense rather than interest income, and this will reduce profits. After that is added or deducted from operating profits, the resultant number is called profit before tax (PBT), and you will often hear this term bandied about in City bars, at cocktail parties, and at the occasional analyst meeting. (If you ever get into one of these, please let us know.)

Finally, not wanting to be left out of the action, the Inland Revenue comes along and takes its piece of the pie. The taxman is everywhere. The UK corporate tax rate currently stands at just 30 per cent, but if a company has some overseas earnings, this rate will vary depending on the local tax laws. As far as corporate tax rates go, the UK has one of the most generous – in favour of companies, that is – regimes in the world.

The end result, or the bottom line, as it is often known, is the net profit. This is also known as profit attributable to shareholders, since they are the owners of the company. This is the amount that can be either distributed to shareholders by means of a dividend payment, or retained in the business for future growth, or a combination of both. UK companies tend to distribute part as a dividend, and retain part of their net profits. Many dynamic US companies, including the phenomenally successful Microsoft, don't pay dividends, preferring to keep the profits within the business, using them to fuel future growth, a strategy which has more than paid off.

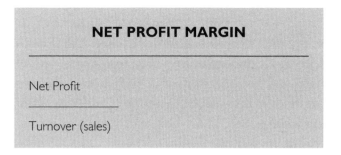

NET PROFIT MARGIN

Net Profit

Turnover (sales)

Here we go again. What's e-Meringue's net margin?

2009: £_____ ÷ £_____ = ____ or ____%[11]
2010: £_____ ÷ £_____ = ____ or ____%[12]

Again, the net margin looks to be going in the wrong direction, because ideally you want to see a company that is eking out better returns for each pound of sales. However, as we've been going down the profit and loss statement, looking at the erosion of first the gross, and then the operating margin, it is hardly surprising that the net margin has also fallen. It's often a slippery slope as we slide down the profit and loss statement.

Companies that can consistently increase their profit margin are usually amongst the best out there. From 1994 to 1998, PizzaExpress have seen their net profit margins rise from an already high 13.8 per cent to 18.1 per cent, and in the same time period the share price has grown from 110p to 857p. That's the equivalent of 67 per cent compounding share price growth per annum – just a bit better than the rates the building society has on offer! Whether they have the brand, expertise and know-how to keep rolling out the PizzaExpress formula across the world as they have in the UK remains to be seen. However, to date they've done a pretty fine job.

---

[11]2009: £3,600 ÷ £40,000 = 0.09 or 9%
[12]2010: £4,050 ÷ £48,000 = 0.084 or 8.4%

What's a good profit margin? Guess what? It really depends on the industry. Just like it does with gross and operating margins. There are no hard and fast rules or quick routes to success in the company analysis game. But, a little knowledge and know-how can take you a long way down that winding road.

Earnings Per Share

This is the little number that usually gets the City chaps really excited, and, in most cases, rightly so. If you run your own small business and make a profit of £10,000 in a year, as the only shareholder, you can do what you like with this money. If you were one of two equal shareholders, you'd get a smaller piece of the pie, half to be precise. When it comes to publicly quoted companies, there are usually many thousands of different shareholders, and many more thousands of shares in issue.

Enter *earnings per share*, or EPS.

EARNINGS PER SHARE

Net Profit

—————————

Shares In Issue

As you can see, the number of shares in issue has increased from 10 million to 11 million in the course of the year. This could have happened for a variety of reasons. One of the most common is that companies issue new shares to employees, under a stock option scheme, and this is reflected in a higher number of shares. Another is that companies sometimes issue shares as payment,

---

E-MERINGUE PROFIT AND LOSS STATEMENT AS AT 31 DECEMBER 2010

(In £,000)

	2009	2010	CHANGE
Net profit	3,600	4,050	13%
Shares in issue	10,000	11,000	10%
EPS*	0.36	0.37	2.3%

*Net profit and shares in issue are in thousands, while earnings per share (EPS) is always an absolute amount. Dividing net profit by the shares in issue gives you the EPS.

---

instead of cash, when buying another company. Sometimes, although this is rare for a UK company, the number of shares in issue actually falls, as the company uses some of its cash resources to buy back its own shares, and then retire them. This has the effect of reducing the shares outstanding, and all else being equal, boosting the EPS number.

Buying Back Your Own Shares

Why would a company buy back its own shares? It does seem a somewhat bizarre concept, but there is method to this madness. The company themselves are always looking for the best place to allocate their precious cash. If they see value in their own shares, it makes sense to buy them, using the same rationale that an individual investor uses. Once bought back, the shares are retired, just like a washed up footballer or cricketer, never to be seen in an annual report again. *All things else being equal*, and that part of the equation is very important, this has the effect of increasing a company's earnings per share, because the denominator in that calculation has fallen. And, since most company's are valued by the stock exchange on a multiple of their EPS, the higher that number, the higher the share price rises, or so the theory goes.

---

e-Meringue have increased their shares outstanding by 10 per cent. That means that there are a greater number of shares in issue, and therefore over which the net profit is spread. In effect, the issue of 1 million more shares has diluted the value of the 10m shares in issue in 2009. This is reflected in the EPS percentage increase between the two years of just 2.3 per cent, compared to a net profit increase of 12.5%.

As we've moved down the income statement, the year-on-year trends we've been seeing haven't exactly filled us with joy. Apart from a 20 per cent sales increase, things seem to have deteriorated from there. This is ultimately reflected in the rather miserly 2.3 per cent increase in EPS. As we've said all the way through, there could very well be some justifiable reasons for this deterioration. The company could deliberately be building itself a stronger long-term business by investing now in things like brand name, marketing, advertising, R&D (although we know they're not spending on this particular item), market share and acquisitions. You only find that out by following the company's progress, be that in the written portion of their annual report, through the press or by actually speaking to representatives at the company. The bottom line is that the numbers can only tell you so much about a company.

And that is the bottom line to the profit and loss section. Now, it's time for a little quiz. Sharpen your pencil for the e-Meringue 2011 *Blankety Blank* Challenge!

Fill in the missing numbers:

E-MERINGUE PROFIT AND LOSS STATEMENT AS AT 31 DECEMBER 2011

(In £,000)

	2011
Turnover	55,000
Cost of sales	-34,000
Gross Profit	___
Sales & Marketing	-9,000
Admin	-4,700
R&D	-500
Operating Profit	6,800
Interest income	20
Profit Before Tax	6,820
Taxes	-2,100
Net profit	
Shares outstanding	11,000
Gross Margin	___
Operating Margin	___
Net Profit Margin	___
EPS	___

Did e-Meringue have a good 2011?

a. It was better than 2010, that's for sure.
b. It was lousy – when are they going to get their act together?
c. Not bad – but the still falling gross profit margin worries me.
d. I can't tell – I need to see their balance sheet and cash flow statement.

Answers – Gross Profit: £21m. Net Profit: £4.72m. Gross Margin: 38.2%. Operating Margin: 12.4%

Net Profit Margin: 8.6%. EPS: 0.43 (d) but if you chose (a) or (c), give yourself half a point.

STATEMENT OF CASH FLOWS

Don't fall asleep now, dear Fool. This final statement is an integral part of a company's accounts, and like the balance sheet and profit and loss, is very important. On their own, the three accounting statements don't mean an awful lot – they should always be read in conjunction with each other. Where the cash flow statement differs from the other two is that it is fact – the balance sheet and income statements have an element of subjective opinion in their make-up. Cash, however, is cash is cash. The bank balance never lies, but your accountant can.

(Accountants are nice people, really, and very truthful. Like any profession, there's the very occasional bad egg. Here's a big Foolish wave to all accountants out there.)

This is an abridged version of a cash flow statement. The whole thing, which includes such delightful items as 'contingent consideration transferred to other loans' (it's true – this comes from the accounts of a real company) is unbearably long and complicated. We'll touch on them very briefly at the end of this little section.

Profit and loss statement earnings and cash flow earnings are not the same. In 2010, e-Meringue saw operating profits of £5.8 million translated into net cash from operations of just £2.7 million. Something look and feel a little fishy? The difference is down to a number of things and let's go through the cash flow statement, item by item, to see why.

E-MERINGUE ABBREVIATED CASH FLOW STATEMENT AS AT 31 DECEMBER 2010

(In £,000)

	2009	2010	CHANGE
Operating profit	5,000	5,800	16.0%
Depreciation	250	300	20.0%
Working capital changes			
(increase) in stocks	-2,000	-4,000	100.0%
(increase) in debtors	-500	-1,000	100.0%
increase in accounts payable	1,000	500	-50.0%
(decrease)/increase in accruals	-500	1,100	-320.0%
Net cash from operations	3,250	2,700	-16.9%

Operating Profit

That's easy. It's the same amount as taken from the profit and loss statement we looked at earlier. Why start with operating profit rather than net profit? That's a debate for Speaker's Corner on a Sunday morning.

Depreciation

Even though I gave them a boost earlier, accountants do often make things difficult for us. They want us to live in a world where, in any given period, income and expenditure are perfectly matched. One of the ways they do that is through this feature called depreciation. If a company goes out and buys a new company car today for £10,000, they have to pay for it now. That money therefore leaves the bank account.

However, that company car is going to last more than just one year. Unless you assign it to one of your more junior employees, one who's recently been convicted for joy riding or ram raiding (has anyone ever told you your personnel selection skills could be improved?), that car should last for at least four years. Because of that, the accountants show it as a fixed asset – remember back to the balance sheet – and then depreciate that asset over its estimated useful working life.

Depreciation is therefore a non-cash charge. The actual cash payment for the car shows up at the bottom of the cash flow statement as capital expenditure, and also reduces the bank account balance. Since depreciation is a value loss, rather than a cash loss, it is added back on to operating profits. The cash flow statement is tracking the flow of *actual* cash. In 2010, we therefore add back the £300,000 of depreciation that was deducted from operating profits in the profit and loss statement.

Got that? Read it again, slowly, if you haven't. If on the second reading, you still only have a glimmer, then press on and come back to it later.

Working Capital Changes

You already know what working capital means, don't you? Flick back to page 105 if you want to give yourself a little refresher course. If you don't want to do that because you're one of those people who's always looking forward and can't wait to finish this book, my saying 'net liquid assets' might jog your memory.

First cab off the rank is an *increase in stocks* of £4 million. Remember we said that higher stock levels were a no-no? Looking at how this is reflected in the cash flow statement reinforces that statement. Money makes the world go round, and surely the higher the cash generated from operations the better. If a company is building up its stock levels, this is a cash expense, and is therefore shown in the cash flow statement as a negative. This is exactly what's happening to e-Meringue. If, on the other hand, stock levels were on the decline, the cash change in working capital would be positive. When searching for potential companies to invest in, what you're looking for is a company with lower stock levels, providing it can still meet sales demand. The ideal scenario is a company which can buy raw materials on credit, sell for cash, and after they've got the cash, make and deliver the product to order. Know any companies with that business model? US personal computer maker Dell Computer Corporation comes pretty close, and that's one of the reasons it's been one of the best performing shares this decade.

Next down the list is *increase in debtors*, or accounts receivable. What underlies these is similar to what underlies stock levels. The less money owed to you the better, which fits with the ideal 'sell for cash' business model. e-Meringue has seen debtors rise. They have booked those sales in their profit and loss statement, but haven't yet received the cash. Therefore, it's not difficult to deduce that this increase in debtors has to be deducted from operating profits when we calculate the movement in cash.

Then we move on to the other side of the balance sheet, and see how changes in liabilities affect the cash flow statement. Can you see how finally all these statements are interlinking? Everything here is related.

Time for a little teaser test.

Without using a calculator, what is the square root of 212? To make things easier, please give your answer to the nearest 2 decimal points.[13]

---

[13]Answer – 14.56

OK, that one was a joke, just to keep you on your toes. Here's the real test.

What's generally better? An increase or decrease in *accounts payable*?

a. Increase
b. Decrease
c. The Great Wall of China

Answer – (a) Those who circled (c) aren't really taking this seriously enough, are you?

Accounts payable are effectively a company's interest-free loans, and therefore you are looking to maximise them. e-Meringue have increased their accounts payable by £500,000, and that is therefore added to operating profit as we calculate how much cash those profits have generated.

The same goes for *accruals*. They refer to benefits – be they goods or services – that a company has received, but not yet paid for. They show up as an expense on the profit and loss statement, and an accrual in the balance sheet. No cash has changed hands, as yet, so an increase in accruals is added on to accounting operating profits. Got that? An example is where, on 30 December 2010, you receive a batch of eggs, but Eggs Benedict PLC fails to invoice you until after your accounting year end. Benefit received. Not yet paid for. 'Dis is good.

Getting the drift? Operating profits are accounting profits, and the cash flow statement then looks at the relationship between profits and the actual cash the business generates.

Net cash from operations

Having started with operating profit – taken straight from the profit and loss statement – added back depreciation and then made the necessary adjustment for working capital changes, we finally get to the elusive *net cash from operations*. This tells us how much cash the company generated in the course of the year from their operating activities.

E-MERINGUE ABBREVIATED CASH FLOW STATEMENT AS AT 31 DECEMBER 2010

(In £,000)	2009	2010	CHANGE
Operating profit	5,000	5,800	16.0%
Net cash from operations	3,500	2,700	-40.0%

As we can see, although e-Meringue's operating profit rose, its cash generation actually fell. Also, cash profits were significantly less than operating profits. Some of the better companies actually monitor the *cash conversion ratio*, aiming to convert at least 100 per cent of their accounting profits into cash.

CASH CONVERSION RATIO

$$\frac{\text{Net Cash From Operations}}{\text{Operating Profit}} = \frac{2,700}{5,800} = 0.47 \text{ or } 47\%$$

This should get the alarm bells ringing, if they weren't already trilling away inside your head. Not only has e-Meringue's net cash from operations fallen in 2010, but their cash conversion ratio is diabolical. Companies can get away with this for a little while, but over the long term, they will eventually be found out. We already saw the warning signs when we went through the balance sheet – rising stocks and debtors, and a falling bank balance.

In any one given year, there can be a very good reason as to why a company is not converting all its profits into cash. A big order placed on 29 December will be added to sales, although the cash has not yet been received for those sales. Come January 29, if you could peer into the company's internal accounts, you'd most likely see that cash safely tucked away in the bank account. Companies that consistently have a cash conversion ratio of less than 80 per cent, however, should be treated with caution. Remember earlier in this chapter where we said that you may be able to flush out any instances of dodgy accounting by looking at the cash flow statement? A company with a cash conversion ratio of less than 80 per cent ought to be treated with caution. For example, are those increases in debtors *real* sales, and will the money ever be collected?

e-Meringue – we've got our eye on you!

Cash flow – The Conclusion

Our look at the cash flow statement is going to end with net cash from operations. However, you should be aware that there are a couple more sections to go before you get to the very bottom line – increase or decrease in cash in the year. They are:

- *Returns on investments and servicing of finance* – to you and me that means interest income and/or interest payments on any loans we have.
- *Taxes paid*
- *Capital expenditure* – the cash paid to buy new motor cars, or machinery, or shops.
- *Acquisitions and disposals*
- *Dividends paid*
- *Financing* – cash received from new shares issued, and movement in bank loans.

All these items are important, because they affect a company's overall cash position. A company may have a cash conversion ratio of 120 per cent, but if they are already massively in debt, the interest expense may push them further into debt, and ultimately kill them. A company which needs to continually update and maintain its plant and machinery, whilst sales are stagnant, will see its capital expenditure chewing into its cash from operations. A company not generating cash after interest, taxes and essential capital expenditure won't have any money left to grow the business or pay a dividend to shareholders.

Gearing

Gearing, or leverage as it is known in the US, is a way of measuring a company's level of debt in comparison to total shareholder's funds. It is usually calculated as

$$\text{Gearing} = \frac{\text{Debt}}{\text{Shareholder's Equity}}$$

The answer is expressed as a percentage. For example, a company with debt of £30 million and shareholder's equity of £110 million would have gearing of 27 per cent. Some companies are very highly geared, some have negative gearing, because they have net cash balances. Ideally you want a company with relatively low gearing, and one that can easily afford to pay off its interest charges every month. We've got a measure for that, called interest cover, which we'll spring on you in the next chapter.

And that's it. When you think about it, all this cash flow stuff is quite simple: a company generating oodles of the stuff is going to knock spots off a company which is seeing its bank balance quickly diminishing.

WHAT HAVE I LEARNT FROM THE NUMBERS?

Just think – not too long ago you probably thought annual reports were useful as door stoppers, and not much else. Now you know differently. As we've glided our way through the balance sheet, then the profit and loss statement and finally on to the cash flow statement, you've learnt:

- how to calculate the gross margin, and what it can indicate about a business
- how to spot a dodgy accountant
- why increasing stock levels are a bad sign
- why companies should have high levels of accounts payable
- how a company with sales increasing by 20 per cent can show EPS growth of only 2 per cent
- how to calculate the flow ratio
- why Marks & Spencer had a poor 1998/99
- about the importance of the cash conversion ratio
- why a company with falling R&D spend is potentially boosting today's profits at the expense of tomorrow's growth
- that David Berger is a mad scientist (the accountant's revenge!)

But the fun doesn't stop here. With a bit of practice, you'll soon be able to pick up an annual report, flick through the three key accounting statements, and quickly make an initial judgement about a company's financials. It takes legendary investor Warren Buffett usually less than ten minutes to decide whether he's interested in buying a business. If you picked up an annual report, skipped straight to the cash flow statement, and saw the company had a cash conversion ratio of 60 per cent last year and 50

per cent the year before, the chances are that report will soon be making a visit to the paper recycling bin.

To some potential investors, all this stuff may seem a bit deep and unmeaningful. However, what you've learnt here will take you a long way along the road to successful individual company investing. We're guessing that you're chomping at the bit, and can't wait to get hold of the latest annual report for Vodafone Airtouch, Sage, Glaxo Wellcome or BT – all great long-term performers. You'll also come across your fair share of dogs, too, but at least now you'll be able to recognise companies with squalid accounts in advance of buying their shares.

We're about to move on and you need a break, so choose any of:

a) Take a deep breath
b) Pump some iron down at the gym
c) Pour a large alcoholic drink
d) Pour a large non-alcoholic drink
e) Phone up your best friend and wow them with your knowledge about gross margins
f) Phone up your best friend and weep piteously down the phone

You can pick more than one of these options and indeed repeat individual options too. When we tested this chapter out on various people, we found many repeating (c) several times and then moving straight to (f). Others just chose (f). Both groups found the process quite helpful.

When you come back, we'll be looking at what we'd *like* to see in the numbers.

CHAPTER 9

What Do You Want To See In The Numbers?

As yet a child, not yet a Fool to fame,
I lisped in numbers, for the numbers came.
Alexander Pope

Having read this far, your mission, should you choose to accept it, is not only to match the returns of the stock market, but to beat them. As you start to build a portfolio for the next ten and twenty years, you'll be wanting to try and identify some great individual companies. You know they exist, and you've so far heard or read about plenty of them. Now is the time to put the theory into action, and go hunting for them. Here, we're going to run through some of the criteria we look for when searching for the superb businesses of today and tomorrow. There's nothing very earth-shattering. It's all just simple common sense.

The first part of this chapter will cover the more quantitative aspects of a good company. These are criteria on which you can actually hang some numbers. The second part of the chapter is much more qualitative. Not concentrating so much on the numbers, it helps you identify the winning companies of today and tomorrow. Some overlap is inevitable, but only because you want market-leading, brand-led companies to also

have perfect financial statements. Do those companies exist? Maybe . . .

THE IDEAL BALANCE SHEET

Having spent the last chapter dissecting the three financial statements, this section should be relatively straightforward. Before we jump into the numbers, it is worth remembering that there's no perfect company. Just like humans, they all have their faults. Speaking of which, here comes our friend, e-Meringue again, along with its balance sheet. Have a look through it again, as we'll be using it as the basis for this section.

E-MERINGUE BALANCE SHEET AS AT 31 DECEMBER 2010 VERSUS 31 DECEMBER 2009

(In £,000)			
ASSETS	2009	2010	CHANGE
Fixed Assets			
Property and Equipment	8,000	11,000	+38%
Less accumulated depreciation	1,000	1,300	+30%
Total fixed assets	7,000	9,700	+39%
Current Assets			
Cash at bank and in hand	2,000	1,300	-35%
Stocks	5,000	9,000	+80%
Debtors	3,000	4,000	+33%
Total current assets	10,000	14,300	+43%
Total assets	17,000	24,000	+41%
LIABILITIES			
Current Liabilities			
Trade creditors	3,000	3,500	+17%
Accrued expenses	1,000	2,100	+110%
Total Current Liabilities	4,000	5,600	+40%
Long-term debt	0	0	0%

Now, what are we after . . .

1. Loads of Cash and Little or No Debt

Again, money makes the world go round. A company with lots of cash in the bank can –

a. invest in new business ventures

b. make timely acquisitions
c. pay off debt
d. pay generous dividends to shareholders

Companies in debt are a completely different kettle of fish. In extreme situations they will struggle to even pay the monthly interest bill on their bank loan. They may have to tap shareholders for more funds just to stay in business. That is not a pleasant prospect. The bottom line is that a cash-rich company with plenty of growth opportunities beats its cash strapped counterpart every time – hands down.

e-Meringue has £1.3 million cash and no long-term debt. That's good. The downward trend in the cash balance is something to keep an eye on, though.

2. Low Stock Levels

Next time you go into the supermarket, forget about tea-bags and toilet paper for a minute. Instead, focus on the amount of stock on the shelves and the number of people in the check-out queue. Although the number of customers in the supermarket is irrelevant to this chapter, it may help you decide whether you want to consider investing in the company, further down the track.

Look at all those tins of baked beans. They are taking up a lot of space. The supermarket doesn't earn a shilling on them until someone buys them. It has probably already paid Mr Heinz or Mrs No-Label for their cans, but has yet to sell them, and therefore turn a profit on those cans of beans as they sit on the shelf. Look at the mushrooms. Are they getting browner and browner? Tonight the supermarket will have to toss them on the compost heap if they haven't sold them before their sell-by date. That's lost revenue for the supermarket.

High stock levels are bad because -

a. while money is tied up in stocks, it's costing the company, through lost interest
b. storing the stocks costs money
c. stocks can deteriorate, become obsolete, or go out of fashion (baked beans excluded – they live forever!)

There are a few ratios you can calculate when analysing a company's stock levels. The most generally used is stocks/turnover.

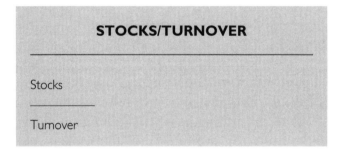

STOCKS/TURNOVER

Stocks
_____
Turnover

Over to you again, Fool. What's e-Meringue's stocks/turnover ratio in 2010?

2010: £_____ ÷ £48,000 = _____ or _____ %[1]

Companies which make large and complex goods – an aircraft manufacturer, for example – have much higher stocks/turnover ratios than a service company, which carries very little in the way of stocks. All things being equal, the lower the stocks/turnover ratio, the better. With a stocks/turnover ratio of 19 per cent, e-Meringue is on the high side, especially given that its stocks are perishable goods.

What we're basically looking for is a

_____

[1] 2010: £9,000 ÷ £48,000 = 0.1875 or 19%

company that has lots of sales and very little in the way of stocks. Have you ever wondered why companies in the support services and software and computer services sectors have massively outperformed the traditional construction, engineering and manufacturing companies? One of the reasons is that the former companies have much lower stock levels. This frees up resources so that they may pursue further growth opportunities. Always remember to compare a company's percentage stock levels with its industry peers when making an assessment as to their stock management. Not all heavy equipment companies are poor long-term investments.

3. *Low Trade Debtors or Accounts Receivable*

You may think it's fine if people owe you money. It may even give you a false sense of security. You think to yourself, 'I'll just buy this new Porsche, and stick it on the credit card. I'll be able to pay it off in the next month, when my friend Bob pays up for that £100,000 bet I won. He should never have offered me 10,000 to 1 on QPR winning the football Premier League title before 2002.'

Now, we all know that

a. QPR will never win the Premier League title, and
b. Bob will never be able to pay his debt, and
c. you're far too Foolish to buy a new Porsche.

(If you're a QPR fan, and wish to disagree with (a), please do so! Post a note on *The Motley Fool UK Investment Workbook* message board at the web site.)

A decent company will hopefully not be

relying on Bob stumping up £100,000 in order to pay off their outrageous debts. But, from this example you can see that high debtors are not what you want to see on a company's balance sheet. You are effectively giving an interest free loan to a third party. Now that's not an efficient use of your cash resources, is it?

The most popular and useful ratio to calculate how efficiently a company is managing its debtors is the days sales outstanding (DSO).

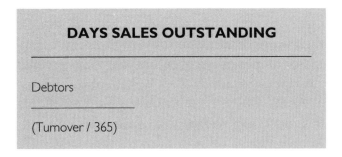

DAYS SALES OUTSTANDING

Debtors
————————
(Turnover / 365)

This takes the current debtors' balance and divides it by the average sales per day. For e-Meringue in 2010

$$DSO = \frac{£_____}{(£48,000/365)} = \frac{£_____}{_____} = \_\_\_\_\_ days^2$$

Most companies give and accept 30 day credit terms. That means you give your customers 30 days to pay you, and you pay your suppliers within 30 days. A DSO of 30.4 days is spot-on for e-Meringue.

The higher the number of debtor days outstanding, the more chance there is of

a. never collecting the money, forcing the

initial sale to be written off as a bad debt

b. creative accounting artificially boosting sales

c. customers having their shelves stuffed with the company's goods, and therefore delaying new orders

Having read this far and now being somewhat of an expert in days sales outstanding, guess how many debtor days outstanding your local corner shop has, and whether that number is good or bad.

DSO: _____
Good / Bad

How did you go? I estimated they have about five days' sales outstanding. Every time I go into the shop, unless I hand over some cash, I don't get my milk and paper. There's no credit for me. They may give credit to some of their regular and reliable customers, but although I'm sure I'd fall into that category, I would be in the definite minority. A company with just five days outstanding is usually a very good one.

4. High Trade Creditors or Accounts Payable

Imagine you were foolish (note the small 'f') enough to lose £100,000 to Bob, rather than the other way around. Presuming you were fully intending to pay your debt – because if you weren't you should never have made the bet in the first place – it's in your best interests to delay paying for as long as humanly possible. That way, you're either still earning interest yourself on the £100,000 you already have, or you're delaying

————————
[2]$DSO = \dfrac{£4,000}{(£48,000/365)} = \dfrac{£4,000}{131.5} = 30.4 \text{ days}$

paying the interest charges your bank will inevitably whack you with when you borrow the money from them. Before paying that debt – how could you be so stupid! – it would show up as an account payable on your personal balance sheet.

Guess what's coming next? Yep, we've got another ratio, this time to analyse accounts payable.

DAYS IN PAYABLES

Trade Creditors

(Cost Of Goods Sold / 365)

Cost of goods sold is a good indicator of the cost of goods purchased during the year. As most of those purchases will be (or at least should be) made on credit, the correlation between trade creditors and cost of sales is a fair one to make.

For e-Meringue;

$$2010 \text{ Payable Days} = \pounds_____ \quad \pounds_____$$
$$\frac{\qquad\qquad}{(\pounds29,500/365)} = \frac{\qquad\qquad}{\qquad\qquad} = \_\_ \text{ days}^3$$

As with trade debtors, most companies give and receive 30 day credit terms. Presuming you got the above equation correct – of course you did – this means that e-Meringue is paying its debts within 43 days of them being incurred. Companies that can legitimately stretch their payable days above 30 are managing their cash resources well. On the other hand, if you see a company that takes 60 days to collect its debts but pays them within 20 days, steer well clear.

As far as e-Meringue is concerned, days sales outstanding of 30 and days in payables of 43 is reasonably good going. Effectively, some of their creditors are funding part of the business.

5. A Low Foolish Flow Ratio

If you thought the above ratios were a bit too complex, or even dare we say a little boring, the Foolish flow ratio conveniently pulls together the salient numbers of a balance sheet. Like all ratios, it has its flaws, and should be used in conjunction with other ratios and analysis, but it easily and conveniently gives you a quick fix on how well (or not) a company is managing the pound notes that flow through its business.

Do you remember the formula? The flow ratio takes current assets, deducts cash balances, and then divides that figure by current liabilities less short-term debt. The lower the ratio the better – it usually means that a company has low debtors and stocks, and high accounts payable and accruals. You preferably want to see companies with a flow ratio of under 1, although there are always exceptions to the rule.

You did this one before, but what the heck, you can never get tired of doing the Flowie. In 2010, e-Meringue's Flowie is;

$$\text{Flow Ratio} = \frac{\pounds_____ - \pounds_____}{\pounds_____ - \pounds_____} = _____^4$$

$$^3 2010 \text{ Payable Days} = \frac{\pounds3,500}{(\pounds29,500/365)} = \frac{\pounds3,500}{80.8} = 43.3 \text{ days}$$

$$^4 \text{Flow Ratio} = \frac{\pounds14,300 - \pounds1,300}{\pounds5,600 - 0} = 2.32$$

What does this tell you about e-Meringue? A high flow ratio means the company is not managing its balance sheet very well. Very high levels of stocks and accounts receivable in relation to its accounts payable and accruals is not a good sign. Remember that things can go wrong with stocks and accounts receivable – there's a chance that stocks will depreciate or perish before they are sold, and that some of your debtors will eventually not pay their dues. It happens all the time. Bigger companies, courtesy purely of their size, usually have lower flow ratios than smaller companies. This is because they usually have strong buying power, and can dictate payment terms and conditions to their suppliers. This inevitably means their suppliers, generally smaller companies, get squeezed, which shows up in a high flow ratio for them.

We don't actively encourage big companies to squeeze their smaller counterparts. We think all companies of all sizes should pay their bills on time, and within the payment terms. Despite that, we've all dealt with companies that don't send their own bills (known as invoices) out on time, therefore automatically delaying the customer payment process. The quicker a company sends out its bill, the quicker it gets paid. Have you ever known there to be a delay in BT sending your phone bill to you? It has never happened to me, and if I don't pay it on time, they send me a nasty red letter threatening to cut me off from the outside world. You'll not be surprised to learn that an investment in BT since its initial flotation has rewarded shareholders handsomely.

Are any of the balance sheet rules and ratios hard and fast rules? Not on your Nellie. Some great companies have, at one stage in their evolution, had high days sales outstanding and/or low days in payables. However, this state of affairs cannot go on forever. Something has to give. The most successful companies will improve their balance sheet management, and that will ultimately result in a lower flow ratio. The companies that don't eventually make this transition will never be truly great companies.

THE IDEAL PROFIT AND LOSS STATEMENT

Where's that perfect company? We're still looking, as you are no doubt still looking too. There are plenty of excellent companies out there, and when trawling through the profit and loss statement, here's ideally what you'll want to be searching for.

1. High Turnover Growth

It all starts with the top line. (You getting into the spirit of this? Nonchalantly bandying about phrases like 'top line' and 'bottom line' is high investor chic.) Very few companies can consistently grow profits over a long period of time without generating sales growth. A company with static sales growth can still grow profits – by cutting costs – but ultimately you can only reduce your cost base by so much. After all, you still have to make and distribute your product and/or service.

Many larger companies physically cannot grow their sales very quickly. You don't expect Unilever, with its global 1998 sales of £27 billion, to be able to double that over the next two years. For the larger companies, you therefore want to be looking for sales growth in the region of 8-10 per cent per annum. Smaller companies on the other hand can grow their sales much faster. Trafficmaster grew its top line by 41 per cent in 1998 as it introduced new products, signed new partnership deals, and expanded quickly. Good smaller companies ought to be growing sales at a sustainable rate of between 15 per cent and 25 per cent, but others will obviously be able to grow even faster than that.

2. High Gross Margin

The gross margin gives you an indication of the cost of making the goods or services that the company ultimately sells. A company selling software products and supplying them to its customers on a CD-ROM will have a very high gross margin, perhaps as high as 90 per cent. That's because the cost to produce each of those CD-ROMs is minuscule in relation to the selling price. This is one reason why Microsoft has been one of the best performing shares ever. On the other hand, a shipbuilding company will have a low gross margin, because giant edifices like the *Titanic* cost a fortune to put together. And we're not talking about the movie here, even though that was hardly made on a tight budget! (US$300 million, to be precise.)

As we saw during our run through the profit and loss statement, the gross margin usually sets the scene for the company's net profit margins. If you start off with a low gross margin, there's a good chance you'll end up looking at a company with a low net margin.

Ideally you want to be looking at companies with gross margins of 50 per cent and above, although there aren't many of those about, particularly in Europe. That usually means those entities will have a reasonably 'light' business model, meaning they don't have too much money tied up in expensive factories or machinery – both fixed assets. Companies with low gross margins can sometimes be hit the hardest when things

start to turn a little sour. Many of the costs involved in manufacturing the product are fixed, meaning you can't cut back on them easily and quickly if the need suddenly arises. Closing down factories is not a cheap option, but if the market for ships dries up (you never knew accountants had a sense of humour, did you?), there is no option.

Does all this mean we don't like traditional manufacturing companies, and particularly shipbuilders? Not really, because some companies excel at what they do, and have very little in the way of competition. However, we do have a bias towards companies with lean business models and high gross margins.

3. Operating Margins above 12 per cent, and rising

If a company has a gross margin of 60 per cent, but an operating margin of 5 per cent, you'd want to know what the heck is going on. Perhaps they are spending large amounts on research and development, building for the future. There's nothing wrong with that, as long as they are spending the money on projects with identifiable growth prospects. Or perhaps they are having a huge marketing blitz, with the ultimate aim of building a world-recognisable brand name. On each occasion, operating margins will be on the low side, but hopefully only temporarily so.

A company with a high operating margin usually has some sort of competitive advantage. In the previous chapter we cited drug companies as a classic example. Utility companies also have traditionally enjoyed a competitive advantage, so much so that until very recently many of them were still monopolies. There was once a time in London when telephone, gas, water and electricity services could *only* be bought from BT, British Gas, Thames Water and London Electricity respectively. As a consumer, you had no other option. These days the markets have been opened up, and choices abound.

The very best companies have high operating margins, yet they keep stretching those margins higher as the years go by. That is often seen as a sign of good management, and since good people run good companies, this is something you want to be on the look out for. Companies that increase sales *and* operating margins in tandem are going to see their net profits roaring ahead, and therefore in all likelihood, their share price will follow suit.

Does this mean you should ignore all companies with operating margins below 10 per cent? No way. Some of the best performing companies run on razor-thin margins. Tesco, which has unceremoniously booted J. Sainsbury from the top supermarket slot, has an operating margin of less than 6 per cent, yet it hasn't stopped the share price from more than doubling in the five years from 1994 to 1999. Companies that compete on price alone, rather than product differentials, are often poor long-term performers. But, if at the same time you are the low cost producer of goods, *and* the low cost seller of those goods, you have a very powerful business model.

THE IDEAL CASH FLOW STATEMENT

This one's pretty easy.

1. A cash conversion ratio above 90 per cent.

Remember the old cash conversion ratio? It compares a company's operating profits (as per

the profit and loss statement) with its net cash from operations (as per the cash flow statement).

For those who have already forgotten this vitally important formula (how could you?!), here it is again.

CASH CONVERSION RATIO

Net Cash From Operations

Operating Profit

We like to see this number as high as possible. Some companies, courtesy of their large non-cash depreciation charge, have cash conversion ratios as high as 160 per cent. As far as we're concerned, the higher this number, the better.

There are the very occasional exceptions to this rule. A company may see a seasonal build-up in its stock levels as, for instance, Christmas approaches. Or a large customer may have inadvertently delayed payment by one day, but on the date the accounts were prepared, a large debtors' balance may have somewhat artificially depressed your cash conversion ratio. That situation should be reversed in the following year's accounts. On a rolling 24-month basis you should see a company's total operating profits being at least 80 per cent of its cash from operations.[5]

We all know how important cash is to ourselves, and therefore also to any business. The

---

[5]By 'rolling' we mean if today's date is 31/12/2010, our rolling 24 months would be from 1/1/2009 to 31/12/2010. Next month, our rolling 24 months would be from 1/2/2009 to 31/1/2011.

greater the percentage of profits that translate into cash, the better. That cash can then be used to grow the business and pay dividends to shareholders. No cash, no growth, and no joy.

You've now got a good checklist of things to look for when you look through a set of accounts. You will never find the perfect company, but some get pretty close, albeit that they are in the definite minority. Don't let that put you off, because when you find a great company, you will definitely cherish the moment. The best companies keep going from strength to strength, and this is usually reflected in their financial statements. Although there will be the odd imperfection in a company's accounts, especially when you're following one over many years, as long as you understand what has caused that deterioration and are comfortable that it is only a temporary blip, you shouldn't be overly concerned.

QUIZ: BASIC CONCEPTS

1. Which of the following situations is preferable?

	CASH	LONG-TERM DEBT
a. Eagle's Golfing Gear	£12m	£125m
b. Popper's Parties	£356m	£5.6 billion
c. Davies' Gold	£851m	£230m
d. Air Exile PLC	£650m	£0

2. What is Eagle's Golfing Gear's gross margin, and do you like it?

Turnover	£250m
Cost of Goods Sold	£115m
Gross Profit	£135m
Gross Margin	_____

3. Calculate the Foolish Flow Ratio for Popper's Parties

Cash	£365m
Current Assets	£823m
Current Liabilities	£621m
Short term debt	£421m
Foolish Flow Ratio	_____

4. What's the stock/turnover ratio for Davies' Gold?

Turnover	£1.6 billion
Stocks	£523m
Stock/turnover ratio	_____

5. Would you buy shares in Davies' Gold?

_____

6. When's the last time you bought some underwear in Marks & Spencer?

_____

7. What's Davies' Gold Cash Conversion Ratio?

Turnover	£5.6 billion
Cost of Goods Sold	£2.6 billion
Operating Profit	£500 million
EPS	35.6p
Net Cash From Operations	£235m
Cash Conversion Ratio	_____

8. Calculate Popper's Parties Days Sales Outstanding (DSO)

Debtors	£440m
Turnover	£2.3 billion
DSO	_____

9. What's the turnover growth for Eagle's Golfing Gear?

2009	2010	SALES GROWTH
£250m	£325m	_____ %

10. Who is the person best placed to look after your financial affairs, and future?

_____

Answers
(1) (d). (2) 54% and Yes. (3) 2.29. (4) 33%. (5) Not based on their stocks/turnover ratio, but I'd need more information. I know the boss is a nice person. (6) How the hell would we know!? Give yourself a point if it was in the last 6 months. (7) 47%. (8) 70 – Yikes! (9) 30%. (10) YOU.

Did you get 10 out of 10, Fool? We hope you did. Of course, if you flunked completely, it might be a good idea if you went back through the last couple of chapters to refresh your memory. Perhaps you read them at bedtime, and dropped off into a sleep-induced haze, but yet still managed to keep turning the pages. Or perhaps your little brother has just moved your bookmark.

Just before we move on to the exciting part – identifying winning companies – the following quote from Warren Buffett, taken from his 1996 Chairman's letter to shareholders of Berkshire Hathaway, makes a perfect prelude to the next section. 'Your goal as an investor should simply be to purchase, at a rational price, a part interest in an easily-understandable business whose earnings are virtually certain to be materially higher five, ten and twenty years from now.'

Let's hop to it, Fools.

LOCATING WINNING COMPANIES

Now that you know what an ideal company's financial statements ought to look like, it's time to go about locating winning companies. The following criteria are not the be-all and end-all of share selection, nor indeed will they guarantee to lead you to the Promised Land. But, they will certainly point you in the right direction, and put you firmly ahead of the pack, and many of the City experts. Unlike them, individual investors have got time on their side, so you don't have to rush into any investment opportunity.

Here are some of the criteria you should be looking for in a company.

1. Brand Name

We've already looked at the importance of brand names. If Orange didn't spend a fortune splashing their name around billboards, radio and televisions, how would you know whether they existed? Some brand names are built largely from word of mouth. Have you heard of telephone banking group First Direct? They are now part of the HSBC Group, and the vast majority of their customers have come from word-of-mouth recommendations. That's a special form of marketing, and obviously by far the cheapest. But, no matter how companies do it, the brand name is important.

In this exercise, we're looking for companies with strong brands. The brand may be specific to a particular product, or it may relate to a service. You'll be familiar with most of those listed below, and naturally, since this is a workbook, there's space for you to list your own brands and companies.

A survey in mid-1999 by Interbrand, a company specialising in valuing brands, ranked Barclays and Lloyds as the two most valuable brands in Britain and Ireland. Retailers such as Marks & Spencer and Tesco were also

BRAND	COMPANY
Vodafone	Vodafone Airtouch
BT	BT
St Michael	Marks & Spencer
Reuters	Reuters
Sky	British Sky Broadcasting
BP	BP Amoco
Carling Black Label[6]	_____
Ventolin[7]	_____
Walls[8]	_____
_____	_____
_____	_____

prominent. The survey excluded all non-UK brands, such as Coca-Cola, Kelloggs and Mars. This finding is quite surprising, as financial service companies fare poorly in worldwide brand rankings. This shows that in the UK, unlike other countries, which cover a much bigger land mass, national and historic brand names tend to predominate.

Moving swiftly on . . .

2. The Best in the Business

Great companies usually keep getting better and better. They have the expertise, the brand name, the know-how and the resources to keep improving the business. Note that we are looking for the *best* company, and this is not necessarily the biggest. The problems facing Marks &

---

[6]Bass

[7]Glaxo Wellcome

[8]Unilever

Spencer in 1999, cited in the 1998 *Motley Fool UK Investment Guide* as an obviously great investment, are an example of how the biggest and the best can also get things wrong. Some would argue that M&S had lost that aura of invincibility somewhat before the profit warning which shocked the City in early 1999. Subsequent to that, the management team have been labelled as arrogant, bureaucratic, and worst of all, it was said they'd lost sight of their own customers. The M&S debacle of 1999 may yet turn out to be temporary. The last thing a company loses is its brand name (see point 1).

Are the companies on your list the best in the business? To help you decide, it's a good idea to know who each company's major competitors are. Just like professional sporting teams, who'd never dream of playing against the opposition without knowing their strengths and weaknesses, so you should know which competitors pose the greatest threats to your companies. Taking our list of companies the next step, please list what you consider to be the largest competitor to each business you've identified. We've taken our guesses – see how you compare.

Now go back through your list. Is your left-hand column full of the premier brands? Or are some of their competitors better companies? Or perhaps there are some companies you've not really heard of, or don't fancy. Place a circle around the top brands on your list.

3. Repeat business

How often do you buy a new lounge suite? Or a new car? Not too often, if ever. I for one have never bought a new car, and in fact don't even own one. What that means is that although Ford, Vauxhall and Rover are great brand names, they

BRAND	COMPANY
Vodafone Airtouch	_____[9]
BT	Cable & Wireless
Marks & Spencer	Tesco
Reuters	Bloomberg (privately owned US based company)
BSkyB	_____[10]
Bass	Whitbread
Glaxo Wellcome	_____[11]
BP Amoco	_____[12]
Unilever	Procter & Gamble (US quoted)
_____	_____
_____	_____

are not necessarily great companies or investments. Once you buy a car, you've got it for a long time. Although it is depreciating in value, you can see, use and touch it. Check in your garage now – is the car still there? Yep – there it is. And guess what? You don't have to go out and buy a new car every time you want to use it.

How often do you use your telephone? Do you watch much television? Do you eat much pizza? Do you drink too much wine? Each of these are examples of consumable products. You can make one telephone call, or one hundred telephone calls. Can you remember who you called on 8 April 1999? Probably not, but your telephone company will, and they'll also remember to bill you for those calls. What happened to last week's pizza? It's long gone, and

next week you'll be wanting to eat another pizza. And the glass of wine you've just consumed with your meal? It's gone too.

Consumers return to repeat business companies day after day, month after month, with open wallets. If they've got a great brand name, even better. Now, shorten your list to include those companies you're familiar with, and those whose products you use on a monthly basis.

COMPANY
Vodafone Airtouch
BT
Tesco
BSkyB
Glaxo Wellcome
BP Amoco
Unilever
_____
_____

4. Operating Profit Margins Above 12 per cent

Remember these things? The operating margin is the amount of money a company makes on every £1 of sales, before deducting taxes and any interest payments. We want to be looking at businesses which are generating substantial profits. Although we recognize that some fast-growing companies are currently deliberately losing money as they invest in the infrastructure and the marketing of their business, these are usually higher risk propositions than your steady, large-cap performers. And, although you'd think otherwise if you spent any length of time in City wine bars on a Thursday night, the steady Eddie

[9]Orange

[10]Granada

[11]SmithKline Beecham

[12]Shell

larger (not to be confused with lager) companies are usually the source of great long-term investments.

Why 12 per cent? The average operating margin for FTSE 100 companies is just a smidgen below 14 per cent, so why aren't we looking for companies with operating margins of 15 per cent and above? Well, while a high operating margin is important, it's not the be-all and end-all. Also, many of the better companies have started out with relatively low operating margins, and slowly but surely increased them as they've become more efficient, and therefore more profitable. If you identify these companies early enough, you can ride them higher as the double whammy of rising sales and rising margins really gives a boost to profits.

How do you find out what a company's operating margin is? You can –

a. get hold of the company's annual report, fire up your calculator, and work it out for yourself.
b. ring up the company and ask them. Many of the bigger companies now have investor relations departments, which are there to help you.

Here's what we came up with;

COMPANY	OPERATING MARGIN
Vodafone Airtouch	26.2%
BT	22.5%
~~Tesco~~	~~5.6%~~
BSkyB	23.8%
Glaxo Wellcome	33.9%
~~BP Amoco~~	~~4.4%~~
~~Unilever~~	~~10.6%~~
_____	_____
_____	_____

Oh dear. We've lost three of our companies. Tesco, BP Amoco and Unilever are all solid companies, and have provided shareholders with excellent long-term returns.

Tesco – 11.6% per annum over the last 10 years.
BP Amoco – 15.3% per annum over the last 10 years.
Unilever – 20.6% per annum over the last 10 years.

As is shown by its relatively low operating margins, Tesco operates in a very competitive industry. In fact, the whole retailing sector always has, and always will be, extremely competitive. There are relatively low barriers to entry, and pricing power is minimal.

BP Amoco is the biggest company in the UK, and is capitalised on the stock exchange at a value well in excess of £100 billion. It is a giant of a company, with a world-wide presence, and BP ranks as the 5th most valuable brand of quoted UK companies. But, nevertheless, like most oil companies, it has relatively low operating margins. Drilling for oil, and extracting it from the ground, is an expensive business.

Unilever was featured as an obviously great

investment in the *Motley Fool UK Investment Guide*. With an operating margin of 10.6 per cent, they just fail to make our cut-off point. Does this mean they are no longer a great company? Not at all. In fact, their operating margin has risen steadily over the last four years, and could yet hit 12 per cent in the relatively near future. We're reluctantly discarding them here, because rules are rules, but we're certainly not writing them off.

You'll usually find companies with high operating margins also have a high return on equity. Oh no, not more ratios! Yes, but you'll like this one when you come across it in a number of pages hence. It's actually a terrific way of valuing a company, which of course is the very next chapter. However, suffice to say here that high operating margins and return on equity are both highly desirable qualities.

5. Interest Cover of More than 10

Whoa! What's this one? It's to do with measuring a company's debt, and its ability to pay the interest on that debt. Put simply, it's a measure of how many times a company can cover its interest expense, and the higher that number the better.

INTEREST COVER

Profit Before Tax + Net Interest Expense*

Net Interest Expense*

---

*Net interest expense means interest receivable less interest payable.

We want to be looking at financially strong companies. And by that we mean businesses that aren't excessively in debt. We realize that many UK companies utilize debt as a cheap form of financing, particularly when interest rates are low. In fact, about 65 of the FTSE 100 companies are in debt. That may get you thinking that UK PLC is riding for a fall, because you've learnt throughout this book about the evils of debt. However, large companies can borrow money relatively cheaply and, used prudently, debt can actually enhance a company's earnings per share.

Despite that, the ideal company is one which has loads of money (cash) and no debt. Microsoft is the classic example. Yet again. It has no debt and billions of dollars in cash.

Looking back at our shortlist, let's see how they rate.

COMPANY	INTEREST COVER
Vodafone Airtouch	12[13]
BT	13
~~BSkyB~~	~~7~~
Glaxo Wellcome	30
_____	_____
_____	_____

That narrows the field even further. Although BSkyB is arguably still in its growth phase, courtesy of digital television, and therefore still spending today's money on tomorrow's

---

[13]This number is calculated using Vodafone's annual report for the year ended March 1999. The merger with Airtouch, which was consummated on 30 June 1999, will see the combined company with a very different interest cover.

growth, interest cover of 7 is a little low for our liking.

In conjunction with high interest cover, you also want to see companies with cash conversion ratios of 90 per cent and above. Like every rule, there are exceptions, and some companies can successfully operate and grow with relatively low levels of interest cover. However, they won't be able to do this for ever, especially if they've got a low cash conversion ratio.

6. *Proven Past Growth Record*

'Past performance is no guarantee of future results.' If you've carefully read the ads for financial services products in the newspapers and magazines, you'll be familiar with that caveat. And in many cases it does prove prophetic, as this year's table-topping unit trusts are often next year's laggards.

However, when it comes to individual companies, and their share price performance, the great performers of yesteryear are often the great performers of tomorrow. Human instinct says that because a share price has gone up 50 per cent in the last two years, it can't do the same again in the next two years. But, this is where human instinct goes out the window, and logical business sense replaces it.

A company growing its profits by 19 per cent a year will double its profits every 4 years. Although 19 per cent profit growth is no easy task, especially for the bigger companies, plenty of them achieve that feat. Therefore, all else being equal (i.e. if the relationship between the company's share price and its earnings, the P/E ratio, remains the same – more of this in the next chapter) the company's share price will double in 4 years.

What are we getting at here? I'm going to re-write the first sentence of this section. **'Great past performance, when it comes to individual companies, is no guarantee of future success, but it jolly well helps point you in the right direction.'** (Dear Editor, we recommend that when the book is published this sentence is put in bold and in large print, just to show the financial services companies that small print is for wimps.)

Let's look at the share price performance of our companies over the past ten years. You can get the numbers for the past five years from a few sources, one being the market-eye (www.market-eye.co.uk) web site. We're lucky enough to have access to a huge database of statistics, and have used the Fool's super-duper Bloomberg information service – can you now see why Reuters didn't make it on to our short-list?

COMPANY	10-YEAR PERFORMANCE
FTSE All Share	166%
Vodafone Airtouch	2140%
BT	335%
Glaxo Wellcome	370%
————	————
————	————

That's impressive going for our two telecommunications and one pharmaceutical giant. How did your companies compare?

At this stage we should comment on the extraordinarily good run virtually all companies in the telecommunications sector have had in 1998 and the early parts of 1999. The pharmaceutical sector also had a good run in 1998 as the market chose to mark those shares higher. As the stock market has recognized the long-term steady growth potential of these companies, so it has rewarded them with share price rises far in excess of their profits growth. Over the very long term, a company's share price should largely move in tandem with its earnings growth. Over shorter periods of time, and these can be anything from one day to three years, the share price can move completely independently of the company's underlying progress, depending on stock market sentiment.

The Final Bit

There we have it. Our sieving process has identified three companies which pass our six criteria. How many got through yours? That's not to say anyone should rush out and buy a part-ownership of any of those companies, because there's still work to be done. Remember the first half of this chapter? Does Glaxo Wellcome have a low flow ratio?[14] Do Vodafone Airtouch collect their debts within 30 days? Is BT's turnover rising by 8 to 10 per cent per annum?

BT, Vodafone Airtouch and Glaxo Wellcome are three giants of the UK stock exchange, all firmly ranked in the Top 10 by market capitalization. They operate in growth industries, sell classic repeat purchase services, and most British people are probably aware of their brand names. Undoubtedly, every single person in the country over the age of 16 has used BT services at some stage in their life. In recent years, they've begun to spread their tentacles to all parts of the globe. In a world seemingly dominated by American companies and brands, telecommunications and pharmaceuticals are two areas where the UK can hold its own at the worst, and lead the world at best. Already Vodafone Airtouch is the biggest wireless telecommunications company in the world.

Why are these amongst the biggest and best companies in the country, and the world? Not only do they generate extraordinary earnings by providing repeat services on a regular basis, but the numbers also stack up. As we saw, some excellent companies fell by the wayside as they passed through our demanding sieves, hopefully leaving you with the *crème de la crème*.

One of the best places for you to start when identifying individual companies is to look at what you know, recognize and use. That's what we've done here, and you've followed along with your choices. You should consider adding any or all of these companies to your portfolio. Along with an index tracking fund, and / or a mechanical strategy such as Beating The Footsie, you'll be well on your way to building a market beating portfolio for the next 10 and 20 years.

As always, be prepared for short-term volatility in your investments, which is part and parcel of the game. Over the long term, and that's what we're all in this for, the market has relentlessly marched onwards and upwards. If you buy quality companies, they will too and stand a good chance of beating the average performance of the market.

A WORD ON SMALL-CAPS

These poor little blighters once ruled the world, but recent times have seen the dream go rather sour – at least as far as the stock market is

---

[14]Flick back to page 129 and have a look for yourself. Does that get you thinking?

concerned. From a relatively recent high point in May 1998, the FTSE Small-Cap index slumped 26 per cent in the next seven months, eventually finishing 1998 down 11 per cent. For comparison, over that same seven-month period, the FTSE 100 lost just 1 per cent, and actually gained 15 per cent over the course of the whole of 1998. This large disparity is somewhat rare.

One of the many great things about the stock market is its longevity, and therefore the great database that it provides us with. The market has lived through two World Wars, umpteen civil wars, the Great Depression, the inflationary 1970s and the go get 'em 1990s. Over such a long period of time, you see trends repeated and repeated, over and over again. If smaller company shares have performed well in the past, you should feel comfortable that they will bounce back again in the future. In fact, the first six months of 1999 has seen the FTSE Small-Cap index grow by a whopping 28 per cent. What was that about the death of the smaller company?

About here we're going to throw in the usual Foolish caveat. Remember, we're not share tipsters or hypesters – you're the best person to look after your financial future – so therefore you should make your own investment decisions. There's no doubting that smaller company shares are a riskier proposition than their larger counterparts. They haven't got the financial strength or the brand name to be considered anything like a certainty to succeed. The world is littered with failed start-up companies, despite many of them having what looked like great business models. Either the concept didn't take off, or management cocked things up, or a big competitor muscled in and took their market right from under their feet. There's no love lost in business and competition – just look at the Virgin and British Airways wars.

It would be foolish (note the small 'f') to bet the whole house on smaller company shares. We all wish we'd found Vodafone Airtouch when it was just a baby, and watched it grow into a giant of a company. But to have the courage, foresight and vision to buy shares in them eight years ago when they first demerged from Racal Electronics, *and to still own them today*, takes a special kind of investor – dare we say a Foolish investor?

Smaller companies have the ability to grow very quickly, and profits growth always translates into share price growth, over the long term. Consider throwing some into your portfolio, but as ever do your homework in the first place – and don't forget to double check it too!

We'll close this chapter by asking you:

In your opinion, what's the present value – as distinct to its market capitalisation – of Glaxo Wellcome's business?

£ _____ million

Have any idea? The stock market places a value on it on a daily basis, but that's not necessarily what you think the business is worth. To help you along the way with that conundrum, Chapter 10 is all about how to value shares. See you there.

CHAPTER 10

How To Value Shares

'Determining the intrinsic value of a company is both art and science.'
Robert Hagstrom

Welcome to the weird and wonderful world of share valuation. Before we dive into advanced discounted cash-flow calculations, residual and intrinsic values, logarithms and financial modelling with a complexity level of the nth degree, here's a little theory behind it all.

This is an imprecise art. The value of a company is one person's opinion. That valuation may or may not be right. Regardless of the valuation anyone puts on a company, at any given time the stock market can and will price the company differently.

In other words, it's all fairly uncertain.

Having read the above paragraph, you must be thinking of skipping straight to the next chapter, or even of using this workbook as an expensive (hey – it's great value at only £9.99!) paperweight. Why bother going through all the valuation malarkey if there is no correct answer to the valuation conundrum? Well, some us around here in Fooldom reckon this stuff is important, and that you *can* have a pretty good stab at

valuing a company. The judgement period for how close you've got to a company's true valuation is measured in years, and many of them. It is not, and this is a mistake many people make, measured by the short-term movements in the share price. As Benjamin Graham, one of the grand old masters of the stock market once said, 'In the short term the stock market is a voting machine: in the long term it is a weighing machine.' Paraphrased, this means that whilst share prices oscillate up and down on a daily and monthly basis for many reasons, generally unrelated to the health of the company, in the long run they largely track the underlying performance – both up and down – of the company. A growing company will ultimately have a growing share price. A shrinking company will obviously do the opposite.

Over the very long term, a company's valuation does matter. A fast-growing company with a great product could be the current stock market's darling. Yet in ten years' time, it may not even exist, as the competition could have effectively put it out of business. On the other hand, it could have built itself up into a powerhouse of a company, surpassing even the expectations of the most optimistic of its investors and have a dominant market position. After all, the massive companies of the world like Glaxo Wellcome and Vodafone Airtouch had to start somewhere.

The price you pay today for a company can determine the return you will make over an extended period of time. A company with sales of £5 million could have a value today on the stock market of £1 million or £100 million. Which is fair? Fast-forward ten years from now and we'll know the answer, because by then the company will have wonderfully succeeded, dismally failed, or more likely performed somewhere in the middle. Fixing this 'fair' value for a share today, based, among other things, on its current share price and its current and likely future earnings is part of what this chapter is all about.

One thing we always stress here in Fooldom is that the quality of the company matters first and foremost. Placing a value on a poorly managed, poorly performing company is almost impossible. We always yearn for great companies. The definition of a great company varies from person to person. You saw our thinking in the previous chapter. Some would say that it is one with a great past record, and one which has predictable earnings. Others would say that a company should be product led – find a company with a great product and the chances are it will also be a great company.

Another important thing to consider in stock market investing, and therefore valuation, is that the company should be within your circle of knowledge and competence. It's no use trying to value a company if you don't know anything about it.

Some investors look for first movers in an important, emerging and growing industry and let the conventional valuation go hang. No matter how expensive the company appears, it is hoped that the results it may deliver down the line will result in the current valuation being dwarfed by the company's potential size. Those kinds of investors are Rule Breakers and for them one of their key investment criteria is that a company should be generally considered astronomically *over*valued. More on this in the chapter on Rule Breakers, Makers and Shakers. Meanwhile, those of a true Rule Breaking bent will still be interested in this chapter, may even apply some of its valuation methods to their shares, but they're not going to get too worried about what today's calculations are predicting for five or ten years hence.

Some people invest in companies that have temporarily (they hope!) hit on hard times. The stock market valuation of these companies often gets irrationally low, and that's when these investors pounce. This strategy is commonly called 'value investing'. Others prefer mechanical investment strategies, such as ones based on high dividend yielding shares – known around here as Beating The Footsie. It's all a matter of horses for courses, and following the style and strategy that you feel most comfortable with. However, ultimately – and this could be 20 years from now – valuation does and will matter.

Finally, if you do read through this chapter and become so fired that you become a valuation fiend, thinking of nothing else, morning, noon and night ('I'm more likely to cut off my right arm'), be aware that, however enthusiastic we are, absolutely none of us can predict the future with certainty. That shouldn't, however, stop us having a go at it, and trying to put the odds of success in our favour. By attempting to put a value on a company, we learn more about it, we think about its business in more depth and at the same time take a peek into one possible version of the future. At the very least, it provides a powerful mental discipline and an often illuminating perspective on the company we're looking at: even if it turns out wrong, valuation is a valuable exercise.

EARNINGS BASED VALUATIONS

The P/E and EPS

It's here, there and everywhere. The good old, trusty P/E ratio. The price to earnings ratio (P/E) is your typical commoner. It is quoted almost willy-nilly in the financial press, and enables investors to get that quick valuation fix they all crave.

You will often see something written in the newspaper like 'Dodgy.com PLC trades at a forward P/E of 10, making it look fully valued' or 'Epic! PLC has a trailing P/E of 30, which makes it look cheap in comparison with other companies in the sector.' But why is Dodgy.com 'fully valued' and Epic! 'cheap' when on face value their P/Es would suggest the opposite? The P/E is a one-dimensional number and needs to be viewed in the context of growth rates, the industry, competition and many of the other valuation tools we shall look at.

THE PRICE TO EARNINGS RATIO (P/E)

Share Price

Earnings Per Share (EPS)

You already know all about earnings per share, and how to calculate it. Nevertheless, when I went to university, I found a refresher course never went astray – when I could be bothered to turn up, that is. But that was then . . . Anyway:

EARNINGS PER SHARE (EPS):

Net Profit (after tax but before dividends)

Number of Shares Outstanding

EPS is another of those widely quoted numbers, as it is inextricably linked to the P/E. Whilst the amount of pure profit a company makes is important, what really counts is the profit per share that a company makes.

To explain, let's take an example. Epic! PLC is an Internet start-up company, offering consumers connection to the Web for free, with an 0800 access number thrown in for good measure. They make money through selling advertising space on their home, or portal, page. The company is already profitable, having signed up 2 million subscribers in their first week alone!

(By the time you read this, in the fast-moving Internet world, this company *will* exist. It will probably be capitalized at £2 billion or more. Remember that you saw it here first. When you examine individual companies all the time, and swap ideas about them on the Motley Fool message boards, you often think that you can run companies and develop their business strategy better than the existing management. Cultivate it, for it ultimately helps make you a better investor.)

In fiscal 2008, Epic! made after-tax profits of £1,000,000. The number of shares in issue is 10,000,000, so their EPS is

$$\frac{£1,000,000}{10,000,000} = £0.10 \text{ or } 10p$$

Epic!'s current share price is 300p, so their P/E is

$$\frac{300p}{10p} = 30$$

But what does that mean? Are Epic! incredibly cheap or wildly overvalued? It is impossible to say just by looking at the P/E on its own. What if I said that every Internet Service Provider (ISP) is now offering free access to the Internet, and a competitor has just begun offering to *pay you*, the consumer, £10 as a lure to take business away from Epic!? Or what if I said that Epic! are forecast to grow earnings by 100 per cent per annum over the next year? The point is that an investor needs a lot more information than the P/E alone to attempt to put a value on to the company.

The higher the P/E, the higher the market values a company. If you took away inflation and growth from the equation, if you paid 30 times earnings to buy the whole company (equivalent to a P/E of 30), it would take you 30 years to recoup that investment. Only then would you start moving into profit. Would you pay 30 times earnings for such a company?

Fair Value

A machine that prints one £10 note per year is offered for sale. Its earnings are £10 per annum, and it has one share in issue. How much would you be prepared to pay for the machine? Clearly, if you could buy that machine for £10 (P/E = 1), you would have a bargain on your hands. Your investment payback period would be just one year, and from then onwards you could just sit back and watch those £10 bills roll in. And, you still own a machine with a residual sale value. Make a mental note – if anyone ever offers you that machine for £10, make sure you buy it.

How would you value that £10 printing machine? I'd be willing to pay up to £90 for it. That's what I see as its fair value. But, don't tell the current owner, because I reckon they'd be willing to sell it to me for a lot less than that. Can you see the stock market connections? If you find a company with predictable earnings and it is selling below its fair value, would you buy it? I would.

It is often said that in a fairly valued situation the P/E should roughly equal a company's future EPS growth rate. That isn't as complicated as it sounds. All it means is that a company on a P/E of 40 should be forecast to be growing its earnings at 40 per cent per year. In recent years, particularly as far as larger companies are concerned, it has become very difficult to find great companies which pass that test. Companies with a P/E of 40 yet growing at an average rate of 15 per cent or less per annum have been commonplace. That doesn't in itself mean they are necessarily over-valued, because the P/E is not the only way to value a company. For example, a company trading at P/E of 40 but forecast with some certainty to grow at 20 per cent per annum for the next ten years may still offer value. Remember – valuation is an art, not a science. And, unlike 5th form mathematics, when your teacher marks your paper, there's no right or wrong answer. In my book, that's scholastic bliss – I'd have got straight A's instead of being regularly sent straight down to the headmaster's office.

Before we leave P/Es and EPS – don't worry, you'll have all these abbreviations licked in no time – it's worth having a word about analyst expectations. Wise brokers in the City are paid handsome salaries to come up with predictions about a company's future growth rate. This is usually done under the guise of EPS forecasts for the next 18-24 months and it often gets written down something like this:

EARNINGS PER SHARE

	2009A	2010E	2011E
ETPhoneHome plc	42.5p	50.0p	55.8p

a – actual

e – estimate

This means that analysts expect ETPhoneHome to earn 50.0p per share in net profits in 2010. If they've got 2 million shares outstanding, that translates into net profits of £1 million (0.50p x 2,000,000).

These earnings forecasts usually turn out to be amazingly accurate, given the hundreds of variables that can affect a company's profits. The brokers who prepare these estimates keep in relatively close contact with the company they are following, so much so that the company gives them 'guidance' about the level of profits the company themselves are forecasting. That this 'guidance' is effectively insider information is Not Very Fair At All and needless to say we at the Motley Fool think this information should be made freely available to all and sundry immediately, and not just to a select few City analysts who act on it for the benefit of their privileged clients. The Internet is the perfect distribution vehicle for this kind of information.

See Box on page 111.

The good news for us private investors is that we do get access to at least the bare numbers of these analyst earnings estimates, and they are freely available on the Internet. In general, they are relatively reliable, especially for the bigger companies that are covered by many analysts. Of course, the estimates are not fool-proof (note the small 'f' in fool-proof). Some companies will exceed earnings expectations, which is usually good news for the share price. On the other hand, shock profit warnings can quickly put paid to earnings estimates, and these usually are bad for the wealth, at least in the short term, of your portfolio.

Some earnings estimates need to be viewed with caution, particularly for the smaller companies. This sector of the market is not as widely covered as its big brother large-cap sector. Some companies have no analysts covering them, because they are just too small to be of any interest to any broker. Others just have one broker following them, and that is usually the 'house broker'. Because the company butters their bread (i.e. it pays their wages), it is unlikely that the house broker will err on the pessimistic side when assessing the company's prospects.

At this point, it is always worth remembering why brokers issue lengthy reports about companies, including earnings estimates. There's usually an investment recommendation attached to these reports, such as BUY, OUTPERFORM, UNDERPERFORM, HOLD, ADD, and even the odd SELL. The aim of these recommendations is to encourage investors, major investors, to trade, and when that happens, the brokers make money. Often, the analysts are acting as little other than highly paid, institutionalised share hypesters. You should therefore take little heed of these trading tips, instead concentrating on the numbers and earnings estimates that are included in the report, if you ever get to see one of these documents.

It is also worth remembering that earnings estimates focus on the short-term prospects of a company. Foolish investors are ideally looking to own shares in an individual company for more than 18 to 24 months. It is over the very long term that the returns from a successful investment really compound up into significant growth rate returns as we saw earlier in the book.

Right, it's out with the pencil again and time for some 'rithmetic. Fill in the gaps:

COMPANY	SHARE PRICE	EPS	P/E RATIO
King Tours	250p	25p	10
Sherlock Holmes PLC	124p	3p	a.____
Wise Hatters	1060p	b.____	18
Crazy Fool Golf	263p	24p	c.____
Hats & Tails (Kilburn)	d.____	18p	28
Wally's Bikes	95p	e.____	18

Answers: (a) 41, (b) 59p, (c) 11, (d) 504p, (e) 5p

Not bad, Fool. You're now a dab hand at EPS and P/E calculations. That may not be something you want to bring up with a handsome member of the opposite sex in the first 30 seconds of conversation, but please accept our Foolish permission to bask for a moment in quiet pride.

And here's one final quiz question:

Why do you think Hats & Tails (Kilburn) trades on a P/E of 28 compared with Shabb. E. Lee., also trying to make a name for itself in the dinner suit business, which trades on a P/E of 10?

The answer is that it's probably because the market expects Hats & Tails to grow much more rapidly than Shabb E. Lee. Only time will tell whether the investing community was right to believe there could be a fast-growing dinner suit business in the heart of Kilburn.

HOW MUCH WILL MY COMPANY BE WORTH: EARNINGS GROWTH RATE PROJECTIONS

This is a technique for long-term investors in solid businesses. For some companies, you can roughly calculate their potential share price over the very long term, as much as ten years. But, it is only applicable to value a company over that time period if it has predictable earnings. Reasonably mature businesses with a past record of growth, strong management and a high degree of certainty about their future growth rate fit this bill. On the other hand, fictitious Epic!, which operates in a fast-moving, competitive and forever changing industry, is probably less likely to have a predictable future growth rate, making this kind of projection much less valuable.

In the following example, for a company called Predictable PLC, the base year is 2009 and the company is forecast to grow both EPS and dividends by 20 per cent per annum for the next ten years. Here's a potential valuation scenario:

EARNINGS GROWTH RATE PROJECTION

YEAR	EPS	P/E	SHARE PRICE	DIVIDENDS
2009	12.0	25	300	7.20 (BASE YEAR)
2010	14.4	25	360	8.64
2011	17.3	25	432	10.37
2012	20.7	25	518	12.44
2013	24.9	20	498	14.93
2014	29.9	20	97	17.92
2015	35.8	20	717	21.50
2016	43.0	18	774	25.80
2017	51.6	18	929	30.96
2018	61.9	18	1115	37.15
2019	74.3	18	1337+	44.58
				231.48

Share Price	1,337.42+
Total Dividends	231.48
Total 10 Year Return	1,568.90
Total Growth	423%
CAGR*	18.0%

*CAGR = Compound Annual Growth Rate

Remember the relationship between the EPS, P/E and share price? If you know two of these numbers, you can calculate the third. What we've done with this valuation model is to forecast out the rise in EPS and presumed that over time the P/E will probably drop somewhat, to 18 in this case. On this basis, we can then go on to calculate what the share price would be in those situations, using the formulae which come next and which we've already explored:

Share Price and Earnings Ratios

$$EPS = \frac{Price}{P/E}$$

$$P/E = \frac{Price}{EPS}$$

$$Price = EPS * P/E$$

By calculating the CAGR, you can compare the annual rate of return with other forms of investment, whether they be building society interest rates, bonds or gilts or other equity investment possibilities. In the case of Predictable PLC, a 10-year CAGR of 18 per cent beats just about every other form of investment going, and presuming you've got your assumptions correct, it could present a great growth opportunity.

What the above table effectively says is that, from a starting, or buying point of 300p, if your growth and P/E forecasts turn out to be correct, your total return will be 1568.90p after ten years. In other words, 300p growing at 18 per cent every year for ten years will come to 1568.90p. Note the change in the P/E ratio can also have a big bearing on the CAGR. In the above example I've assumed it falls from 25 in 2008 to 18 in 2019. If instead it had have risen to, say, 35 with all other assumptions unchanged, the CAGR would have risen to a whopping 25 per cent. Just from that little example you can see what a difference a change in the company's P/E can do to your share returns. If you enjoy using computers, you can set up a template like the above table in a computer spreadsheet and play around with different valuation models. Alternatively, paper, pencil and a calculator do just as well. For example, what if

Predictable grew at 20 per cent for 5 years and then dropped to 10 per cent for the next five years? Or, what if they traded at a P/E of 25 in 2009 but only grew at 15 per cent per annum for the next ten years? A little sensitivity analysis can give you a range of possible valuations and CAGRs. Ideally you want to have an idea of the low point, most likely point, and upper valuation point.

But wait one moment. How do you calculate the annual growth rate, the 'CAGR' which we've been bandying about in such a cavalier fashion? Actually, it's easy. You can either use a calculator, pencil and paper or else a computer spreadsheet. Let's start with a computer spreadsheet:

The total growth is simply calculated as

$$(1568.90p / 300p) - 1 = 4.23 \text{ or } 423\%$$

Say the total growth of 423% is in cell E24 of your spreadsheet. To calculate the CAGR, you'd enter this formula.

=(E24+1)^(1/10)-1
=0.18 or 18.0%

That formula takes the 10th root, with 10 being the number of years over which you are calculating the growth rate. Written differently:

300p *1.18 *1.18 *1.18 *1.18 *1.18 *1.18 *1.18 *1.18 *1.18 *1.18 = 1568.9p (It actually equals 1570.15p, the discrepancy being due to small rounding differences.)

Whoa! Come back, Fool! Don't run away. This stuff really is quite simple. If you are struggling, think back to the delights of square roots.

What's the square root of 4?

———————

That was easy – the answer is of course 2. We know this either because we've still got it tattooed on our wrists from the time we cheated in the maths exam in the second year, or because we could manually deduce that 2 * 2 = 4.

What's the cube root of 64?

———————

This one's not so easy. Again you can probably deduce the answer, and figure out that it's 4 (4 * 4 * 4 = 64).

A company grows its earnings per share from 10p to 17.3p over 3 years. What's its CAGR?

———————

For someone like me, who's worked with calculators for a long time, off the top of my head, this one's virtually impossible without a calculator or spreadsheet. However, it is not that difficult, if you take it one step at a time.

Step 1. 17.3p ÷ 10p = 1.73

Step 2. Cube root of 1.73 = 1.20 (I used a calculator or spreadsheet for this one[1])

Step 3. Subtract 1 to give 0.20

Step 4. Multiply by 100, to give 20

Step 5. Add a little '%' sign to give CAGR = 20%

It's easy once you've done a few for yourself. Guess what that's the cue for?

———————

[1]The cube root of 1.73 on your scientific calculator: 1) Key in 1.73. 2) Press 'shift' or 'inv'. 3) Hit the 'x^y' button. 4) Press '3'. 5) Press 'equals'. 6) You should have the answer. 7) Whoop for joy.

CALCULATE GROWTH RATES

	SHARE PRICE	EST. TOTAL RETURN	YEARS	CAGR
ETPhoneHome	300p	1569p	10	18%
Popper's Parties	250p	750p	6	20%
Mr Rik's Curries	120p	805p	4	a._____
Roly's Pies	526p	652p	7	b._____
FoolShop	333p	874p	5	c._____
Wally's Bikes	95p	235p	8	d._____

Answers a. 61% (wow!) b. 3% c. 21% d. 12%

Before moving on, I will repeat, however, that a company's earnings growth rate projected valuation depends largely on the assumptions you use, and this type of valuation is best suited to larger companies with predictable earnings. And be aware too that some people don't ever use this kind of model, as they don't find it very helpful. As ever, why not come and discuss this on the UK Investment Workbook message board at the Fool UK?

Also, as with all the valuation models and tools we look at, it should not be used as the *only* method to value a company.

THE FOOL RATIO (PEG)

The Fool Ratio is a popular and simple tool which looks at the relationship between a company's earnings growth rate and its price to earnings ratio (P/E). It is known as the PEG in this country, and was popularised here by Jim Slater, author of *Beyond The Zulu Principle*, and stands for price to earnings growth Factor. It is at its most effective when looking at smaller growth companies. Like any ratio and valuation tool, it has its limitations, and we'll look at some of them at the close of this section.

Remember when we were looking at the P/E ratio we said;

> It is often said that in a fairly valued situation the P/E should roughly equal a company's future EPS growth rate.

This means that if a company's P/E is 10 and its earnings per share are growing at a rate of 10 per cent per year, you might start to think it fairly valued. So, you ask, if this is the case and everyone knows this, surely every stock would be fully valued and bargains would never exist. All investors, including those highly paid, perennially under-performing professional fund managers, should at least be able to match the market average. Shouldn't they? Well, shouldn't they?!

But we don't live in a perfect world. At least not one where England wins the Ashes (anytime recently), money grows on trees and every stock you ever buy instantly soars and keeps on sailing up and up. As humans, we have many different opinions on a variety of topics. We support different football teams, wear different clothes and we have contrary views on individual stocks. This lack of uniformity creates opportunity.

Ah, but back to the Fool Ratio. As investors, we aim to buy quality stocks at sensible prices. If the Magic Umbrella Company (Kilmarnock) PLC (MUCK) had a P/E ratio of 80 (which is very high), but with the lack of rainfall due to the greenhouse effect was expected to grow at a rate of only 5 per cent per annum, you might say that MUCK looked a smidgen over-valued. However, if MUCK were priced at a P/E ratio of 15 and their magic umbrellas suddenly became the latest, most chic, *I have to have one*, fashion accessories for the billion or so inhabitants of China, you might wonder if in fact the stock is looking under-valued and investigate further.

Of course, as we said the P/E ratio is only one method of assessing a company's value. In the example above, MUCK may have a huge cash hoard built up over many years of selling people umbrellas with the guarantee that they will prevent you being caught in torrential downpours at inappropriate times. So, although MUCK may seem expensive based on earnings, the cash stockpile may be worth more per share than the market currently values the company.

So how's this Fool Ratio/PEG thing calculated?

FOOL RATIO

Price To Earnings Ratio (P/E)

Earnings Growth Rate

We've already covered the P/E, so you know how to work that one out. The earnings growth can be calculated by looking at a company's forward earnings estimates. These are freely available on the Internet, and as we saw earlier, typically look like this:

EARNINGS GROWTH RATE

Current Share Price 260p

	2009A	2010E	2011E
MUCK PLC	13p	19p	25p
Growth %	30%	46%	32%
P/E	20	14	10

A – actual

E – estimate

Faced with this scenario, you may well be wondering how the Fools are going to get out of this one. Is the earnings growth 30 per cent, 46 per cent or 32 per cent? Perhaps, having studiously read the previous section, you've already worked it out for yourself.

What about if we set out a table like this? Would that help?

CALCULATE GROWTH RATES

	CURRENT EPS	FORWARD EPS	YEARS	CAGR
MUCK PLC	13p	25p	2	_____

In the previous section, just as you calculated growth rates based on total returns, you can use the same principles to compute a compounded average growth rate for EPS.

Step 1. 25p ÷ 13p = 1.92

Step 2. Square root of 1.92 = 1.39 (using a calculator or spreadsheet)

Step 3. 39% = CAGR

Incredibly, you just computed something called the 'compounded average growth rate for EPS'. Was that not worth the cover price of this book, alone? Phone your mum, go on, you know she'd be proud of you.

We now know the current P/E (20) and the earnings growth rate (39), and therefore we can calculate the Fool Ratio.

$$\text{Fool Ratio} = \frac{20}{39} = 0.51$$

If you were happy that MUCK PLC passed your strict quality of business criteria, had a sound balance sheet and a high cash conversion ratio, would you buy them, knowing their Fool Ratio is 0.51? I don't know about you, but I'd be very tempted to look closely at them as a potential buy, because a Fool Ratio of 0.51 indicates that the shares are trading at significant discount to their growth rate.

When using the Fool Ratio, always bear in mind that maxim – 'In a fairly valued situation the P/E should roughly equal a company's future EPS growth rate.' If MUCK PLC shares were to follow that maxim, they'd trade at a P/E of 39, or a share price of 507p (EPS 13p x P/E 39 = 507p). That's a whopping 95 per cent above the current share price of 260p. Wow!

As a rule of thumb, here are our Fool Ratio guidelines. They are not set in stone, they are merely guidelines and add but one piece of the jigsaw to your investing decision. However, that can be a useful piece.

FOOL RATIO	SUGGESTS
Below 0.60	Look To Buy
0.61 to 1.00	Consider Buying
1.01 to 1.50	Fairly to Richly Valued
1.51 or more	Potentially Overvalued

Proceed with Caution

Before you go rushing out and buying every company you can find with a Fool Ratio under 1, you need to be aware of its limitations. Not every company can be evaluated using this tool – it usually works best for smaller companies, but they also generally happen to be riskier investment prospects.

When P/Es get quite high – above 20 to 25 – the Fool Ratio is less effective. Over time, P/Es will eventually revert to the norm. For example, a company with a Fool Ratio of 0.94 may look attractive. But, if it came about because the company's current P/E is 66 and its current growth rate is 70 per cent, even after two years of stellar earnings growth, the share price will remain unchanged if the shares are reverting to a normal P/E. As such:

	2009a	2010e	2011e
Share Price	100p	100p	100p
EPS	1.52	2.58	4.38
P/E	66	39	23
Growth %		70%	70%
Fool Ratio	0.94		

If we're looking for a standard against which to measure ourselves, at the time of writing, in mid 1999, the companies in the FTSE 100 index have a prospective P/E of about 23.

The Fool Ratio also isn't appropriate to use on so-called 'recovery' shares. A company which has recently fallen on hard times, and has therefore had its earnings depressed, may have a low Fool Ratio. However, recovery companies don't usually pass the quality company test, and besides can hardly be considered upwardly mobile growth companies.

Finally, although earnings estimates are mostly reasonably accurate, they can sometimes turn out to be horribly wrong, the result inevitably being a share price tumble. Like all individual valuation techniques, there's more to valuing and analyzing a share than the Fool Ratio alone.

Got the Fool ratio sorted? Good. Let's move forward.

SALES BASED VALUATIONS

The Price to Sales Ratio (PSR)

Every time a company sells a customer something, it is generating revenues. Whether or not a company has made money in the last year, there are always revenues. Companies that may be temporarily losing money, have earnings depressed due to short-term circumstances (like product development or higher taxes), or are relatively new in a high-growth industry, are often valued off their revenues and not their earnings. Revenue-based valuations are achieved using the price to sales ratio, often simply abbreviated PSR.

The price to sales ratio takes the current market capitalization of a company and divides it by the last twelve months' sales.

The Price to Sales Ratio (PSR)
Market capitalization
_____
Trailing (last 12 months) Sales

The market capitalization is the current market value of a company – you already know this – arrived at by multiplying the current share price by the shares outstanding. This is the current price at which the market is valuing the company. For instance, if our example company Epic! PLC has 10 million shares outstanding priced at 300p per share, then its market capitalization is 10,000,000 * 300p (or £3) = £30m.

Some investors add the current long-term debt of the company to its current market value to get the market capitalization. This is known as the enterprise value. The logic here is that if you were to acquire the company, you would acquire its debt as well, effectively paying that much more. This helps you make a better comparison between PSRs of two companies. One may have fuelled its sales growth by taking out an enormous debt burden, versus one having lower sales growth but which has not added any debt.

For a quick fix on trailing sales, you can take the number as reported in the company's last published annual report. Say Epic! had 2009 sales of £10 million, then what's the PSR?

$$\frac{£}{£} = \underline{\qquad}$$

Did you get it? But what does it mean? You may impress your work colleagues by saying that Epic! trades at a PSR of 3, but if they're savvy, they will retort: 'Why, Jessica, kindly inform me exactly how that compares to other companies in the same industry and while you're about it, pray specify whether you are referring to a PSR calculated using market capitalization or enterprise value. When in possession of said information, I shall then give you my response, but not before. Good day, madam.'

Can you see your work colleagues saying that? Perhaps not, but you never know.

What if I said that Epic!'s arch rival Titanic!

traded at a PSR of 15? Would that give you any clues? It would certainly mean that the market rates Titanic! at a much higher level than Epic! It could be that Titanic! has higher operating margins, better growth prospects, courtesy of a better product and better management. This will be reflected in the relative PSRs of the two companies.

The PSR is often quoted as the basis for the price when companies buy other companies. If you have ever heard of a deal being done based on a certain 'multiple of sales,' you have seen the PSR in use. This is a perfectly legitimate way for a company to value an acquisition.

Uses of the PSR

The theory goes, as with the PEG, that the lower the PSR, the better. Ken Fisher, author of *Super Stocks*, is most famous for using the PSR by looking for companies with PSRs below 1 in order to find value stocks currently overlooked by the market. This is actually a pretty good indicator of value, according to the work that James O'Shaughnessey has done on mechanical investment strategies in his book *What Works On Wall Street*, which we talked about earlier.

The PSR is a valuable tool, and is often used to value fast-growing, loss-making businesses. A company which has yet to turn profitable cannot be valued on the basis of its earnings using the price to earnings ratio (P/E). It doesn't have any earnings, right? Companies such as loss-making telecommunications and Internet entities can be valued on a multiple of their sales, and that can be compared to companies in a similar line of business, or at a similar stage of development. For example, Freeserve, the pioneering free Internet Service Provider (ISP), was valued at a PSR of approximately 123 times forecast sales at the time of flotation, which is FANTASTICALLY

HIGH by conventional standards, but may reflect the vast and almost unknowable potential of the Internet for the companies which make the first, the most decisive, and the most creative moves to exploit its opportunities.

The PSR only gives investors an indication of a company's valuation. As with most valuation tools, it should be interpreted in conjunction with other factors, such as the competitive environment in which a company operates, the barriers (or lack thereof) to entry for competitors, and the gross profitability of the company and its peers.

What exactly constitutes a good PSR depends on the industry in which a company operates and its stage of growth. Companies with low margins and quick turnover of products, such as supermarkets and distributors, traditionally trade at low PSRs. They are in a competitive business, and each pound of sales contributes a relatively low amount to the company's profitability. On the other hand, the big pharmaceutical companies traditionally trade on much higher PSRs, as they have greater barriers to entry into their business and each pound of sales contributes a higher amount to its profitability.

Don't fall into the trap of comparing the PSRs of two companies in two entirely different industries.

Over time, studies have shown that companies revert to a 'normal', or average PSR applicable to the industry in which they operate. For example, big supermarkets, courtesy of their low margins and competitive environment, usually trade on a PSR of about 0.5. If a smaller, faster growing competitor came along, and was justifiably trading at a higher PSR, you could estimate a future valuation for that company.

Here's how to do it and it's similar to the earnings growth rate projections we did earlier. Eat-It-Now is the hot young pretender to the

Tesco, Sainsbury, Safeway, Asda crown. Their shops are springing up everywhere and the kids won't let you go anywhere else ('Eat-It-Now! Eat-It-Now! Eat-It-Now!'). Eat-It-Now, you see, has amazing video games fitted to their shopping trolleys for kids to play as you wander round and that's just one of their many innovations. This is a coo-oo-ool company and it's valued at a PSR of 2, very high for a supermarket. Their sales growth, you think, might be as much as 20 per cent per year, a lot for a company like this. You're getting hot for Eat-It-Now, you're going to do a PSR-based valuation ten years out, your pulse is racing, your palms are getting sweaty, your breathing is getting faster. Oh my! Praise the Lord and pass the ammunition, there's a valuation coming on:

(in £ thousands)	SALES	MARKET CAP	PSR
1998	1,000	2,000	2.0 (base year)
1999	1,200		
2000	1,440		
2001	1,728		
2002	2,074		
2003	2,488		
2004	2,986		
2005	3,583		
2006	____		
2007	____		
2008	____	____	0.5

PSR Valuation for Eat-It-Now

Sales growing at 20 per cent per year, PSR 2.0 to start and 0.5 in ten years. We've started off putting in the sales growth each year, but you go on and fill in the blanks, if your hand, quivering as it is with excitement and anticipation, is steady enough.

How is it going? Did you have to get your calculator out? You'll find the answers to the sales growth column at the bottom of the page.[2] Now we know what we think sales are likely to be in 2008 and we are presuming Eat-It-Now will drop back to the average PSR of around 0.5 (the average could have changed by then, of course), so we (that means you) can now calculate what its future market capitalization would be:

2008 market cap = 2008 PSR x 2008 sales

If you've already peeked at the bottom of the page, you'll have seen that 2008 sales is likely to be £6.192 million:

2008 market cap = 0.5 x £6.192m
2008 market cap = _____

---

[2]2006 sales: £4.3 million. 2007 sales: £5.16 million. 2008 sales: £6.192 million.

Yes, that's right, just £3.096 million. But in 1998, market cap was £2 million. That means that the total growth is:

(£3.096m ÷ £2m) – 1 = _____
Now multiply this by 100 to give growth over the ten years of _____%

Total growth in the market capitalization, or price, of the company over this time is just 55 per cent. Hmm, so what does that come down to in terms of compound annual growth rate? Flick back a couple of pages if you can't remember the calculation.

No? What do you mean you can't be bothered?! You're not allowed to say that. Oh, alright, just this once, because it's you, here it is for possibly the last time (answers at the bottom of the page):[3]

   Step 1. £3.096m ÷ £2m = _____
   Step 2. Tenth root (10 years, yes?) of Step 1 = _____ (use a calculator or spreadsheet)
   Step 3. Subtract 1
   Step 4. Multiply by 100
   Step 5. Add a little '%' sign to give CAGR = _____%

A bit disappointing, hey? Twenty per cent growth every year in sales and yet the actual growth in share price every year was just 4.5 per cent and all because the company eventually reverted back to the average PSR of the industry, 0.5, from the PSR of 2.0 at which it started. You would have been better off putting your money in the building society than have it earning a somewhat riskier 4.5 per cent per annum by investing it in the above business. Although Eat-

It-Now is growing sales very quickly (20 per cent per annum), ten years from now it will likely be trading closer to the average PSR for companies in its sector, unless it remains an innovator or the average PSR changes.

Before you leave the PSR, here's a thought. Why not figure out your own PSR? How much in terms of sales do you think you are worth to your organisation every year? If you're not directly involved in sales, just make an estimate of your sales value. Go on, be wild! You're worth a lot. We know you are and we won't tell.

For instance, if you're an accountant working for a large international firm, you may be billing clients £200 an hour (genuinely) and yet be on a salary of, say, £50,000. Assume you billed clients for just 6 hours a day, then that's £1200 a day, £6000 a week and roughly £300,000 a year. That puts you on a PSR of:

50,000 ÷ 300,000 = 0.167

Hmm. Less even than a supermarket. You'd better have a chat with your boss.

YIELD BASED VALUATIONS

The Dividend Yield

The dividend yield is the percentage of a company's share price that it pays out as dividends over the course of a year. It is calculated as:

---

[3]Step 1: 1.548 Step 2: 1.045 Step 5: 4.5%

DIVIDEND YIELD

$$\frac{\text{Dividend}}{\text{Current Share Price}}$$

The dividend yield expresses the annual dividend of a share as a percentage return on investment at the prevailing market price. When Epic! declares a 6p per share dividend, a person holding 1000 shares in the company will receive a cheque for £60. Depending on a person's particular tax circumstances, either they have no further tax to pay or will have to fork over some additional money to the taxman.

The Epic! dividend yield would be calculated as

$$\frac{\text{6p   (Dividend)}}{\text{300p (Share price)}} = 0.02 \text{ or } 2\%$$

Most profitable companies in the UK pay regular dividends to their shareholders. Some pay more than others, depending on their growth prospects, cash balances and dividend policy. You will find that the majority of companies increase their dividends each year in line with the increase in their underlying profits.

In the US, many of the biggest and fastest-growing companies don't pay a dividend. This is because management aims to increase returns to shareholders by investing all of that money back into the business, rather than handing it back to shareholders. Examples of non-dividend paying companies include Berkshire Hathaway, super-investor Warren Buffett's investment company,

Dell Computer Corporation and Microsoft. All three are incredibly successful companies, proving dividend yield is not the be-all and end-all of share valuation. In fact, you could say that a really successful, top-flight company should be better able to make use of shareholders' money than shareholders themselves. There is almost no way that if Microsoft had paid dividends, a Microsoft shareholder would have been able to invest those dividends at a rate which would have matched Microsoft's share price returns. Share-holders have been better served by letting Microsoft use the cash they generated to enhance the business, than by taking it as a dividend payment.

In the UK most loss-making companies don't pay dividends, especially the loss-makers who are growing sales quickly. They want to invest their money back into the business, as they are building a solid base from which future profits will be generated. Since its stock market flotation in 1996, mobile phone company Orange has never paid a dividend, and is not forecast to pay one until after 2000. Yet, this fact hasn't stopped its share price from rapidly rising as its subscriber base has exploded.

Looking at a company's dividend yield is another way of valuing it. Investors may compare a company that is paying an 8 per cent dividend to the current building society rate of 6 per cent and figure they'd be better investing in the company than putting their money in the bank. Caution as ever is required, for companies that fall on troubled times will cut their dividend, and with it their share price will probably fall, too, hence leaving the unwary investor with a capital loss as well as a cut in their expected income. As always in investing – and actually in life too – you get paid to take risks.

The whole *au contraire* nature of the

mechanical Beating the Footsie strategy, dealt with in Chapter 6, revolves around investing in companies with the highest dividend yield. The theory goes that these big companies have seen their share price hammered to a point where their dividend yield becomes quite high. The income, or dividend, makes up a large part of the overall return.

One final word of warning which may seem obvious – when a company has a dividend yield that looks too good to be true, it usually is!

RETURN ON EQUITY

Return on equity (ROE) is one of the most important weapons in any Fool's armoury and Warren Buffett is one of its great champions.

In her excellent book *Buffettology* Mary Buffett, former daughter-in-law of Warren, goes into great detail about the valuation techniques that the Buffett uses. She concentrates largely on a company's ROE when determining its value.

RETURN ON EQUITY

$$\frac{\text{Net Profit}}{\text{Shareholders' Equity}}$$

We looked at shareholders' equity back in the balance sheet section and you'll remember that it refers to the amount of cash shareholders have contributed to any given business. It is defined as a company's total assets less its total liabilities. In your own personal balance sheet, it

was the equivalent of your net worth. Since it is the shareholders who actually own the company, and not the directors, their equity represents the owners' claims against a company's assets. ROE gives you an idea of how much profit is being generated for every pound that is employed in the business.

By relating the earnings generated to the shareholders' equity, an investor can see how earnings are being created from the existing assets. If the return on equity is 20 per cent, then 20 pence of assets – in the form of profits – are created for each pound that is invested in the business. Clearly, the higher a company's ROE, the better the company, all other things being equal. Which company would you prefer to invest your hard earned money into – one that makes £5 profits from assets of £100, or one that makes that same £5 but from assets of only £20?

We always encourage Fools to think of themselves as part owners of a business when they purchase shares in a big company. You are buying more than a share certificate, and more than a quoted price on the stock exchange. Money that is spent by your company is partly your money. When you see directors awarding themselves large bonus payments when they are hardly deserved, that's partly your money they are pocketing. A lavish head office – yep, that's your money again.

Because big businesses often produce detailed and complicated accounts, and each individual shareholder owns but a tiny, tiny portion of that company, it is easy to lose sight of the big picture. The following example may help your understanding of the concept of shareholders' equity and ROE.

Ally's Abode

You inherit £150,000 and decide to buy a house for cash as an investment. An independent valuation of the house confirms its value at exactly £150,000. Straight after the purchase of that house, your balance sheet looks like:

ASSETS	
One House	150,000
SHAREHOLDERS' EQUITY	
Share Capital	150,000

Like all balance sheets, assets = liabilities + shareholders' equity. In this case, the liabilities are nil. Your £150,000 spent on the house is effectively the amount of share capital you've put into your little business. As this house is an investment, you expect to make a return and you rent the house out to a load of students and receive £12,000 per annum, after all taxes.

What's the Return on Equity? _____

In this case, it is clear that your return on equity is 8 per cent (net profit of £12,000 ÷ shareholder's equity of £150,000 x 100 = 8%). We are assuming your students are model tenants, pay all their bills, and don't leave you with expensive repairs and maintenance bills (as if that really happens!). Your profit and loss statement at the end of year one would simply look like:

Income	15,000
Less Tax @ 20%	(3,000)
Net Profit	12,000
Less Dividends	0
Retained Profits	12,000

And your balance sheet at the end of year one would look like:

ASSETS		
One House	150,000	
Cash At Bank	12,000	
		162,000
SHAREHOLDERS' EQUITY		
Share Capital	150,000	
Retained Earnings	12,000	
		162,000

As you can see, after Year 1 you've created an additional £12,000 worth of assets, in the form of cash at the bank. Also, as a shareholder, you've now got a claim over £162,000, and since this is a one-person company, this is effectively equivalent to your net worth.

Year 2 begins and your starting shareholders' equity is £162,000. With inflation running at 5 per cent per annum, if you leave the annual rent bill unchanged at £12,000, you will slowly start seeing the real value of your income eroded. Also, if you only managed to receive total income of £12,000 versus your starting shareholders' equity of £162,000, your ROE falls from 8.0 per cent to 7.4 per cent. Look:

$$ROE = \frac{£12,000}{£162,000} = 0.074 \text{ or } 7.4\%$$

Looking back to Year 1, if you'd have paid the net profit of £12,000 out in dividends to shareholders (i.e. yourself), your starting equity would have been £150,000 and the Year 2 ROE would have been based on that lower starting point. Virtually all companies retain at least some earnings to invest back in the business in the hope of growing the business. A good company will increase its ROE. Any company can grow its earnings, but only the better ones can grow their ROE.

Great companies usually have a high ROE. The average return on shareholder's equity over a long period of time has been about 12 per cent. That may seem quite low but, over time, competition is a great leveller. Just look at the number of mobile phone re-selling shops that have popped up on High Streets across the country in recent years. Even my local dry cleaning shop is now selling them in the back corner of the shop. Does that say something to you about the returns available in this business? They're likely to be pretty high. However, as more and more of these shops open – remember the barriers to entry are relatively low – returns will come down as competition intensifies. Eventually, some of these shops will be driven out of business. Competition, as we've said, is a wonderful leveller, although obviously very painful for the losers, and is the very basis of the capitalist system.

Companies with high ROEs include

- Glaxo Wellcome
- Vodafone Airtouch
- Lloyds TSB
- Sage
- PizzaExpress

All of these have been great long-term investments for their shareholders.

Before leaving ROE, let's go back to the thorny topic of purchased goodwill, which we briefly discussed in Chapter 8. This is an accounting term and occurs when one company acquires another. It is the difference between a company's net asset value and the price which it is purchased. In the above example, net asset value of the company called Ally's Abode is £162,000. If Hector's House PLC bought Ally's Abode for £200,000, the purchased goodwill would be £38,000 (£200,000 – £162,000).

Up until December 1998, Generally Accepted Accounting Practices (GAAP) allowed UK companies to treat purchased goodwill as a deduction to shareholder's equity. This meant the classic ROE calculation often came up with numbers that were artificially high. Acquisitive companies often looked as if their ROE was well over 100 per cent, whereas the true figure was much less. Fools should keep an eye out for these types of companies, and manually add back purchased goodwill to get the true shareholder's equity number, and therefore the ROE.

Return on Equity Valuations

Long-term investors, as all Fools are, should not be concerned with earnings forecasts for this year or next. The challenge for investors is to identify great companies with superb economics and wonderful long-term growth prospects and ideally buy them at sensible prices. When valuing shares using ROE, we like to look at a company's potential valuation ten years from now.

This sort of valuation is only applicable for companies that have a high degree of predictability of earnings. Looking ten years out for Internet start-up companies, or high technology concerns that have rapidly depreciating products which are obsolete in a matter of months, it is almost impossible to predict what sort of a returns they will be earning. That's not to say that you should never be invested in those types of companies, it's just that using a 10-year ROE model is not suitable. Likewise, companies that are currently going through rapid periods of growth should not necessarily be valued as if that rate of growth will be maintained for a year, let alone 10 years.

Clive's Canny Carvings (CCC)

CCC is a newly floated company, starting with owner's equity, or shareholders' funds, of £1000. From that investment the company made an after-tax profit of £200, giving CCC a return on equity of 20 per cent (£200/£1000 = 20%). Of that £200 attributable to shareholders, CCC decides to pay out 40 per cent, or £80, as dividends.

Summarizing that:

Starting Equity £1000

Net Profits £200 (ROE = 20%)

The £200 profit is divided into

a) £120 retained earnings, or 60% (£120/£200)

b) £80 distributed as a dividend, or 40% (£80/£200)

CCC is a very predictable business, and has been achieving steady profit growth over a number of years prior to flotation. Clive has a nice little niche business, and there is little threat of serious competition that would dent his returns. CCC is an ideal business with which to project forward a valuation based on its return on equity, taking into account its dividend payout and retained earnings ratio. Here's how a 10-year projection would look:

YEAR	EQUITY	PROFITS	DIVIDEND	RETAINED
0	1,000.00	200.00	80.00	120.00
1	1,120.00	224.00	89.60	134.40
2	1,254.40	250.88	100.35	150.53
3	1,404.93	280.99	a._____	168.59
4	1,573.52	314.70	125.88	188.82
5	1,762.34	352.47	140.99	211.48
6	1,973.82	394.76	157.91	236.86
7	2,210.68	442.14	176.85	b._____
8	2,475.96	495.19	198.08	297.12
9	c._____	554.62	221.85	332.77
10	3,105.85	d._____	248.47	372.70
Total Dividends			1,652.37	

How did you get on? Before we reveal the hidden location of the answers, we'll first give you a clue, just in case you're struggling.

Clue

In year 0, the £120 retained earnings are added to the initial £1000 equity to give a new starting position of £1120. A 20 per cent return on that starting equity gives a year 1 profit of £224, of which 40 per cent is paid out in dividends (40% × £224 = £89.60) and 60 per cent is retained in the business (60% × £224 = 134.40). This scenario continues for the full ten years.

The answers are at the bottom of this page.[4] We didn't hide them very well, did we?

Over the course of the ten years, CCC's equity has risen from £1000 to £3105.85. That gives a compound annual growth rate (CAGR) of exactly 12 per cent. Not surprising, really, given that the company earned a steady 20 per cent on equity throughout the ten years and retained 60 per cent of it – 60 per cent of 20 per cent equals 12 per cent.

Say that CCC traded at exactly the value of its shareholders' equity – also known as book value – in year 0 of £1000 and at book value again in year ten of £3105.85. If you bought the business in Year 0 at its initial book value of £1000, your total return over ten years would be £3105.85 plus dividend income of £1652.37 = £4758.22.

What would be your total growth and CAGR? These are easy by now, aren't they?

Total growth = (£_____ ÷ £1,000) – 1 = _____ or _____%[5]

Since you've got this manual CAGR calculation sussed, we're going to take the quick route on this one, using computer spreadsheet terminology.

CAGR[6]

Step 1. $(£4{,}758.22 \div £1{,}000)\verb|^|(1/10) =$ _____

Step 2. Subtract 1 (this is my favourite step)

Step 3. Multiply by 100 (this is my second favourite step)

Step 4. Throw on the percentage sign, giving you CAGR of _____%.

You get it – your CAGR would be 16.9 per cent – a very good return, and much better than what you'd get by sticking your money under the bed or in the building society.

(Note. You will notice that we've ignored most taxes, including any possible Capital Gains Tax, and any further tax an investor may have to pay on his dividend income. We're deliberately trying to keep things simple.)

If CCC were quoted on the stock exchange, it may be valued quite differently to book value. Companies are traditionally valued by the City at a multiple of earnings, or the P/E ratio, which we've already discussed. Taking the exercise a little further, here are some more assumptions based on the Year 0 numbers:

Shares in issue 2000

EPS 10p (£200 profit/2000 shares)

Share price 180p

P/E 18 (180p share price ÷ 10p EPS)

Market capitalization £3,600 (180p share price × 2,000 shares)

With profits expected to grow at 12 per cent

---

[4] a) £112.39, calculated as profits of £280.99 x dividend pay-out ratio of 40% = £112.39.

b) £265.28, calculated as profits of £442.14 x retained earnings ratio of 60% = £265.28.

c) £2273.08, calculated as Year 8 starting equity of £2475.96 + year 8 retained earnings of £297.12 = £2273.08

d) £621.17, calculated as starting equity of £3105.85 x return on equity of 20% = £621.17

[5] (£4,758.22 ÷ £1,000) – 1 = 3.76 or 376%

[6] Step 1. 1.169 Step 2 0.169 Step 3 16.9 Step 4 16.9%

per annum, and the company trading at a price to earnings ratio (P/E) of 18, many investors may automatically assume the company is fully valued or even overvalued. That is because, it is often said, in a fairly valued situation, a company's P/E will equal its growth rate. What would its Fool Ratio be, and what would it indicate?

CCC's Fool Ratio is _____ and this indicates the company is _____.

Either you've committed this one to memory, or flicked back to page 151. We did the latter, and came up with a Fool Ratio of 1.50, which indicates the company is richly valued. We also re-read the Proceed With Caution box while back there.

On a 10-year ROE perspective, however, investors may see a slightly more favourable valuation for CCC. Let's presume over that period CCC trades at an average P/E of 20, having hit a high of 35 in Year 3 and a low of 12 in Year 6. In Year 10, CCC's profits are £621.17 – see table on page 161. Assuming a P/E of 20 on those profits gives a market capitalization of £12,423.40 (20 x £621.17). Add to that the dividends of £1652.37 you've received, and your potential total return is £12,423.40 + £1652.37 = £14,075.77. The CAGR – you definitely know how to do this now – based on a £3600 market capitalization starting point is an impressive 14.6 per cent.

At this stage it always makes good sense to calculate the potential high and low points of a company's valuations. With a Year 10 P/E of 12, the CAGR would fall to 9.7 per cent, and at the top end with a P/E of 35, your CAGR would increase to a whopping 20.6 per cent. You may decide that the upside potential outweighs the downside, and buy all, or a part of, CCC.

The mix between retained earnings and dividends is a very important determinant of total returns. For example, if CCC retained 100 per cent of its earnings, leaving them in the business to compound at the return on equity rate of 20 per cent, over 10 years the book value would increase to £6191.74 for a CAGR of exactly 20 per cent. In a stock market situation, if you then whacked a P/E of 20 on to year 10 profits of £1238.35, your £3600 would increase to £24,766.95, for a CAGR of 21.27 per cent. This is a big difference to the 14.6 per cent CAGR we calculated when 40 per cent of earnings were paid out as dividends. Think back to the compound interest example in Chapter 2 for a moment to see just how big a difference it is. A £2000 investment at 14.6 per cent for 10 years will give you £7814. Meanwhile, at 21.27 per cent, you'd be looking at £13,758.

This type of profit projection works on relatively few companies. It is most effective with mature, established companies and ones that can sustain above average returns over a long period of time.

AND FINALLY . . .

Wow – that was rather heavy stuff. We've listed all these different valuation techniques in the belief that at some stage in your investing career you'll make use of some or all of them. At the very least, they should help you understand how the stock market values companies over the very long term. Using what you've learnt here, when looking at a company, by using more than one valuation technique, you'll come up with a range of values for a business. That range may be as wide as 25 per cent (say you value a company between 1200p and 1500p), but at least that gives you some feel for the potential current valuation of the company.

Littered throughout this chapter are caveats about valuation, and it just wouldn't be right if we didn't repeat a couple of them here. You can do all the valuations in the world and still not be a successful investor. Strange as that may seem, since you've just read (you were reading, weren't you?) 10,000 words on this stuff, but it's very true. It is impossible to place a definite value, with any degree of confidence, on a great many of the 2000 quoted companies on the London Stock Exchange. Does that mean you should only invest in companies on which you can place a definite valuation? No. Definitely not. See the Rule Breakers, Makers and Shakers chapter for another view of the investing world entirely.

Getting the quality of the company right is the number one valuation technique. Trying to value 'dogs' – as notoriously poor companies are known – is like trying to grow grass in January. It's impossible, and pure guesswork. Stick to the quality, well managed companies, who have an excellent past record of growth and profitability, and ones in which you feel confident enough to be sure that the future will be as good as the past.

Always make your own investment decisions. Don't blindly follow the magazine and newspaper tipsters – if you do and the investment goes bad, the tipsters aren't going to take any responsibility. In fact, it's likely you'll never see the company mentioned ever again in the offending publication. It's amazingly uncanny how often the winners are revisited. You can just

see it – 'We tipped Powderduff PLC last September at 250p, and shares have now risen to 305p. Oh how fantastic we are, and err . . . don't forget to buy a copy of this great publication next week.' As for the losers, they become amazingly anonymous. Unlike the tipsters, you *are* accountable – but luckily only to yourself and/or partner.

Having done all your homework and research, and finally decided to take the plunge, at the time of purchase make sure you make some notes. Keep your valuation papers or spreadsheets. Set targets for the growth of the company. Keep a note of the current earnings estimates and various valuations. Obviously you'll already have the company's latest annual report – hang on to it. If you're really keen, write yourself a brief buy report, detailing why you're buying the company and why you think it will be a good investment, as we do when one of our online real money Fool portfolios buys a company. It will be a valuable reference point, and learning experience, whether the investment goes well or not so well.

So, that's share valuation done to death. Next step in this workbook wonderland is the seductive chapter titled Perfecting Your Portfolio. You see, once you've checked the three accounting statements, identified some great companies, and valued them (if that's your style), it's time to consider putting them into a portfolio of shares, and one whose value you hope will march forward over time. Onwards, Foolish soldiers . . .

CHAPTER 11

Perfecting Your Portfolio

'The pursuit of perfection, then, is the pursuit of sweetness and light.'
Matthew Arnold

Having read this far, you should now be ready to put together a portfolio of shares that will help secure your long-term financial future. Gosh, just think that if you started this investment lark at the tender age of eighteen, you may even be able to retire before you hit the half-century mark. That's 32 years of compounding returns. If your late Great Aunt Helda left you £10,000 on your eighteenth birthday, and you Foolishly invested that in the stock market, you should have amassed almost £400,000 by the time you're fifty. That should to help pay for the fiftieth birthday bash!

The £400,000 is based on a compounding return of 12.2 per cent, the same rate as shares have returned from 1919 to 1999. If you beat the index, and achieve a compounding return of 15 per cent per annum – which is far from impossible – your nest egg would be £875,000. Ah, the power of compounding interest. Bet you never knew that a 2.8 per cent per year difference in your investment return could be worth so

much money to you until you read the section earlier on compound interest. Nor did we until we started doing these calculations. WOW!

Just Think

While we're playing with some numbers, consider instead if Aunt Helda had kicked the bucket on the day you were born. Apart from being a sad moment for your family, in 40 years' time you would be a millionaire if your parents had Foolishly invested this money in the stock market on your behalf. You'd certainly be toasting your late Auntie at that particular birthday party.

But, who wants to stop investing when they're 40, 50, or 90? OK, you do want to enjoy the fruits of your labour at some stage in your life, but you can do that *and* keep investing. The chances are that you'll be having so much fun that you'll want to keep investigating individual companies, looking for the acorn that will turn into an oak tree. The next Vodafone AirTouch, or Glaxo Wellcome, or Tesco is out there somewhere. Why, you've probably already uncovered quite a few over the past years. When the time comes to splash out on that world cruise, or holiday house, or putting the kids through school, simply liquidate part of your portfolio, and leave the rest to continue to grow and grow. When your time comes to wave goodbye to this planet and all who sail on her, you'll both have had a rewarding and enriching life, and you'll be able to help secure the long-term financial future of your descendants, just like Aunt Helda did for you.

Having read the above couple of paragraphs, and the rest of this book, you may be thinking that we Fools are evangelists, a band of born-again investors. You may be thinking this is some sort of 'get rich quick' scheme, and are waiting for the catch. Well, there is a catch. It's called time, patience and just a little skill. Nothing more is required. History shows that you can get rich by investing in the stock market, but it takes many, many years of compounding returns to reach those glorious levels we've just been ogling at. If only all of us had the foresight to start investing earlier in life, us included! But, all is far from lost, as it is never too late to start investing money in shares.

Back to the nitty-gritty of building a winning portfolio. Before you dive in, however, we suggest you do this on paper, and not risk your hard-earned money until you're confident of success. There are many pitfalls along the way, and that's not counting the inevitable stock market fluctuations. You see, as well as stock picking skill, you also need to be able to control your emotions. Can you sit there and watch 20 per cent of the value of your portfolio wiped out in the space of a few months? Believe me, Fools, this will happen more than once over an extended time period of 20 years or more. However, the good news is that these 'corrections' often create excellent buying opportunities. On top of that, history has shown that the stock market always recovers, and continues its relentless march forward. Love it or hate it, that's capitalism for you.

One of the biggest mistakes many novice investors make is having too many shares in their portfolio. Whilst it is a great feeling to ring up your broker, or log on to their web site, and confidently place a buy order for Faxes Are Us PLC, *and* Phone Us PLC, *and* Drinkup.com PLC, *and* Calendar City PLC . . . you'll end up with relatively small holdings in lots of companies. Whilst this may impress your friends, the chances are that your portfolio isn't going to be the real winner you hoped it would be. Remember you are buying a business, not a share price. You want to be able to keep up to speed with developments in that company, looking at and assessing its progress at least twice a year. If you've got 25 companies in your portfolio, that means on average there will be at least one major announcement concerning them every single week of the year, and probably a lot more. That's too much to keep up with.

Some investors have very focused portfolios, owning major positions in, say, only five companies. This is Warren Buffett's style. He often has 30 per cent of his portfolio invested in just one company. The fact that the one company is Coca-Cola, one of the greatest long-term investments of our time, is no coincidence. To make large investments in one company, you have to be absolutely sure of your facts, and have the emotional steel to live with the inevitable bumps a focused portfolio brings with it.

For the average Foolish investor, we reckon a portfolio of between eight and fifteen individual companies is about right, with fifteen being a fraction on the high side. It is true that a more diversified portfolio lessens the risk of loss, but it is also true that a really diversified portfolio lessens the chance of truly exceptional performance. With a heavily diversified portfolio, you will probably end up largely tracking the performance of the main indices, but probably not beating them. Therefore, why own fifteen or more individual companies, with all the dealing charges that go into buying and selling those shares, when you can buy a very low cost index tracking fund and match the returns of the FTSE 100? There's the fun and educational factor to consider, but I've yet to meet anyone who enjoys losing money.

Having read the above, and the first 80 pages of this workbook, you took the plunge and decided to buy shares in ten companies. You put together the following portfolio.

YOUR PORTFOLIO, AS AT 1/1/2010

COMPANY	SHARES	BUY PRICE	COSTS	TOTAL COST
Large Cap – The Ballast				
British Telecommunications	200	1050p	£26	£2,126
Vodafone Airtouch	150	1330p	£25	£2,020
Glaxo Wellcome	100	1850p	£24	£1,874
Unilever	320	580p	£24	£1,880
Medium Cap – The Growers				
Hays	280	625p	£24	£1,774
Dixons	100	1150p	£21	£1,171
Misys	200	560p	£21	£1,141
Sage	80	2100p	£23	£1,703
Smaller Cap – The Acorns				
Trafficmaster	400	375p	£23	£1,523
e-Meringue	300	385p	£21	£1,176
Total			£232	£16,388

(A Foolish note: Don't buy any of these companies without doing any research. These are most definitely not share tips. They are merely illustrative.)

What's the first thing that strikes you about this portfolio? To me, it's the familiar names that make up the ballast of the portfolio. You've probably heard of each one of these companies, or seen their brands. You have witnessed and even participated in the huge growth of the Internet, and know that British Telecommunications must be a beneficiary. Why, have you looked at your phone bill recently? You've also bought yourself and the rest of your family a mobile phone, and marvelled at their convenience. You've also noticed lots of other people using them, so know they are getting more and more popular. The market leader is Vodafone Airtouch, so this was an easy decision for you.

The mid-caps are not necessarily household names, but have all got impressive past growth records. You found that out by reading the newspapers, by talking to others verbally – yes, person to person, something we Fools still do occasionally – on the Motley Fool message boards, and also by generally keeping your eyes peeled for companies that impress you.

Finally, there's the small-caps. Your new company car was fitted with a Trafficmaster device, and you were so impressed with its traffic management system that you bought the company – or part of it anyway. You know e-Meringue pretty well, having learnt *all* about them in this workbook. Despite the reservations you had about their financial statements, you nevertheless purchase shares in them because you absolutely adore their meringues, as do the rest of your family, and to some extent you're in 'just for the ride'. You realise this is not the Foolish thing to do, but you are going into them with your eyes wide open, and know the risks.

The mix of the portfolio, and the number, or lack of, individual companies is also important. Let's break that down by category.

CATEGORY	% OF PORTFOLIO	STERLING TOTAL
Large Cap – Ballast	48%	£7,900
Medium Cap – Growth	35%	£5,789
Small Cap – Acorns	17%	£2,699

It's no coincidence that the large-caps make up the biggest portion of your portfolio. These are solid companies with solid growth prospects. Over the long term, you should see their share price march forward as these companies continue to grow. They are not going to go out of business anytime soon, and hence form a very solid base to your portfolio.

Some Fools may prefer to mix some mechanical strategies in the portfolio, and these could be in addition to or even take the position of the ballast. In fact, given the returns these strategies have made over the years, you'd perhaps be foolish (note the small 'f') *not* to include them in your portfolio.

Note the costs of buying each individual company. Your friendly online broker will usually charge a minimum of about £15 to trade shares, although this may get lower in the near future. Some companies also have a maximum charge, and this can be as little as £20. In the US, you can buy and sell shares for as little as US$5 a go, with no upper or lower limit. The UK government also gets a piece of the action whenever you buy shares. Called stamp duty, this charge is 0.5 per cent, and is levied on every purchase. Here at the Fool we consider this charge to be preposterous. On the one hand the government wants to encourage us to save for our long-term futures – and we all know by now that investing in the stock market is the best vehicle to achieve this aim – yet on the other hand it is penalising us for doing so. If individual investors are funding their own retirement, and not relying on the government, we're doing the country a favour. Why therefore penalise us with stamp duty? Which brings me on to another Foolish battle cry:

'Down with stamp duty!'

This is an easy one to remember. Every time you buy a share, think of our battle cry.

Let's move on now we've got that off our chest.

The total costs of assembling the portfolio are £232. More importantly, this amounts to only 1.4 per cent of the total cost of the portfolio. Presuming you get your stock picking right in the first place, and the total portfolio appreciates in line with your expectations, as the years go by this percentage – as a proportion of the total value of your portfolio – will only fall. This is in contrast to people who trade shares on a regular basis. They are not only shown to under-perform the market, but they also end up lining their broker's pockets. That's not Foolish.

The portfolio has only ten separate companies. Although the amount invested in this mock portfolio is 'only' £16,388, it could be appropriate for a portfolio up to £1 billion. (At this point, George Soros should feel free to skip the rest of this chapter.) On the lower side, you can start a stock selection portfolio with as little as £2500. This would be spread over five ballast-type companies, with each selection being a minimum of £500. The costs to buy £500 worth of shares in a company could end up being as low as 1.5 per cent, depending on which broker and type of broker you chose. It would also end up being as high as 3 per cent or 5 per cent. Remember the difference between annual returns of 12.2 per cent and 15 per cent per annum, compounded over 40 years? Every

percentage point counts.

You should be able to keep up with the progress of all ten companies in this portfolio. The large-caps will hopefully need less maintenance than the smaller-caps, but nevertheless you should keep up to speed with developments. Any more companies than fifteen and you'll really be struggling to keep on top of things.

e-Meringue

You bought your shares at the beginning of 2010 in e-Meringue at 385p. Flick forward to the performance table on the next page and take a look at how they performed during the year. Come the end of 2010, the shares now trade at 260p. Ouch! That hurts. It's a paper loss of £396, or 33.7 per cent. And you thought that all shares went up in value? Think again. This can be a tough game. Naturally you've been following the progress of e-Meringue over the course of the year, and have seen its weakening share price. In fact, during the year the shares traded as low as 150p, or a 50 per cent loss, before recovering to 260p by the year end.

The chances are that this share price fall hasn't happened by accident. During the year there could have been a shock profit warning issued by the company. Or sales growth could have slowed. Or management decided to diversify from meringue making into Chinese hedge funds, losing a lot of shareholders' money along the way. Or operating margins could have fallen. Or was it just a bad year for shares in general? Only by looking at the overall performance of your portfolio, and comparing it to a benchmark, will you know if it's the latter.

Your Portfolio – 2010

Come December 2010, you check the share prices of your portfolio, getting them either from the newspaper or from the Motley Fool web site. (Come on, 2010, it'll have to be the web site. Don't tell us you'll be using the *newspaper* to track the progress of your shares!) You then plug them into a simple spreadsheet, or jot them down on a nice piece of ruled paper. You'll need to keep records of this stuff for the taxman, so make sure you do it well. The back of a fag packet just won't do!

OVERALL PERFORMANCE

COMPANY	NO. OF SHARES	BUY PRICE	TOTAL COST	PRICE NOW	VALUE NOW
Large Cap – The Ballast					
British Telecommunications	200	1050p	£2,216	995p	£1,990
Vodafone Airtouch	150	1330p	£2,020	1210p	£1,815
Glaxo Wellcome	100	1850p	£1,874	1720p	£1,720
Unilever	320	580p	£1,880	650p	£2,080
Medium Cap – The Growers					
Hays	280	625p	£1,774	650p	£1,820
Dixons	100	1150p	£1,171	1300p	£1,300
Misys	200	560p	£1,141	650p	£1,300
Sage	80	2100p	£1,703	1900p	£1,520
Smaller Cap – The Acorns					
Trafficmaster	400	375p	£1,523	345p	£1380
e-Meringue	300	385p	£1,176	260p	£780
Total			£16,388		£15,705

Oh dear. It doesn't look like 2010 has been a great investing year for you. To offset that, perhaps something positive happened: you got married, had a child, or found a great new job instead. There's more to life than sitting watching your share prices go up and down on a minute-by-minute, or even month-by-month basis.

Anyway, you've only got four winners and six losers. On the upside, good old Misys has served you well, and Unilever has had a good year too. e-Meringue has been the real dog. Investors have been selling Vodafone Airtouch, and haven't been too enamoured with Sage this year. Either it's not been a great year for shares in general, or you've done a poor job of picking individual companies.

Let's look at the percentage returns for the year.

PERFORMANCE BY SHARE

COMPANY	TOTAL COST	PRESENT VALUE	PERCENTAGE RETURN
Large Cap – The Ballast			
British Telecommunications	£2,126	£1,990	-6.4%
Vodafone Airtouch	£2,020	£1,815	-10.1%
Glaxo Wellcome	£1,874	£1,720	-8.2%
Unilever	£1,880	£2,080	10.6%
Medium Cap – The Growers			
Hays	£1,774	£1,820	2.6%
Dixons	£1,171	£1,300	11.0%
Misys	£1,141	£1,300	13.9%
Sage	£1,703	£1,520	-10.7%
Smaller Cap – The Acorns			
Trafficmaster	£1,523	£1,380	-9.4%
e-Meringue	£1,176	£780	-33.7%
Total	£16,388	£15,705	-4.2%

In 2010, you've managed to convert a starting sum of £16,388 into £15,705, or a loss of £683, or 4.2 per cent. e-Meringue has been a disaster, losing you £396. Your biggest winner, in sterling terms, has been Unilever, which appreciated by a total of £200. The rest of the shares bounced about a bit, but because you had more losers than winners, and two of them were your biggest holdings, BT and Glaxo Wellcome, your portfolio ended 2010 in the red.

As you analyze the portfolio's performance, you should have a look at the performance of your shares by category – the ballast, growers and acorns. Often this can help you pinpoint where you went wrong, or in which sector your area of expertise lays. It could be that you've misallocated funds, or that you're better at picking the acorns than the ballast.

PERFORMANCE BY CATEGORY

CATEGORY	TOTAL COST	PRESENT VALUE	PROFIT/(LOSS)	PERCENTAGE RETURN
Large Cap – Ballast	£7,900	£7,605	(£295)	-3.7%
Medium Cap – Growth	£5,789	£5,940	(£151)	2.6%
Small Cap – Acorns	£2,699	£2,160	(£539)	-20.0%
Total	£16,388	£15,705	(£683)	-4.2%

Nearly £400, or 58 per cent of your near £700 total loss came about because of your investment in e-Meringue. Still think they taste good? The ballast didn't have a great year either, but thankfully the growers held things together for you, rising 2.6 per cent over the course of a difficult year. Looking at the table above, it looks like you've done a lousy job of picking smaller companies. Trafficmaster also deflated, leaving the so-called acorns down almost 20 per cent for the year. You also haven't done too well with your larger companies either, although there's less cause for concern there because you should be able to rely on these giant companies to remain excellent long-term investments. After all, that's why you bought them in the first place!

This ain't supposed to happen, is it? We Fools have been telling you all along that the stock market is the place to invest, and that it is a wealth creation scheme. If that is the case, you're probably asking 'Why have I lost money?' There may be a perfectly valid reason.

Have you noticed one vital statistic that's been missing from all our tables to date? It's tragically not going to bring back your lost £683, but it will help you compare the performance of your portfolio to the total universe of shares.

Go on, write down the deliberate error below. What information haven't we provided you?

_____

Exactly right. The performance of the FTSE All Share index. It tracks the share price performance of the UK's 800-odd largest companies, and is a good benchmark against which to measure the return of your portfolio. You should also use the FTSE SmallCap index to compare the results of your Acorns against, because the two indices sometimes move in completely different directions to each other. For example, 1998 saw the FTSE All Share make large gains (11 per cent) whilst the FTSE SmallCap had a nightmare, losing 10.5 per cent.

The FTSE 100 index, affectionately also known as the Footsie, is the most popular and widely quoted index, and can be substituted for the FTSE All Share. When your TV or radio newsreader says 'Footsie up, Footsie down, put your right leg in, put your right leg out', they are talking about the FTSE 100 index. It measures the performance, by weighting, of the biggest 100 companies in the UK. Some index tracking funds mirror the performance of the FTSE 100 index, and some follow the FTSE All-Share index. Some years the All Share wins, and in others the Footsie wins. There is no clear pattern of success for either one index or the other, so to our minds there is little mileage to be gained or lost in choosing an All Share index tracking fund over a Footsie one.

When comparing your portfolio's performance to the indices, it could be that the market gained 10 per cent in 2010, meaning you've had a more than disappointing year. You may be better off scrapping individual stock picking altogether, and plumping your money into an index tracking fund. That way you can be guaranteed to match the returns of the market, and at the same time you'll beat the investment returns made by most managed unit trusts. On the other hand, the market could have lost a whopping 20 per cent in the year, in which case you'd be feeling rather pleased with yourself, having lost just 4.2 per cent.

No-one likes to lose money, but measured over relatively short time periods, such as one year, it could very well happen. Remember your investing life should be measured in terms of many years, and not just one year. Even the very best investors have down years, but they more than make up for it in the years they win. Whilst the market has gone up an average of 12.2 per cent since World War I, it hasn't done so in a straight line. The Great Crash of 1929, followed by the Depression of the 1930s saw as much as 90 per cent wiped from the value of shares. The bear market of 1973/74 saw shares lose well over half of their value. Old market hands (*really* old market hands in the case of 1929) will tell you how difficult it was to live through those times, watching helplessly while your paper worth was being decimated. However, those investors with patience, and who could sit out those bad times, were rewarded in the long term – for example, after the carnage of the previous two years, 1975 was one of the best years ever for shares. As we

follow through this exercise, always bear in mind that one investing year is still only a relatively short time period over which to measure your overall performance.

Let's see how your imaginary portfolio actually performed against the indices in 2010.

VERSUS MARKET PERFORMANCE

	31/12/2009	31/12/2010	PERCENTAGE RETURN
FTSE All-Share	3400	3150	-7.4%
FTSE Small Cap	2980	2810	-5.7%
Your Portfolio	£16,388	£15,705	-4.2%

You beat the market! Congratulations! It may be hard to get really excited when you actually lost money in the year, but it hopefully shows you've got the skill to beat the market on a consistent basis. And, as we all know, the market will march up over time, and if you can beat it in most years, your first million may not be as far away as you think.

Letting Time Work for You

We love throwing a few numbers out there, just to show the power of time and compound interest. Just £200 saved per month, in an index tracking fund growing at 12.2 per cent per annum, will see you hit the million in 33 years' time. Even if you start saving when you're 27, having spent much of your twenties frequenting snazzy wine bars and the backs of black cabs, £1 million at age 60 is nothing to sniff at.

Your imaginary portfolio is down, but

certainly not out. It could be just that 2010 was one of those bad years for shares overall, and that 2011 will be a much better year. Remember share prices often move independently of company performance. e-Meringue may have had a storming year, with excellent sales and profit growth, yet the market saw fit to punish the share price, for whatever reason. In fact, on every market day the prices of hundreds of shares move despite there being no news whatsoever about the company. Looked at on a daily basis, the stock market is an auction house, where the laws of supply and demand affect a company's share price. We're looking out five, ten, twenty and more years' time for our return period, not one year, or, much worse, between the hours of 9.30 am and 4.30 pm on a single trading day.

As to why 2010 was a bad year for shares, it could be for any number of reasons. Try these for size;

- The stock market in general was considered over-valued at the beginning of 2010, having risen by an average of 16.5 per cent per annum over the past four years.
- The inflationary outlook has worsened, meaning Alan Oscroft, ex-Fool and now Governor of the Bank of England, was forced to unexpectedly raise interest rates. Stock markets hate this – remember the crash of 1987? – and they collapsed in mid-2010 before staging a mini-recovery towards the end of the year.
- The Prime Minister, Lulu Tubby, was involved in a sex and drugs scandal, and this depressed the market.
- Investors switched their cash out of the UK market and, knowing that the Moon was a growth market, threw money at this emerging (and high) market.

- A newspaper column said the market was wildly over-valued, and that everyone should sell up and head for the Mediterranean.

What are you going to do? The market is clearly unsettled, for whatever reason, and you've lost money. Tempted to throw the game away and cash out? Before you do, reflect once again that these knocks are just part and parcel of being an investor in the greatest wealth creation vehicle ever invented: the stock market. And, don't forget that you've beaten that market this year.

While you may need to take some remedial action, and we'll look at that next, always remember that time is on your side. You went into all this thinking long term, and one year simply does not count as that.

ALL SORTS OF RETURNS

In the above example, we've looked at the returns over a one year period. Horror of all horrors, 2010 saw our imaginary portfolio on the slide, but we're not fazed – we've got a lot of years left yet to build our fortune. Let's have a look at the various types of returns that you'll want to be calculating.

1. **Annual Return**. We've just done that one. It's the gain or loss you've made over just one year. If your annual return is 12 per cent, it means that your investment gained 12 per cent in the year. In this case, your portfolio lost 4.2 per cent, which is calculated as

$$\frac{2010 \text{ End point } £15,705}{2010 \text{ Start point } £16,387} -1 = 0.416 \text{ or } 4.2\%$$

2. **Total Return.** This is the total appreciation (or depreciation, but we hope that's not the case over the long term) of an investment. Your imaginary portfolio lost 4.2 per cent in its first year. That's the same as saying the portfolio is worth 95.8 per cent of its starting point, in other words 100 per cent minus 4.2 per cent = 95.8 per cent. Next year, 2011, from a starting point of £15,705, let's say your annual return turned out to be 16.5 per cent (2011 is shaping to be a good year for shares, but don't hold us to it!) You want to calculate your total return for the two-year period. Here's how:

1 = portfolio value at starting point
1 x 95.8% = 0.958 (value after Year 1)
0.958 x 116.5% = 1.116 (value after Year 2)
1.116 − 1 (starting point) = 0.116
or 11.6% = total return

You can do the same calculation using the pound sterling amounts.

£16,388 x 0.958 = £15,700* (value after Year 1)
£15,700 x 116.5% = £18,290
£18,290 − £16,387 = £1,903
£1,903 ÷ £16,387 = 0.116
or 11.6% = total return

* Note that the difference between £15,700 and £15,705 in the tables on the previous page is due to rounding errors, because instead of losing 4.2 per cent, the imaginary portfolio actually lost 4.16768 per cent.

3. **Average annual return.** This is the same concept as the compounded annual growth rate, or CAGR, as discussed in Chapter 10. Let's briefly go over another example. There's a bit of root work here, but thankfully we're not talking about drilling at any nerves below your teeth. Imagine your portfolio has risen 159 per cent over the past eight years. You simply need to take the eighth root of [1 (your original investment) + 1.59 (the rise in value)] = 2.59. Using a scientific calculator, like the one on your computer, tap in 2.59, then 'shift' or 'inv' and then '8' and then 'equals' and you should get the answer, 1.126. That's a return of 12.6 per cent per annum over an 8-year period, and a lot better than what you'd get from your friendly building society! To check that number is right, you could multiply 1.126 by itself 8 times, and see what you get.

4. **Return versus the market.** We've done the above calculations on your portfolio. You should always do the same calculations for the overall market too, to see how you are comparing. If the market is up a total of 65 per cent over five years and your portfolio is up only 42 per cent, you're losing. You'd be better off investing your money in an index tracker. If the market is up only 36 per cent over five years, on the other hand . . .

What's the CAGR; market up 36 per cent in five years . . . ?

_____[1]

and you're up 42 per cent, you're doing mighty fine. Conventional Wisdom hasn't caught up with these simple calculations or, more to the point, they conveniently leave them off their marketing literature. You, on the other hand, are being Foolish and not kidding yourself. If you are failing to beat the market, it's not the end of the world, because you can transfer your funds into a

_____

[1] 6.3%

cheap index tracker, relax and live happily ever after! We love happy endings here at the Fool.

Industry Doublespeak

In 1999, a major fund company, Mercury Asset Management (MAM), was still sending out deeply flawed promotional marketing literature. How so? They were displaying four snazzy graphs of the performance of their funds. The first two (three-month performance history and one-year performance history) showed the funds' performance against the index, which they roughly matched, or even beat. The second two graphs of three- and five-year performance, however, strangely dropped the index. Back-of-the-envelope calculations carried out at the Motley Fool revealed the reason: the index had beaten the MAM funds resoundingly over those longer periods.

Smelly? Yes, smellier than a two-week-old haddock on a Caribbean beach holiday.

WHAT NEXT?

First things first. You should always look to be constantly adding new cash to your portfolio. That's an easy decision to make. If you are saving money into an index tracking fund on a monthly basis, that's an ideal way to add funds to your portfolio. If on the other hand you are running an active portfolio, you'll need to save up the money over a few months so that you have an economical amount (minimum £500) and can then buy shares in another company, or add to an existing holding. Whichever way you're saving, and you can obviously do both, it's great that you're adding to your nest egg.

You should look to be taking care of your actively managed portfolio. A portfolio needs mothering over time. Whilst here we are looking at a snapshot of your imaginary portfolio after one year, you should have been following the progress of your companies as the year progressed. At the very minimum you'll have seen each of your companies release two sets of results – interim and final. The chances are your company will have made a trading statement at its Annual General Meeting (AGM), and if they've made an acquisition or disposal, you'll also have heard from them.

If you've done your homework right in the first place, the large-caps, or ballast, shouldn't need too much looking after. Is BT still growing sales, profits, cash-flow and dividends? Are they still expanding abroad, always looking to extend their long tentacles? Is Vodafone Airtouch continuing to dominate the world's wireless communication channels? Are they paying down their debt? Does Glaxo Wellcome still have a great product line, with more potentially block-busting drugs in its pipeline? Are their debtors falling and their creditors rising? These are huge companies, with global reaches. Management should be continuing to do a great job with the core businesses, and also be looking for future growth prospects. After all, that's what you, as shareholders, pay them to do. Of course, it is not always plain sailing, even for the biggest and best companies in the world. The year 1999 has been an *annus horribilis* for Marks & Spencer, that king of the British High Street. Who would have thought that such a great company, with a wonderfully powerful brand name, would see their profits halve from 1998 to 1999? Rentokil Initial, a company whose stated aim is to grow earnings by 20 per cent per annum, saw its share price plummet in 1999 when it warned that earnings for that year would 'only' grow by between 10 and 15 per cent. Even the very best companies can get it wrong. If you have major concerns surrounding any of your large-cap shares, consider selling them. However, this is a decision that should not be taken lightly, because these big companies have the ability to recover, courtesy of their huge financial resources, giant sales and powerful brand names.

The growers need a bit more tending to than the large-caps, but hopefully not too much. By definition, they are fast-growing companies, and therefore quite highly valued by the market. That should remain the case, unless there's a general market sell-off, which is out of your control, or they suddenly stop growing. In the latter case, be prepared for the share price to take a big fall. You therefore have to look out for warning signs that growth may be slowing. That may be a slowing of sales growth or a change in market conditions, such as the entry of a major competitor. Barring that, your company should still be doing all the right things regarding its balance sheet and cash-flow. Telltale signs of problems to come can sometimes first be spotted by a deterioration of the balance sheet. If, for example, debtors are suddenly on the rise without any good reason, it could be that problems are brewing for the company. (Having worked through this book, you now understand what all these terms mean, something you may never have believed before you started.)

The final step is to consider the progress of the acorns, or small-caps. e-Meringue was your biggest disaster, leaving you nursing a 33.7 per cent loss over the past twelve months. Was it that the market was playing one of its tricks, and marked down the shares to what you consider being an irrationally low level? Or was there a shock profit warning? Or has the company run up

a debt problem because it has not been generating enough cash?

Ask yourself the following questions about e-Meringue:

- Is the growth story still intact?
- What's their competitive position?
- What are other people saying about them at the Motley Fool message boards?
- Are you having trouble sleeping at night because of the fall in share price?
- How much do you *really* like their meringues?
- Is there a better place for your money?

At this stage, the hardest thing to do is to take the emotion out of the investment. Analyze the questions above, and the many more which you'll also have, and make a rational business decision. Remember that, in the short term, the share price is often divorced from the company. e-Meringue may be progressing superbly, but the market has decided it is worth 33 per cent less than what you paid for it just twelve months ago. You may have overpaid for the shares in the first instance, and that mistake is now coming back to haunt you. However, that may not necessarily be a reason to sell the shares. If however things don't look too promising for e-Meringue, consider selling, even if it is at a loss. Forget the buy price, because that is history. Admit that you made a mistake, get out of that company, wear the wound proudly and *don't look back*.

SELLING A SHARE

When exactly to sell a share is the trickiest investment decision you'll ever make. It is a far harder decision than the buy – that's because there are lots of buy signals, but very few sell signals. On the buy side, if you're looking at a great company, with great financial statements, great management and a wonderful future – *and you can buy it at an attractive price* – that's an easy decision to make. But, what if this company, once you've bought it, is going through a bad patch, as all companies do, from time to time? Do you sell it straight away, or wait for the potential recovery? The recovery may never happen, in which case your decision to sell would have been the correct one. But, if you sell at the bottom point in a company's cycle, when the share price will also be at the bottom, you will feel like a chump should the company recover its past glories.

What if your company now looks over-valued? Do you sell it? And how do you judge whether a company is overvalued? Many companies have looked habitually overvalued, yet their share price has kept marching forward.

Here at the Motley Fool, we realise this is the most difficult of investment decisions to make. You will never get it right all of the time, that's for sure. Experience, as with all things in life, is invaluable, and you will always learn the most from your mistakes. We all make mistakes and we will all continue to make mistakes, but as long as we learn from them and try and minimise our errors as our investing life continues, we'll be doing well.

As a guide, we suggest the following five selling rules, which cover most scenarios.

1. Sell if you made a mistake by buying the shares in the first place.

You may have bought shares in a company that you hoped was going to be the 'Next Big Thing'. It was probably a bit of a speculative buy anyway or, heaven forbid, you bought it after your ex-mate tipped it to you. Or, you hadn't read this workbook, and didn't realise that a company with sharply rising debtors and falling creditors was one that was potentially storing up future problems for itself. You have another look at the business this company is in, and decide you don't really understand it, so you sell the shares. If you do your homework properly in the first place (i.e. before you buy the shares), this rule should hopefully not be invoked too often.

2. Sell if the company's story has changed, for the worse.

Companies evolve. They hopefully keep on growing and growing over time. But sometimes things go wrong. Suddenly you're looking at quite a different company from the one you first invested in. It may have made an ill advised acquisition, a diversification which took it far away from its core business. You may find that the industry your company operates in is fast deteriorating. The coal and steel industries may have been good ones to invest in many years ago, but these days they are capital-intensive, low-growth industries. Laura Ashley, that veritable British household name, is a classic example of a deteriorating company. This has been reflected in its share price, now languishing at about 15p, compared to a high of 211p in 1996.

3. Sell if you've got a better investment opportunity for your money.

Sometimes you will identify a compelling new opportunity, usually in the form of an equity investment. You should always be looking forward, focusing on the opportunities ahead rather than prior performance. Not having enough liquid funds to add new cash to your portfolio, or because you don't want to over-diversify, you need to sell an existing holding in order to buy the new one.

The difficult part of the equation is choosing which company to sell. One of the biggest mistakes investors make is waiting for one of their losers 'just to get back to break even'. As we've said previously, forget the buying price. If the business is weak, and the shares are not ridiculously cheap, you should sell. Most great investors run their winners and cut their losers.

Having said that, you could also sell a share that you think is considerably over-valued, so much so that the potential future returns look low. However, be aware that some companies are perennially over-valued, as measured by traditional valuation techniques, and that you could find the shares still keep rising and rising long after you've sold them.

4. Sell if one or two companies dominate your portfolio.

Obviously you are hoping this situation came about because you had one or two big winners, not eight big losers!

Again, this one comes with a caveat. Some of the best investors have extremely focused portfolios, and will be happy to be in this situation and to let things carry on from there. These are individuals who are extremely confident investors, feel happy about the companies which dominate their portfolio, can control their emotions, and don't mind shocking volatility in their portfolio's short-term performance.

Since there are very few super-investors out there, we would suggest that you consider taking some profits if and when one or two companies dominate your portfolio. This could happen when one company represents, say, 33 per cent of your portfolio. You will know when the time to sell has come, because you'll be feeling uncomfortable about the dominance this one share is having over your portfolio. The ideal scenario is that you'll be able to combine this rule with rule number 3, and have an excellent replacement candidate already lined up.

5. Sell if you need the money.

This option should only come up if you've done your planning in the first instance. If you were going to need the money in less than three years' time, and ideally five or more years, it shouldn't have been in shares in the first instance. However, presuming you've been invested for that length of time, and you want to spend the money on a new house, yacht, or holiday, go ahead and do it. However, be aware that, courtesy of the power of compounding returns, you make the largest gains in the later years of your investments. Any interruption to that process can affect those returns.

When <u>Not</u> To Sell

1. Because you read in the newspaper that shares in general are over-valued.

Here at the Motley Fool, if we had a pound for every time we've read that a market crash is just around the corner, we'd be well on our way to our first million. They do happen – crashes that is – but only very occasionally. We are often reminded about the October 1987 crash, where over 20 per cent was wiped off the value of shares in one day. In the ensuing twelve years, as of writing, we've witnessed nothing like this again, despite many doomsday pundits predicting the worst. There have been market corrections, like the one in 1998 where the FTSE 100 lost 25 per cent from mid-July to October, a period of just two and a half months. It has subsequently recovered, of course. Despite these occasional natural corrections, and they are probably good for the long-term health of the stock market, the value of shares continues to march relentlessly forward.

No-one can successfully, and consistently, time the market. That means selling all their shares when the market hits a high point in a particular cycle, then buying them all back when the market falls to its low point. There was a graphic illustration of the price of failure in Chapter 5, where we looked at the market moves associated with the 1998 correction. Unfortunately there's no little leprechaun conveniently ringing a bell to tell you when the market reaches a particular high or low point.

Because it is impossible to time the market, we recommend that you stay invested through the natural peaks and troughs. It is not pleasant to see the value of your investments fall by 25 per cent in the space of a few months or less, but if you can't stand the thought of seeing your investments fall by 25 per cent and feel you'll be tempted to sell out, you shouldn't be invested in the market at all.

Just before we leave this sub-section, it is worth noting that market corrections can often throw up wonderful buying opportunities. Share prices are often slashed across the board, completely regardless and independent of the underlying performance of the company. Brave and knowledgeable investors can step in and buy, when others fear to trade. The other way you can benefit from a temporarily falling market is through your monthly contributions into an index tracking fund. These funds are split into millions of units, and you will own a number, or percentage of the units. When the market falls, the value of these units also falls. So, if you are contributing a set monthly amount into your index tracking fund, you will actually be able to buy more units when the market falls, known as pound cost averaging and dealt with in Chapter 5. This should turn to your advantage when the market eventually rises again. Remember, we're talking really long term here.

QUIZ TIME

This is your old favourite true-or-false game. I used to love these at school, as on average I'd be virtually guaranteed to get at least 50 per cent correct. Here's my tip for success – choose 'true' every time.

1. You love investing in shares, and following the Fool's advice, feel a minimum of 30 shares in your portfolio should make you sufficiently diversified.
   True   False

2. You can't begin investing in the stock market yet because you haven't got £500 saved up.
   True   False

3. Melinda Messenger has worn a Fool's jester cap.
   True   False

4. If one of your large-cap ballast shares under-performs the market in any given year, you should sell the share immediately.
   True   False

5. You know you need to pay your credit card bill off, but the only way you're going to do that quickly is if you make a fast buck. The stock market is the best place for you to do that.
   True   False

6. Graham Norton has worn a Fool's cap.
   True   False

7. You should never sell your losing shares, because one day they will come back to the price you paid for them. You're never going to lose money on any individual share.
   True   False

8. Jon Snow has worn a Fool's cap.
   True   False

9. All this Foolish stuff is too difficult for you. You should trust your financial future to the experts because they know their stuff and have got your best interests at heart.
   True   False

10. I've got more chance of winning the lottery than winning in the stock market.
    True   False

11. I need to put the kids through school in two years time. Those building society interest rates are so low it's almost criminal. I'll whack my money in the stock market, because those Fools say I'm guaranteed to make 12.2 per cent per year for the next two years.
    True   False

12. Every answer to this quiz is true.
    True   False

13. Margaret Thatcher has worn a Fool's cap.
    True   False

The answers to every question were false, except for three of them – question numbers 3, 6 and 8. Yes, that's right – Melinda was present at the 1998 Creative Freedom Awards, where the Motley Fool scooped the Best Electronic Media award, and kindly posed for a photograph complete with jester cap. Thanks, Melinda, and we hope you enjoy the book.

Graham Norton presented the Motley Fool with the best personal finance site award at the 1999 *New Media Age* awards and kindly wore the hat. Jon Snow, too, ended up with one on at the 1999 Investor Relations awards dinner.

Margaret Thatcher in a Fool's cap? Mmm. Not very likely.

We'll just clarify one answer, because we hope you thought most of them were obviously false. Number 2 – you can actually start investing as little as a few tens of pounds a month into an index tracking fund.

ADDITIONAL PORTFOLIO MUSINGS

We've covered quite a lot of theory in this chapter. At this stage you may be wondering whether this portfolio building stuff is really worth the trouble. You've heard about market crashes, bad investments, difficult buy *and* sell decisions, and seen our imaginary portfolio lose money in 2010.

There is nothing more satisfying than when you make a successful investment. Even if it is an index tracking fund, you've seen how some of the amounts can add up, given time. And time is the investor's best friend. Picking shares in an individual company and watching its share price soar is the best feeling an investor can get. Not only are you making money, but you're having great fun too.

And having fun is an important part of life. You don't want to be hunched over a newspaper each night looking for the tiniest morsel of news, in the hope that you'll find the next Vodafone Airtouch. You don't want to spend your whole day glued to a computer screen, switching between emotions of great jubilation and huge despair as the share prices of individual companies oscillate on a minute by minute basis. In ten years' time, it won't matter whether e-Meringue gained or lost 5p one day back in 1999.

Education and Folly go hand in hand. This workbook, and the Motley Fool web site, aim to provide you with the tools and knowledge to make your own investment decisions. We exist to help you, and are completely independent of any other organisation, be they financial or media based.

Setting up an Online Portfolio

While we're talking about the Motley Fool web site, instead of using paper or a computer spreadsheet to track the performance of your portfolio, you can set it all up at **www.fool.co.uk** – no more manual entries, and you can watch your portfolio updated manually before your very eyes. What *did* we do before we had computers? Of course there's nothing wrong with tracking your portfolio by using good old-fashioned pen and paper, and if that's what you feel most comfortable in doing, who are we to tell you any different? You're a Fool anyway, and therefore will make your own decisions.

Our perfect portfolio may not be your perfect portfolio – after all, you should make your own financial decisions anyway. Try not to make daily, weekly or even monthly portfolio performance – as opposed to portfolio management, which *is* important – become the be-all and end-all of your investment experience. It can be a little depressing at times when the market is soaring, and your portfolio is tanking. The temptation then could be to throw money at the hottest sector and forget about what you've learned about balance sheets, cash flow statements and valuing shares. You might subscribe to one of the many tip-sheets after reading how their imaginary portfolio of shares rose 63% in the last month. It's very hard to divorce yourself from the emotions of the stock market roller-coaster, but to be successful, that's exactly what you've got to do. Remember always to concentrate on the business, and not the share price. And always think long term.

As much as we'd love it if you spent all day clicking around the Motley Fool site, checking out the busiest message boards in the UK, seeing what Fools are saying about the state of life, the market and the universe, if you spent sixteen hours a day doing that, you'd hardly be living a fulfilling life. We don't want to see that.

Finally, remember to manage your portfolio, NOT have your portfolio manage you.

CHAPTER 12

America!

'America is the only nation in history which miraculously has gone directly from barbarism to degeneration without the usual intervention of civilization.'
Georges Clemenceau

When we started the UK Fool, we were surprised at how few of the UK users were going on to visit and use the US Motley Fool site, which was superior in so many respects to our own that it shames us to think of it. They just didn't seem interested. Surely, we thought, the nation which has given us *Baywatch*, Jerry Springer and the bottomless coffee pot in restaurants deserves more consideration than *this*? Following a brainstorming session of the entire company[1] in the early days of our existence, we decided there were probably a variety of reasons. These were amongst them:

- Our UK users were simply not familiar with American companies
- It never occurred to them that investing in the USA was a reasonable thing to do
- They were put off by US jargon
- They were put off at the thought of US share

---

[1] Read: 'Bruce and I had a chat over a pizza one night.'

scams and stockbrokers going bust
- They had no idea how to actually go about buying US company shares
- They were worried about the currency risk

All these are legitimate, understandable concerns, but we are going to cast them aside for just a moment as we once more chew the tops of our pencils in consternation and cast our eyes down for another *leedle* quiz:

Fill in the country for each question:

a) _____ has probably the most stringent financial reporting regulations in the world.

b) _____ has the largest stock market in the world. By far.

c) _____ is chock-full of consumer companies with worldwide brands.

d) _____ is currently leading the technological revolution sweeping the world.

e) _____ has a strong reputation for fostering enterprise and innovation.

f) _____ is renowned for its shy, retiring citizens who hate to create a stir when abroad.

g) _____ has more company information available to private investors than any other country.

h) _____ arrived late for both the first *and* second world wars.

Yes, the answers are all 'America', except question 'f', of course. We're not quite sure what the answer to that one is. Perhaps 'Gabon'. (Have *you* ever seen a Gabonese making a fuss abroad?)

In the world we now live in, wired and in touch, it seems folly to us (note the small 'f') not to even consider investing in the United States. Its economy is booming, it is full of great companies which are shaping the way we live, shop and do everyday things and – get this – they speak English over there. Sort of, anyway. If you have read the book thus far without the aid of a dictionary, you are incredibly fortunate. It means that one of the major barriers to investing in the US has been bypassed. We hate to put up obstacles to anyone investing, but frankly, if you do only speak the Western Balti dialect of Tibetan, it probably isn't such a good idea to be thinking about logging on to the Internet and investing in stocks online in the US because you won't be able to understand much of what is going on. (We would, however, love to have a chat with you about the karmic implications of stock market investing, either on the Fool message boards or by email: **karmicinvestor@ fool.co.uk**. Feel free to write in Tibetan.)

Pray peruse the following list of companies – assembled in no particular order – and then tell us that you haven't heard of all of them or that you have never used the products of at least 50 per cent of them:

- Johnson & Johnson
- Ford
- Campbell Soup
- Hewlett-Packard
- Microsoft
- Gillette
- Boeing
- Intel
- DuPont
- McDonald's
- Disney
- Nike
- Yahoo!
- Pfizer
- Coca Cola

It was a good bet, wasn't it, that you recognised pretty well all these and had used the products of many of them at one time or another? If you were to take a sprinkling of top UK or European companies and try the same test in the US it wouldn't work in quite the same way. While we do have some global franchises on this side of the ocean, we don't have them in the same breathtaking numbers and diversity. America, let's face it, is the spiritual home of capitalism.

You really do know a lot more American companies than you think (even if you don't know about them yet, you can easily learn about them via the phenomenal resources of the Internet) and by the end of this chapter you will be convinced that you want to at least consider investing some of your retirement capital in the US. That's by the end of this chapter, but by the time you finish this book, we'll have you saluting an American flag, getting the family together for

Thanksgiving and singing 'Yankee Doodle Dandy' before breakfast. You can count on it.

In answer, then, to another of the points raised above, more and more British people are already investing in the US and not only is it a reasonable thing to do, it's also *highly* Foolish. Another question which troubles many people is the currency question: if your money is in dollars, what happens if the exchange rate changes for the worse over the years and this eats into your returns? Consider, though, that many of the companies you may consider investing in in the US are world-beaters, likely to provide world-class returns in the years ahead, making currency fluctuations less important. Further, both the pound and the dollar are strong currencies, backed by powerful economies. You'd be unlucky indeed if the US dollar were to be decimated by South American-style hyperinflation, just when you wanted to take your money out. The economic facts of life these days are that if the US goes under, we will all shortly follow. Currency considerations shouldn't deter you from investing at least some of your long-term money in the US.

Feelin' groovy? Pumped? Hot for it? Man, you is one stockpickin' dude. Read on, brother . . .

FINDING A US BROKER – 'TIS SIMPLE

Using a US online discount broker is the easiest, cheapest way to buy US stocks. You may find a UK broker (either on- or offline) who can buy US stocks for you within your UK account, but it will likely be expensive and involve a certain degree of hassle. Alternatively, one of the UK online brokers at the time of writing has just opened a UK, dollar account facility, allowing UK residents to buy US stocks at reasonable prices. Doubtless there will be more very soon.

If you decide you want to use a US-based online broker invest in US companies at the click of a button, as easily as if you were based in Groundhog, Kentucky or Hopeless, North Dakota, then the first place to stop – *bien sûr!* – is the Motley Fool. At the UK site you'll find a section on choosing a US discount broker, and at the US site a much larger one on the same issue, naturally with a slant towards US residents. For comment, opinion and other people's thoughts, the brokers' message boards in the UK and the US are there to help.

Briefly, the way it works is this:

• Decide on the broker you like the look of
• Download the application form and a W-8 tax form from their web site
• Print them out
• Fill them in
• Send them off
• Send money over to the US brokerage account by bank transfer
• Start investing

The W-8 tax form is the form to use if your home country has a reciprocal tax arrangment with the US (the UK has) and means the US tax authorities cream some tax off the dividends your US companies pay you.

As far as guarantees go, you'll find most US brokers are insured up to $500,000 of your assets, or even more. Share scams occur in the US, as they do here, but a Fool who isn't investing in penny shares and acts not on rumour, but only on information widely available in the public domain, has nothing whatsoever to fear.

Once your account is open and you have your password, you're free to start investing.

But in what?

In what?

IN SPIDERS, M'LUD

They're immensely ingenious, dogged, practised killers with black hairy legs (eight) and a tendency to scuttle which seems to make people dislike them, sometimes more than it should.

Spiders are the name of a type of investment known as 'Standard & Poor's Depository Receipts', symbol 'SPDR'. This is a type of pooled investment which tracks the performance of the S&P 500 stock market index, made up of the major industrial heavyweights of the US. Unlike index-tracking funds (which also exist in the US, notably the mighty Vanguard 500 fund), these can be bought and sold at any time of the day through a normal brokerage account, which is why we mention them here.

We're all about simplicity at the Fool and nothing could be simpler than taking part of a collective stake in the driving force of the US economy. A stake in SPDR is pretty well a stake in the US. If you don't know much about the US, or don't want to know much about the US, but do already know that every other TV programme seems to be American these days and why do we have to have all these American words creeping into English, hey, I mean America just seems to be taking over the world, I mean who do they think they are, well honestly . . . If that's the type of person you are – or even if you're not – then Spiders may just be an excellent investment for you. They allow you to hitch your coat-tails to the US market without getting too involved in the details of it all and without taking up very much of your time (say, one minute to buy them). Like the index tracker, this is a 'fire and forget' investment.

Over time, the US market will undoubtedly provide excellent returns, as both it and the UK market have done over the whole of this century. Spiders are a Foolish way of latching on to the coat tails of that growth.

OR IN THE FOOLISH FOUR

If you read through the Beating the Footsie section earlier in the book and said to yourself, 'Mmm, I'll have some of that robot-style investing, I will. Yes, with clotted cream and lashings of jam, Aunt Fanny!' then what follows may be right up your alley. If it didn't grab you, then the following chapter on Rule Breakers, Makers and Shakers could be what you're after. If that doesn't grab you, try one more chapter at random elsewhere in the book. If *that* doesn't grab you, we have specially designed the pages of this book to be suitable for composting. Simply tear it up, throw it on and, er, activate the compost pile by, you know, urinating on it.

But you did like Beating the Footsie, so here you are at the Foolish Four. That's good. Much, much better than composting. The Foolish Four is the grandaddy of Beating the Footsie.

In the same way as Beating the Footsie selects the highest yielders from amongst the FT 30 to hold for a year, before rebalancing into the next selection, the Foolish Four follows a similar, but more complex strategy with the 30 stocks of the Dow Jones Industrial Average. The principle remains exactly the same, though, that the high yielding stocks are 'unfairly' punished by the market, but that their value will rebound over the course of the next year or so, as these are some of the stocks which are most integral to corporate America. Combine this rebound with an already hefty dividend and you have an attractive, outperforming investment, which will pound the market. You're likely to recognise a fair few of the Dow stocks as they are mostly companies with major international operations:

Philip Morris

General Motors

Eastman Kodak

Sears

Goodyear Tire & Rubber

Chevron

Caterpillar

Minnesota Mining & Manufacturing

International Paper

JP Morgan

DuPont

Exxon

Union Carbide

AT & T

Boeing

Merck

Citigroup

Procter and Gamble

Alcoa

United Technologies

Coca Cola

Disney

Allied Signal

Johnson & Johnson

General Electric

McDonald's

Hewlett Packard

Wal-Mart

American Express

IBM

'Dividend yieldology' – the UK Fool's pet name for this subject – is much more highly developed in the US than it is in the UK. This means that the ins and outs of the 'Official Foolish Four', also known as the F4.2, the dividend yield strategy the US Fool follows on its web site, are exceedingly interesting (honest, they are), but is a bit too complicated to go into here. Suffice to say that in backtesting, the Official Foolish Four has been pounding the market to an average tune of 19.56 per cent from 1961 to 1998. The High Yield Five, exactly analogous to Beating the Footsie and which can easily be chosen by any UK investor without recourse to a computer or online access, has returned 16.11 per cent in backtesting over the same period. Meanwhile, the Dow Jones Industrial Average (the Dow 30) has returned 12.19 per cent on average and the S&P 500, 12.32 per cent.

This means that $10,000 invested into each of these strategies in 1961 would have looked like this in 1998, disregarding any charges or taxes:

Official Foolish Four (F4.2):	$8,876,963
High Yield Five:	$2,913,663
Dow 30:	$790,515
S&P 500:	$827,025

What is so striking once more is the tremendous difference between the total return of the Official Foolish Four and the High Yield Five; just 3.5 per cent difference in annual return has meant a threefold difference in the amount of money in your pocket at the end of the day. Still, the High Yield Five is no slouch, has the merit of great simplicity and, Fool, is all you're getting here today. In the pipeline is a *Motley Fool Guide to Investing in the USA*, which will delve more deeply into US mechanical strategies, but in the meantime you'll find much more on the Foolish Four, along with current rankings, at the US Motley Fool site.

If you want to choose the High Yield Five and you're not online, you'll be slipping on your mac and popping down the newsagents right about . . . now . . . to buy a copy of the *Wall Street Journal (Europe)*. 'Ye what, missus? The Wall Street who?' Alright, maybe you'll have to pop along to somewhere a bit bigger than the tobacconist's on the corner. Once you've got it, flick to the financial pages, check the list of Dow 30 companies hasn't changed and then list out the companies with their yield next to them.

COMPANY	YIELD
1._____	_____ %
2._____	_____ %
3._____	_____ %
4._____	_____ %
5._____	_____ %
6._____	_____ %
7._____	_____ %
8._____	_____ %
9._____	_____ %
10._____	_____ %
11._____	_____ %
12._____	_____ %
13._____	_____ %
14._____	_____ %
15._____	_____ %
16._____	_____ %
17._____	_____ %
18._____	_____ %
19._____	_____ %
20._____	_____ %
21._____	_____ %
22._____	_____ %
23._____	_____ %
24._____	_____ %
25._____	_____ %
26._____	_____ %
27._____	_____ %
28._____	_____ %
29._____	_____ %
30._____	_____ %

As before, all you now have to do is take the top five (or ten if you have substantially more money and are aiming for a more diverse, hence less volatile, holding of shares), buy them in equal pound amounts and hold them for a year. Your top five, then, are:

Company	Yield
1._____	_____ %
2._____	_____ %
3._____	_____ %
4._____	_____ %
5._____	_____ %

At the end of the year, you'll be reallocating them in the same way as in the Beating the Footsie chapter.

And that's it. Dead simple. These stocks, picked from among the most solid companies in the US, will doubtless provide an excellent, market-beating return if the strategy is followed, as all stock market investing strategies should be, for the long-term.

A DASH OF AMERICAN JARGON

Finally, the jargon need not put you off either. You pick it up pretty quickly and there really isn't that much difference between the UK and US jargon. Below is a short exercise (get your ruler and pencil out of your pencil case) which asks you to match terms with their explanations. It covers the major US investing terms which foreigners find baffling and is designed to show that it isn't too difficult. Oh? You even find UK terms baffling at this stage? Don't worry – there's a big glossary at the back of the book and you'll be surprised how much of the exercise below is frankly a set-up anyway (er, sorry, 'how much of this exercise you can figure out by a process of elimination').

10-Q	A type of index-tracking security
10-K	A company's symbol; e.g. Microsoft's ticker is MSFT (= British 'EPIC')
CFO	Goes well with chips; subject of a war, 1976
IPO	Broker who advises on stock purchases (= British 'Advisory broker')
Stock	Selling a stock you don't own, hoping it will go down
DJIA	US index of 500 large stocks
Discount broker	The opposite of 'short': buying a stock and hoping it will rise
COO	Chief Executive Officer (= British 'Chief Executive')
COD	US company reports service
Full-service broker	Pooled investment of shares (= British 'unit trust')
Edgar	Company's quarterly report
CEO	Chief Financial Officer (= British 'Finance Director')
Short	Company's annual report
Long	Broker who only acts on orders; cheap (= British execution-only broker)
Ticker	Initial Public Offering, a company's first share offering (= British New Issue)
S&P 500	Oldest US index; contains 30 industrial companies
Mutual fund	Share
Spider	Chief Operating Officer (= British 'Operations Director')

Answers:

10-Q	A type of index-tracking security
10-K	A company's symbol; e.g. Microsoft's ticker is MSFT (= British 'EPIC')
CFO	Goes well with chips; subject of a war, 1976
IPO	Broker who advises on stock purchases (= British 'Advisory broker')
Stock	Selling a stock you don't own, hoping it will go down
DJIA	US index of 500 large stocks
Discount broker	The opposite of 'short': buying a stock and hoping it will rise
COO	Chief Executive Officer (= British 'Chief Executive')
COD	US company reports service
Full-service broker	Pooled investment of shares (= British 'unit trust')
Edgar	Company's quarterly report
CEO	Chief Financial Officer (= British 'Finance Director')
Short	Company's annual report
Long	Broker who only acts on orders; cheap (= British Execution-only broker)
Ticker	Initial Public Offering, a company's first share offering (= British New Issue)
S&P 500	Oldest US index; contains 30 industrial companies
Mutual fund	Share
Spider	Chief Operating Officer (= British 'Operations Director')

CHAPTER 13

Rule Breakers, Makers and Shakers

'The golden rule is that there are no golden rules.'
George Bernard Shaw

RULES

Rules, rules, rules. Who makes them? Do we really have to follow them? How many of the world's really great companies owe their success to following rules? Did Coca-Cola follow the rules? Did Microsoft? Did America Online? No, of course they didn't; they broke them. Then, they cast them aside and wrote their own rules.

Many good companies do indeed owe their success to following existing rules, concentrating on their markets, constantly improving their products and services, honing their efficiency, organically expanding their businesses, and becoming some of the best in their chosen market niches. Evolution in the natural world is based on a random process, that of spontaneous mutations, which may make individuals better adapted to a particular environment than their predecessors, but let's call this process whereby companies change in response to their environment an evolutionary process. It does

have many parallels with the changing structure of businesses, even though one cannot talk of volition and intention to change in the natural world in the same way as one can in the business world. The life of a species, or a company, can come dramatically to an end when conditions change; when the niche disappears. In the world of business, this is, more often than not, due to technological change.

Try writing down six products or animals which were unable to adapt to new conditions or which were overtaken by other products or species exploiting the existing conditions better:

1. _____
2. _____
3. _____
4. _____
5. _____
6. _____

Did you write down the brontosaurus? (It's

the one that's thin at each end and thick in the middle, in case you've forgotten.) Or the gas lamp? The stegosaurus? The electric telegraph? The diplodocus? The steam engine? What have these things got in common? Well, half of them walked very slowly and ate plants, of course, because they were herbivorous dinosaurs. But the other half are examples of technologies that were superseded and which led to the elimination of entire market niches. So, the thing that all six have in common is that they're all dead. Now what happened to all those companies that made gas mantles, Morse keys, and conical pendulum steam governors? They are gone, because the rules they played by were broken. They were broken by Mr Edison, Mr Bell and Herr Diesel (amongst others).

The thing which finally killed off the dinosaurs may well have been a huge meteorite impact which altered climatic conditions overnight. The reason this was fatal for them and not the smaller mammals is that the dinosaurs were unable to adapt to this rapid, cataclysmic change in their environment, which changed the rules they played by overnight. Think about it. If you need to munch through eighteen tons of bog weed a day to survive, you're bound to have trouble switching to other foodstuffs when the bog weed suddenly vanishes. If you're a nimble little mammal, the size of a rabbit, on the other hand, losing your primary source of nourishment is going to be much less of a problem as you'll be easier able to switch to something else. (The place will be littered with dinosaur carcasses for a start!)

Evolution – Darwin Turns in His Grave

You might think this is totally off-topic (and you'd be right), but evolution is one of the most mis-understood ideas in the world today and has been since it was first proposed by Alfred Russell Wallace and Charles Darwin in the mid-nineteenth century. We thought, therefore, we'd take the opportunity here to lay a few misconceptions to rest. Interestingly, however, this particular section was subject to the greatest number of rewrites of any in this book, the result of a spirited debate between its two authors, David Berger and Alan Oscroft. This means that you may not agree with what's written here either. Read through and see what you think. If you have any strong opinions, or even feeble ones, **Evolution@fool.co.uk** is the address to send them to.

Why are we worried about all this? Because people often think that animals or plants 'choose' to try and evolve to better exploit a particular environment. Often in people's writings is the implicit idea that beings 'try' to evolve into something better or more effective. There is a sense that evolution somehow has an intention and a direction, that in some way it is a guided process. This is wrong and a dangerous misconception, especially if this distorted concept is applied to other worldly phenomena unrelated to biology and lends them a degree of moral authority as a result.

Evolution in the natural world consists of two complementary processes. The first is a random process, brought about by spontaneous genetic mutation. The vast majority of such mutations are disadvantageous, and make the individuals who possess them less likely to survive. Every now and then, though, a beneficial mutation comes along, and makes an individual more likely to survive. Here's where the second process comes into play. It is called Natural Selection and is devastatingly easy to understand. Quite simply, individuals with beneficial mutations have a greater chance of living long enough to pass on their genes to their offspring. Just like the difference a couple of percentage points in your investment returns make over the long term, mutations only need to make individuals a tiny bit better in order to give them a survival advantage over their fellows.

Giraffes have long necks because those proto-giraffes (presumably deer-like creatures) in pre-history who *happened to have* longer necks could nibble leaves higher up the trees than their fellows and that *happened to be an advantage*, allowing them to thrive more than their fellows and thus pass on more copies of their genes on into the next generation. (In other words, the more advantage you can extract from your environment, the more and better offspring you will have.) Over millenia, this *selective advantage* led to the evolution of a species of animal with ridiculously long necks. There was never any 'intention' to evolve and if Gerald the Half-a-Giraffe hadn't happened to have been born with an unusually longish neck (he was teased unmercifully, by the way) 3 million or however many years ago, and that hadn't happened to have been an advantage, there would be no giraffes today. Evolution is kicked off through the utterly random process of mutation, a genetic lottery, throwing out a myriad of mutants, a very few of whom just happen to be better suited to life than their peers.

There, we feel better now.

_____

For most species and most companies that have existed, or will ever exist, the ongoing process of evolution ultimately leads to their extinction. Eventually, if you're not nimble enough, someone else will exploit your environment better than you and you'll be left wondering who has been eating all those nice berries you used to find so tasty. For many species, and companies, that have perfected the exploitation of their own individual niches, the ability to

change has long been lost. One day a smart new upstart will come along and start a revolution; they will either exploit a new niche or an old niche in a more effective way, elbowing you out for ever. They will rewrite the rules. That's the real secret to long-term success in business, especially in today's world. Adapt to changing environments. Adapt, adapt, adapt! Break the old rules, and then make the new rules.

In their newest, and for many the most exciting, Motley Fool book *Rule Breakers, Rule Makers*, David and Tom Gardner take a detailed and revealing look at the entire process, starting with Rule Breakers, examining the 'Tweener' stage, in which a company has broken the old rules but not really made the new ones yet, and ending with the world's truly great Rule Makers. And, as you have probably come to expect from the Motley Fool by now, their money is where their mouths are. The Motley Fool US site is host to, among others, two real-money portfolios; the Rule Breaker portfolio and, yes, you've guessed it, the Rule Maker portfolio. We'll take a closer look at each stage below, and we'll also have a look at how the US Fool's portfolios are doing, but for now, why not just take a few moments to ponder, to think about the overall process of company evolution, of adaptation.[1] Don't you think it sounds logical? You should do, because it really is.

Now, it is all very well going on about how great companies make it big. But how do we, as individual investors, identify them, these Rule Breakers and Rule Makers? Do they share any common characteristics that we can logically evaluate? Well, no, unfortunately they don't, so

_____

[1]Here at Fool HQ, we're also taking 30 seconds to honour the memories of Alfred Russell Wallace and Charles Darwin.

close the book now and go and put all your money in the building society. No! Wait a minute! Come back! Only joking. The answer is a clear, but qualified 'Yes'. Why is it qualified? Because, unlike mechanical strategies such as 'Beating the Footsie', it isn't always black and white. There are many shades of grey, and a fair amount of subjective opinion is needed, which shouldn't surprise you too much. If you really want to find the companies on the leading edge, you have to take more risk.

So let's think for a few moments about how rules figure in our personal investments. The strategies discussed in this book so far all involve some kind of rules. Objective rules are, of course, the mainstay of keeping emotion out of our investment decisions, something which reaches its apotheosis[2] in mechanical strategies such as Beating the Footsie. How else would we be able to avoid the popular hype and the Wise nonsense that surrounds the financial services industry? What, then, are the rules for guiding us towards these Rule Breakers and Rule Makers, and how reliable are they? We'll have a look at each in turn.

RULE BREAKERS

What is it that constitutes a genuine rule breaker and that separates it from the many other companies that have new ideas every year? New ideas are ten a penny, after all. Remember Clive

---

[2]Remember *The Good Old Days*? Remember the way the audience would go, 'Whooooooooh . . . !' when the bewhiskered Master of Ceremonies would say a word like 'discombobulating'? Right now, we'd like you to say 'Whooooooooooh . . . !'

Sinclair's LED wristwatches, his computers with keyboards and tape streamers that were never quite reliable enough? And finally, the ill conceived and ill fated C5 that was going to revolutionize personal transport? A successful Rule Breaker? Nope.

There are six key attributes that identify a true Rule Breaker, and we'll look at them now. And while you are reading through these rules, consider Sinclair and see if you can work out which rules that company lived up to. There's a space below to fill in your answers and the reasons for them. Oh, and one other thing to remember — these rules were worked out with respect to American companies, so don't worry if you can't think of any British or European companies that obey all six rules. We will be thinking about applying the rules to Europe a little later, so please bear with us for now.

1: Top Dog and First Mover

The company needs to be the top dog and first mover in an important and emerging industry. Why was it that small furry mammals took over from the dinosaurs? Did they have any intrinsic qualities that destined them for success? Qualities that could not have been found in, say, small reptiles or amphibians? No, they made it because they were the top dogs and first movers. And once they had moved and filled the empty evolutionary niche left by the dinosaurs, that was it – there was no room for any other group. And was it an important and emerging industry? It certainly was: it was survival.

2: Sustainable Advantage

A Rule Breaker needs to have a sustainable advantage over its competitors in order to capitalise on its first mover status. This advantage can be gained from a number of things – business momentum, patent protection, visionaries, or inept competitors. These are all competitive advantages. The classic example of a company with a strong, sustainable advantage is Microsoft, and their first competitive advantage was gained through inept competition, in the shape of the oft-quoted Apple Computer – a company who make great products, but who never had the business sense to license their designs and their software and so capture the market.

3: Strong Price Appreciation

A Rule Breaker's share price should be on a roll, showing that the company really is getting some of the appreciation it deserves. Ideally, it should exhibit a Relative Strength better than at least 90 per cent of the market. That is, its share price should have grown better than 90 per cent of all other companies.

4: Smart Management and Good Backing

This one might seem obvious. All companies must have smart management to stay solvent at all, mustn't they? Wrong! Think about Apple Computer again for a moment. They did not have smart management when it counted, and they blew their chance to dominate the world of personal computers. Good backing is needed too; smart companies attract smart money, so have a look at who is behind the investment. Is it someone you respect? Someone with a good track record?

5: Strong Customer Appeal

Now this one really is obvious if you think about it. Great companies need great products if they are to attract a loyal customer base, inspire repeat purchases, and command a premium price for those products. Can you think of any companies whose products have this kind of customer appeal? How about Coca Cola? They must surely be up there with the very best, don't you think?

6: Grossly Overvalued

What? Yep, that's rule 6. Well, actually, rule 6 states that the company must have been reported as grossly overvalued by the financial media. If you can't find at least one report making this claim, then skip the company and keep looking.

Those are the rules then, so what about Sinclair? Was Sir Clive's company a Rule Breaker?

SINCLAIR – A RULE BREAKER?

RULE	YES / NO	WHY / WHY NOT
1. Top Dog and First Mover	_____	_____
2. Sustainable Advantage	_____	_____
3. Strong Price Appreciation	_____	_____
4. Smart Management, Good Backing	_____	_____
5. Strong Customer Appeal	_____	_____
6. Grossly Overvalued	_____	_____

Interesting exercise, hey? Well, each of the company's products was pretty much the first in its field at an affordable price and computers were definitely an important and emerging industry, even back then. So perhaps we'll pass Sinclair on Rule 1. Rule 2? Hmm, they never got sufficient momentum behind their sales really, did they? And they enjoyed none of the other attributes of sustainable advantage either. Rule 4 is a big miss too, don't you think? An eccentric inventor might be great for thinking up technical wizardry, but driving the company? No thanks! Rule 5? Sinclair never made the connection in people's minds between the company name and a feeling of excellence, and the reason for that is clear; the products were not excellent. Innovative, yes, but they were Ratner-esque in quality. They were the funny little gadgets that early nerds played with, but you'd never actually *use* one.

Rules 3 and 6 were not applicable to Sinclair, of course, because it was never a public company. And that brings us on to one more rule. It's more of a meta-rule really (and all that means is that it is a rule about the rules,) so let's call it Rule 6½. What Rule 6½ states is that if a company is not public, and therefore cannot satisfy Rules 3 and 6, but it clearly fulfils the other rules so strongly that it has you drooling to get at it, then get in when it floats. In fact, if you can think of a company like this, then put this book down immediately and go and queue at the broker's office, now!

THE US RULE BREAKER PORTFOLIO

How is the US Fool's Rule Breaker portfolio doing? You will need to check the web site for the latest details, but the progress as of late June 1999 is as follows:

COMPANY	BUY DATE	BUY PRICE	PRICE NOW	% CHANGE
America Online	5 August 1994	0.91	106.75	11645.61 %
Amazon.com	9 September 1999	6.58	111.69	1597.57 %
Iomega Corp	17 May 1995	1.28	4.13	222.16 %
Excite@Home	4 December 1998	56.08	94.75	68.95 %
eBay	26 February 1999	100.53	148.75	47.97 %
Trump	30 April 1997	8.47	4.88	42.44 %
Starbucks	2 July 1998	27.95	37.38	33.70 %
Amgen	16 December 1999	42.88	55.63	29.74 %
Caterpillar	23 February 1999	46.96	58.94	25.49 %
Chevron	23 February 1999	79.17	95.81	21.02 %
DuPont	20 February 1998	58.84	70.50	19.81 %
Goodyear	23 February 1999	48.72	58.31	19.70 %
3Dfx	8 January 1998	25.67	16.25	-36.69 %

Some pretty impressive results there, don't you think? And if you are wondering about Trump, and how a falling share price can bring a profit, then don't worry – you're not going mad. The portfolio is currently 'shorting the Donald', as they like to call their strategy of profiting from the poor performance of Donald Trump's stock. We know that breaks the Rule Breaker rules, but, hey, that's Rule Breaking for you. Check out the web site for more details.

If you really are super-observant, you will have noticed that the Rule Breaker portfolio holds Caterpillar, Chevron, DuPont and Goodyear, amongst a variety more interesting, rule breaking stocks. These four are old-style industrial giants which wouldn't fit at all into the mould, but for the fact that the Rule Breaker is also holding the Foolish Four to balance out the high volatility of its other stocks. These shares constitute a Foolish Four selection of high dividend yield stocks.

Shorting a Stock

'Short' selling essentially involves borrowing a stock you don't own and selling it with the aim of buying it back at some point in the future at a lower price. At that point, the stock is returned to its original owner and you pocket most of the difference. Of course, if the stock price goes up, you lose. It is a strategy which depends on identifying stocks whose performance is likely to be poor and is a common strategy in the United States. In the UK, it is currently hard for private investors to find a stockbroker who will allow them to short a stock.

The US Fool counts shorting as one of its investment strategies, but only with a small proportion of their portfolio and recommend it only for more experienced, 'hands-on' investors.

RULE MAKERS

That's how to break the rules, then. But to break them, they have to be there in the first place. So who made the rules, and how do we identify these Rule Makers? You won't be surprised to hear that the Gardners have formulated rules for identifying Rule Makers too. These are a bit more formal than the Rule Breaker rules, and there are far more of them. So let's put the actual rules aside for a moment, and first, let's see if we can think of any obvious Rule Makers ourselves, intuitively. These are companies which call the tune for their particular industries. All their competitors have to play by the rules they set. It's an enviable position to be in. See how many you can think of. Try for six again:

1. _____
2. _____
3. _____
4. _____
5. _____
6. _____

OK, how did you do? Difficult, hey?
How about the following?

- Microsoft
- PepsiCo
- Hammurabi
- British Telecommunications
- Amstrad
- Marks & Spencer
- Cisco

What do you think? If you chose Amstrad, go to the bottom of the class. They might have had a pioneering range of computers at one time, but they only pioneered the price. Nobody ever made the rules just by competing on price (and before you all raise your hands and cry, 'Ah, but didn't transistors compete on price with vacuum tubes and help make the new rules?' we will quickly exclude technological change that drives prices down, we are just talking about plain simple price-cutting here).

Go to the top of the class if you chose Hammurabi. One of the finest Rule Makers in history. But go straight back to the bottom of the class again if you think you are going to buy some Hammurabi shares – he was an ancient Babylonian law-maker, not a company. Tough.

What about Microsoft? Now we're getting there. You will probably agree by now that Microsoft once made the grade as Rule Breakers, but they have largely moved on since those days (though they may have some rule-breaking left in them.) The company that makes the software that controls around 80 per cent of the world's computers must surely be making some rules, right? We certainly think so.

Cisco? 'Who are they?' some of you may ask, although many of you who use the Internet will already know. Cisco are the company that make boxes called 'routers' that connect together the physical fabric of the Internet. They join up all those wires and all those computers in a sensible way, and allow fast communication between them. If the millions of computers out there make up the railway stations of the Internet, and the miles and miles of wire make up the tracks, then routers (and other similar boxes) make up the junctions, the signal boxes, and the timetables. And who makes them all? Cisco don't have a complete monopoly, but they dominate the market so much that many people, even in the industry, would be hard pushed to name their competitors. The name 'Cisco' is synonymous with the word 'router' in many people's minds. Rule Maker? Most definitely.

200 THE MOTLEY FOOL UK INVESTMENT WORKBOOK

Just as a brief aside, by the way, have you noticed how computers and technology keep popping up here? That's no surprise really, and it simply isn't because the authors are techie geeks. Think back to Rule Breaker rule number one for a moment, the 'important and emerging industry' bit. That explains it for Rule Breakers, but it is also important for Rule Makers – rules are usually made when an emerging industry starts to mature, aren't they? Great Rule Makers, like Coca-Cola, sometimes keep their kingly status for decades, but getting in when the usurper is consolidating its position can reap the highest rewards.

What did you think of PepsiCo? How many times have you gone a whole day without seeing a bottle of Pepsi, or a Pepsi ad somewhere along the way. Very rarely, we'd wager. How about when you jet away on your holidays? Have you ever been to any country where Pepsi is not sold? Very unlikely. So, do Pepsi make it into the exclusive Rule-Maker club? The hell they don't! That's because they are only the second best at what they do. Their international presence and their worldwide sales may be enough to make most companies green with envy, but they don't come close to Coca-Cola. Coke is the Number 1 soft drink in the world, and by a large margin. Coca-Cola's turnover in the quarter ending September 1998 was a massive $4.7 billion. That's just a single quarter. This domination shows in the share price too – comparing each company's share price with its actual sales, Coca-Cola's shares are valued at about three and a half times that of PepsiCo's. So, you get a zero if you said, 'Yup, PepsiCo's fine by me,' but you're a hero if you thought, 'Hey, Coke's the number one, not Pepsi.'

OK, we've found three Rule Makers now, so let's take a gentle diversion before we look at the other companies on the list. Currently we have decided on Microsoft, Cisco, and Coca-Cola. What do these three have in common (apart from all three making products that computer nerds can't live without)? Does the word 'monopoly' spring to mind? It should. Now, it's true that none of these three has a genuine total monopoly on anything, but each one has a very significant competitive advantage that gives it near-monopoly status. The monopolies enjoyed by Microsoft and Cisco are pretty obvious, but is Coke a monopoly? Coca-Cola, even if it has other large competitors in terms of products, has the world's best known brand name. This brand name superiority, alone, is enough to make millions of people ask for 'coke' when all they really mean is 'a cola-type beverage'.

So, we have identified the most important attribute of a Rule Maker. A monopoly, or near-monopoly status is required. Back to the list then. How about good old Marks & Spencer? For years considered by many to be a cut above their competitors, but did they ever hold a monopoly on knickers and good quality food? Not really. They may have been at or near the top of the list, but their turnover was only ever a small proportion of the total for their market sector. And what competitive advantage they did have was easy for others to erode, and erosion is exactly what has happened, as the High Street supermarkets have all introduced higher quality food ranges in addition to their usual 'pile 'em high, sell 'em cheap' philosophy. M&S don't make it, then.

On to the last company in the list, British Telecommunications. Do they make Rule Maker status? Do they have a monopoly? They certainly have no sort of worldwide monopoly, but what about in the UK? The easy answer is 'No', as there are some clear competitors – Cable & Wireless, Vodafone, Orange and the various cable companies spring to mind. But, it isn't really that clear cut. BT have huge capacity in their telecommunications backbone, and could, if they were allowed to, deny access to other companies and cut prices too. This would make a number of current smaller players completely non-viable. So why don't they do this? Because the telecommunications regulator Oftel won't allow them to, but Oftel may lose its power some day. In terms of turnover, BT are by far the largest telecommunications company in the UK too – with a 1998 turnover of £15.64 billion, it is way ahead of Cable & Wireless, with £2.25 billion, and Vodafone, with £2.41 billion. So, maybe BT do enjoy some monopolistic attributes.

On to the actual rules for Rule Makers then. A lack of space prevents us from describing all the rules here, so if you are really interested, you will need to buy a copy of *Rule Breakers, Rule Makers*, and you should definitely visit the US Fool web site. But we will summarize the categories of rules, and there are four of them. Many of the categories look at measures like gross margins, net margins, cash and debt levels, and the Foolish flow ratio, which we've already examined, but each category looks at them in different ways (and throws in some occasional extra stuff too). All that aside, it's an excellent read, as much a book about business philosophy as investing.

We will briefly examine the four categories in increasing order of importance (that is, the least important first). **Brand** identity comes first. To be a Rule Maker, a company needs to have a familiar, open brand, that promotes optimism. There are seven categories here, with one point each, so a there is a maximum of seven points to be had.

Next in order of importance is the company's current **Financial Location**. Where is it at now? What are its margins, its cash and debt

levels. Does the company have mass-market appeal and inspire repeat purchasing? Seven measures here too, but with up to two points each. Maximum: 14 points.

Next comes **Financial Direction**, which compares the direction a company is moving in. Is it getting better from year to year? Are its margins improving? Is debt falling? There are six measures in this category, each carrying up to 3 points. So there is a maximum of 18 points is to be gained.

Finally we come to the most important, **Monopoly Status**, which we have already considered to some degree. In this category, the same key attributes are considered again, but this time in relation to the company's competitors. There are five measures of monopoly status, each of which carries a maximum of 4 points. So up to 20 points can be scored.

This all adds up to 59 points maximum. So, to make it up to a nice round number (and to add a bit of fun, too) there is one extra point to be had, awarded simply for your own personal enjoyment of the company's products and services. Love Coke? Give them a point. Hate Microsoft? That's a zero, then.

A perfect Rule Maker company, then, will score 60 points, with the real top-tier Rule Maker companies scoring between 50 and 60 points. Second tier companies score between 40 and 49 points, and, though not quite the cream, might still make great investments.

The US Rule Maker Portfolio

Just like the Rule Breaker portfolio, you can check the web site for the latest performance figures, but the following is a summary in late June 1999:

COMPANY	BUY DATE	BUY PRICE	PRICE NOW	% CHANGE
Microsoft	3 February 1998	39.13	85.00	117.20 %
Cisco Systems	23 June 1998	58.41	119.38	104.37 %
Gap Inc.	1 May 1998	34.37	69.25	101.49 %
Intel	13 February 1998	2.34	54.94	29.76 %
Pfizer	3 February 1998	82.30	99.25	20.60 %
American Express	26 May 1998	104.07	124.63	19.75 %
Yahoo Inc.	17 February 1999	126.31	144.44	14.35 %
T. Rowe Price	6 February 1998	33.67	35.00	3.94 %
Schering-Plough	21 August 1998	47.99	45.91	-4.35 %
Coca-Cola	27 February 1998	69.11	63.50	-8.11 %

Nothing quite as spectacular here as some of the Rule Breakers, but a pretty impressive portfolio, nonetheless.

RULE SHAKERS AND THE UK

Something that you might have thought about as you read this chapter is how American are the measures we have discussed so far, and how they may not be applicable to UK and other European companies. At the Fool UK, we have actively been pondering this too, as we have been doing the groundwork for our next real money online portfolio. What we want is a portfolio containing some of the best companies around, but we also want to concentrate on European companies too (there wouldn't be much point just duplicating the US portfolios now, would there?).

Carefully examining the Rule Breaker rules, we find that there really are precious few Rule Breakers in Europe. It seems that the good old US is the first to break the rules just about every time (and how often have you heard that old lament on how great we are at technical innovation this side of the Atlantic, but how much better the Americans are at commercial exploitation of ideas?). We are convinced that there are European Rule Breakers, though, even if we may have to bend a rule or two to find them. Think about Rule 6, for example, which states that a company must be considered over-valued to be a true Rule Breaker. That one is, perhaps, the most 'American' of the six rules, and perhaps the hardest to apply in Europe; financial reporters over here aren't quite as vociferous as their American counterparts (although even that august publication *The Economist* did carry a leader not so long ago telling us why Internet companies were sure to crash in value).

What about Rule Makers, then? Analyzing UK companies by following the US Rule Maker rules to the letter, we have been finding that no company comes close to the first tier (50-60 points), with very few even approaching the second tier. One of the problems appears to be that UK companies simply do not achieve the gross or net margins that set US Rule Makers apart from the pack.

So what are we going to do, then? Well, we are working on different methods for finding top British and European Rule Makers. We will still stick to the US Rule Maker principles, of course, but we are looking for measures that are commonly associated with the best of European business. Our rules then (which will evolve over time, as we learn from our experience and benefit from the input of the many Fools out there who email us and contribute to our message boards) will probably be similar in nature, it's just the numbers that will be different.

'Why Rule Shakers?' we hear you cry. We've been researching the new UK portfolio for quite some time now, and we decided pretty early on that we can't really use either the 'Rule Maker' or 'Rule Breaker' titles, as we won't be sticking to exactly the same rules – we don't want to cause confusion beneath all those jingly belled caps out there. And we're not quite breaking the Rule Maker rules either, we are just bending them a little, so what should we call the portfolio?

We agonized for many months, tossed aside numerous suggestions and even tortured several interns in the hope of finding some inspiration. Then, one auspicious day at Fool European HQ, David Berger came bursting out of the bathroom following a short 'comfort' break, crying, 'Rule Shakers, that's it!' He categorically refused to disclose how this inspiration had arisen, but thus was the name born and so did it go on to be adopted. Verily.

By the time you read these words, the UK Rule Shaker portfolio should be up and running (and maybe even in profit, who knows?) and you will be able to follow its progress on the Fool UK web site.

Here's to many years of Rule Making, Breaking and Shaking.

CHAPTER 14

Final Foolishness

'Goodness is the only investment that never fails.'
Henry David Thoreau

You're pretty much at the end of this book now. It's remarkable how quiet it is when you close the cover of any book for the last time and direct your gaze thoughtfully out of the window. With a Mills & Boon or Barbara Taylor Bradford romance (Bruce reads these), one's thoughts drift towards what might have been, of how Jennifer's life would have turned out if she had submitted to the charms of the dashing scamp, Alexander Sprague rather than the steady Hartley Fortesque. Sigh.

Reading a thriller, a few reflective moments are in order to allow the pulse to slow down and the adrenalin to subside after Craig Donaldson, veteran of too many wars, has saved the world. Again.

The end of a Jeffrey Archer book is infused by feelings of wonderment and disbelief: so strangely compelling and so awesomely profitable for the author!

Closing the covers of a Delia Smith cookbook or a *Lonely Planet Guide*, you are left with a feeling of the possible, a feeling that maybe you can do some extraordinary things. Maybe, you reflect, looking out on a rain-soaked Parsons Green, it really is within your power to bake a sun-dried tomato and feta cheese tart or to travel around a developing country for six months on local transport and with nary a thought for a change of underclothes.

Humbly, we hope that a similar feeling of the possible is rising up within you now, that perhaps you may feel a little more in control, a little more capable of learning to manage your own money than you did before you started. The journey, you see, starts here, right when you go to put this book down. Naturally, we hope that you have been inspired, if you're not there already, to join the online world and visit and take part in the Motley Fool community. The interchange going on there can help fill that noiseless void which often seems to occupy the space after a book has been finished. But even if that's not a possibility for you, there are many things for you to do in the coming weeks, months and years to keep you firmly in charge of your money, rather than the other way round.

One of the most important things is not to let inspiration set goals and targets which you know in your heart of hearts you won't be able to keep. Don't let managing your money go the way of so many other resolutions you may have made in previous years. It's too important for that.

So, whether you sweated blood on this book from cover to cover, or flicked straight to this page like a debutante, take a couple of minutes now to set down three aspirations which you'll aim to fulfil in the next 3 months and which will set you on the path to managing your own money. Think of three small and practical aspirations, smaller than you think you can achieve, then cut them in half, trim them a little more and inscribe them with a flourish below:

My Three Small, yet Noble and Foolish, Practical Aspirations for the Next Three Months

1. _____
2. _____
3. _____

Did you note down, 'Keep track of my monthly over/under', 'Identify how much I can set aside for regular investing' and 'Set up and follow a paper portfolio'? You could have noted down many other things, depending on your level of knowledge and confidence, but if you chose these three small, relatively low maintenance items, you were on to a good start. Keep your three small, yet noble and Foolish aspirations under rolling review. The process of becoming a Foolish investor is a continual one of aspiration for improvement and learning. Without that attitude, it can become a dead, drab, painful

process and if that happens you will soon lose interest and be back to square one, beholden to a group of professionals whose aims are so different to your own.

Above and beyond those regularly updated practical aspirations, as you become a more active Foolish investor and as time marches you relentlessly towards the ultimate check-out counter from the superstore of life, you should ask yourself more general questions like these:

1. Are you better off than when you started?
2. Are you fulfilling all the long-term goals you set for yourself earlier on in the book?
3. If not, why not?
4. How can you continue to improve your financial status?

To help define the answers to these general questions and keep you on track, here is a checklist for your regular review, which we've divided into three parts: Big Picture Questions, Investment Review, Personal Questions.

BIG PICTURE QUESTIONS

These shade into those questions you used to ask yourself at late night parties in college, with Leonard Cohen playing in the background and a girl locked in the bathroom, sobbing.

Do the long-term goals I've set for myself still seem appropriate?

_____
_____

Were those goals too ambitious? Or not ambitious enough?

_____

_____

Did I overlook anything when I set these goals for myself?

_____

_____

Have I just inherited a mining empire/shipping line/burger chain from a previously unknown – and now dead – relative which means I can upgrade all my goals from Ernie of Ilford level to Sultan of Brunei status?

_____

_____

Have I become a wandering Hindu ascetic, eschewing all money and material goods and wishing nothing more than to end my days by the side of the Ganges?

_____

_____

In what other ways should I be changing my long-term goals?

_____

_____

INVESTMENT REVIEW

The nitty gritty.

Are the reasons I chose the particular investment vehicles I did still valid?

_____

_____

Do I expect too much from my investment strategy? Or too little?

_____

_____

What have I learned about my risk tolerance? Do I force myself to jump out of aeroplanes when I'd really rather be taking a stroll in the park?

_____

_____

Should I be taking more risk in my portfolio? Or less?

_____

_____

Is it time to sell some of my holdings? If so, why? And what would be the tax consequences?

_____

_____

Has my net worth improved, or – gulp, be honest – got worse?

_____

_____

And the most crucial question: Have I beaten the FTSE All Share Index?

_____

_____

If yes, then what did I do right and how will I keep doing that?

_____

_____

If no, what did I do wrong and how will I rectify that?

_____

_____

PERSONAL QUESTIONS

Truth or consequences.

What do I know now about investing that I didn't know three months or a year ago? How should my next decisions reflect this new knowledge?

_____

_____

Have my spending habits changed? Have I learned to live within a budget?

_____

_____

Now that I'm a little older, should I adjust my spending and investing habits?

_____

_____

What else do I need to learn?

_____

_____

Where can I go to improve my skills?

_____

_____

How can I contribute to helping others?

_____

_____

Is it finally time for me to cease torturing small furry animals?

_____

_____

A LIFE OF INVESTING

Mistakes really aren't all bad. That's a good thing, because you are going to make them. Plenty of them. Having read this book and taken to heart a little common sense about investing, you still won't be immune, but you're less likely to make any devastating, reckless ones. As long as that's the case, reckon that mistakes are your biggest opportunity to learn and shape your investing behaviour for the better in future.

As you reflect on your mistakes (and, we hope, successes) over the coming months and years, go back through the book and take some of the quizzes again. See if you get the same scores. Reread parts of the book and decide whether you agree or disagree with them, whether they can be improved upon and how. Be critical and in so doing hone your investing knowledge and skills.

Continue to look at your goals and also your budget. Is there more of your income you could usefully free up for investing, without hammering your lifestyle into the ground? Alternatively, now that you have things a little more securely on track, is it time for a minor splurge on something which may enhance the quality of your life?

Finally, investing is fun, not just a number-crunching series of balance sheets. It has life. There is a joy in the art and craft of fashioning your portfolio and then tending it like a garden. Sometimes, plants which you thought would never take, flourish beautifully and others which by all accounts should have been suited to the soil, the climate and the aspect wither and die. Like gardening, investing is always a surprise and that is much of its attraction. Like gardening, too, investing needs a certain amount of patience and dedication and delivers its rewards over the longer term.

A FINAL THOUGHT – CHILDREN

Children are an excellent place for this book to take its bow. Of course, you may not have any, for very many valid reasons. But you may still want to read on, for few of our lives are not touched by children in some way, shape or form, whether they are those of relatives, those of friends or simply children we come across in our professional lives.

The reason for writing about children here in such an important part of the book, the final bit, is that children are pretty extraordinary creatures. They tend to be wonderfully straightforward and refreshingly adept at picking up on twaddle and blather. They are also outstanding at absorbing new ideas, making them their own and then innovating with them in ways at which stuffy old adults can only marvel. Despite all this, however, they learn practically nothing about money and finance at any stage in their education or upbringing, unless an enlightened adult takes it upon themselves to teach them.

Getting the drift?

You are now, officially, that enlightened adult. You may not feel so and you may make a humble attempt to decline this honour: 'No, honestly, really, I couldn't, not me, I'm no good with children, I can't sing nursery rhymes and I can't *stand* answering questions which start with "Why" all the time, and all that drool from the toddlers, ugh . . . '

Decline and then decline some more, old friend. Yes, we'll even be charmed by the gesture and the self-deprecating sentiment which it implies, but you can't get away from the fact that you know much more about all this stuff now than does your common or garden grown-up and that that knowledge could make a tremendous difference to the lives of children with whom you come in contact. Imagine if you had understood the power of compound interest as a child (for whom, of course, it holds the most power), had understood that investing in the stock market was not some dark and deadly pastime, but a positive statement of belief about the way our society runs and a worthwhile personal undertaking too. Imagine if as a child you had understood the difference between a public company and a private one and had had some feel for what makes a good company and what makes a bad one. Imagine, too, if you had understood that saving and investing wasn't the ultimate purpose, but merely one facet of a rich and diverse life. Finally, imagine if you had understood about the pernicious nature of higher rate debt.

All this knowledge would have given you a breathtaking opportunity to shape your life for the better from a young age and even if you had decided to forget everything you knew for a few wanton years in your twenties, here's betting it would have come back to you sooner, rather than later.

Get children involved with investing. Try having them nominate and follow companies they know and understand, perhaps creating a company scrapbook with press clippings and a chart of its share price. Have them surf the Web with you (they'll know exactly where to click the mouse to get the information you've been searching for for hours). Talk with them about business in general, about what makes a good one, about what the purpose of a business is, about how to improve it. Get them to think creatively about business – and why not? After all it is a creative enterprise – and you'll fire their imaginations.

Finally, with those special children in your life, start contributing on their behalf to some kind of regular savings plan. As time goes on, they will become more and more interested and increasingly competent to take on the responsibility for their savings themselves. When you reach that point, you'll have given a gift far greater than money itself.

And in a chapter where gardening and investing have been brought together as kindred pursuits, the last word goes to the late Clay Jones, former host of the old *Gardener's Question Time* on BBC Radio 4:

A very good day to you!

The Fool's Guide through the Jargon Jungle

No-one likes jargon, but if you come across any terms you don't understand, you may find them explained below. Perhaps one or two of the definitions in here may bring a wry smile to your face. Not a belly laugh, nor a throaty roar of delight or even a hearty chuckle, you understand, just a wry smile. Still, if that happens, that's not bad for a collection of explanations of financial terms.

10-K The official filing of end-of-year accounts a US company makes with the **NYSE**.
10-Q The official filing of quarterly accounts a US company makes with the **NYSE**.
20-F A document prepared for the US SEC by a foreign company listed on the **NYSE** that tells you everything you need to know about a company. It is often more detailed than the report and accounts.
80-SLAM A proprietary Motley Fool name, referring to the breathtaking amount of **commission** (sometimes 80 per cent) charged on

many **Wise** investment products in the first years of their existence. See **endowments**, **Additional Voluntary Contributions** and **front-end loading**.
Accountant An actuary who wanted a more exciting life.
Additional Voluntary Contributions (AVCs) Many try and enhance their **occupational pension schemes** by paying into one of these plans. Watch out for the hefty charges and dismal underperformance, though. Like **personal pension plans**, they attract **tax relief**.
Adjusted earnings Companies don't have to produce adjusted earnings, but can choose to do so to clarify their results if the statutory figures are distorted by **exceptional items**.
ADR American Depositary Receipt. Americans are funny about directly holding foreign shares and prefer instead to trade a receipt from a US bank that holds the underlying shares. Although normally the ratio is 1:1 (i.e. 1 ADR = 1 share), sometimes it isn't. BT, for instance, can be traded as an ADR in the **US**.

Advisory stockbrokers Stockbrokers which offer advice on which shares to buy and sell. We don't favour using them. See **execution-only stockbroker** and **churning**.

Alternative Investment Market (AIM) AIM opened in 1995 for small, growing companies. It's less difficult to be listed here than on the London **Stock Exchange** and shares are higher risk and more likely to be difficult to buy and sell. See **Liquidity**.

America See **US**.

American Depositary Receipt See **ADR**.

Amortization An annual charge taken through the **profit and loss statement** to allow for the fall in value of an asset. This term is often used in conjunction with an **intangible asset**.

Analyst A financial professional who analyzes securities to determine a 'fair' or 'intrinsic' value for those securities. The term is generally applied to almost any professional investor who does research of some kind.

Annualize Taking an item measured over a certain period and restating it on an annual basis. For instance, if it costs £10 million every month to run a factory, the annualized cost is £10 million x 12, or £120 million, since there are twelve months in a year. Simple.

Annual Percentage Rate (APR) When you borrow money, this rate should always be quoted to you. It's the percentage rate which your loan will cost you each year, including all charges. Incredibly, APRs for credit cards can run around 22 per cent.

Annual Report A yearly statement of a public company's operating and financial performance, punctuated by pictures of families enjoying the firm's products and/or services.

Annuity The investment you purchase with your pension fund, which will provide you with a regular income in your retirement. Because it is aimed at providing you with income, the majority of the fund is invested in bonds and government securities. The annuity seller has to guess how long you will live and pays you an income accordingly. When you die the money stays with the annuity seller. Should you die very shortly after purchasing the annuity, this fact leads to a situation colloquially known as a 'Bummer'. The law currently requires a pension fund to purchase an annuity before you are 75.

Appreciation Increase in the price (or value) of a share or other asset. Appreciation is one component of **total return**. Payment of an income, in the form, say, of a **dividend**, is another.

Arbitrage The process in which one bank rips of another one by selling it something at the wrong price. OK, that was a bit facetious, even if it's pretty accurate. It's the process by which small, local price differences in something are exploited and thus evened out. For instance, Unilever trades on the Amsterdam, New York, and London stock exchanges. At any given time, depending on local trading conditions and currency movements, the same shares may be trading at the equivalent of three different prices.

Associate A company that has between 20 and 50 per cent of its shares owned by another is deemed to be an associate. The parent company is assumed to have some management input and is allowed to account for its share of the profits reported by the associate. This is usually more than the cash it actually gets.

Australian-type mortgage As it sounds, a type of mortgage common in Oz. Interest due is calculated daily as opposed to yearly, which can make a significant difference to the cost for those on a repayment mortgage. Also more flexible and allows periods of both under- and over-payment of the mortgage to suit the borrower's changing financial circumstances.

Balance Sheet An important financial report regularly issued by companies. It details, at a particular moment in time, exactly what the company owns and what it owes. It provides a breakdown of the capital structure of the company between debt and equity and analyzes the composition of its assets.

Bank of England Set up in 1649, the 'Old Lady of Threadneedle Street' has responsibility for regulating the banking industry and since 1997 sets interest rates to help the government meet its inflation targets. The stock market hangs on the Bank's interest rate pronouncements.

Bankruptcy When a company owes more than it can pay, or when its debts exceed its assets, it's bankrupt. Occasionally, this situation can exist for sometime before a bank decides enough is enough and calls in its loans.

Bear So you think that the market is headed south? You're bracing yourself for a crash or correction? You feel that shares will soon be taking a tumble? Guess what – you're a bear! Bears are investors with pessimistic outlooks, as opposed to **bulls**.

Beating the Dow The US grand-daddy of our very own **Beating the Footsie**.

Beating the Footsie A mechanical investment strategy, based on buying large-cap shares with a high **dividend yield** on a regular, rotational basis. Like Beating the Dow, it has been historically very successful.

Beta A measure of share **volatility**. High Beta stocks tend to exhibit greater price movement.

Bid-offer spread The difference between the bid price (at which the holder can sell shares) and the offer price (at which the holder can buy shares). On occasion this can be quite large and depends on the **equity**'s underlying price, **liquidity**, **volatility** and a number of other factors. Many

unit trusts also have a bid-offer spread and effectively this amounts to an extra exit charge when the investor sells.

Big Bang The first big shake-up of the stock market in October 1986. This marked the end of single capacity, in which jobbers bought and sold shares for their own account and stockbrokers acted as agents only. Afterwards brokers could hold and trade shares and many of them were wise enough to do so at the time of the 1987 crash. This was followed in 1996 by the introduction of **CREST** and then in 1997 by **Big Bang II**.

Big Bang II 20 October 1997. The use of a computer-driven trading system (called **SETS**) to cut out the middlemen in share trading, who match buyers and sellers.

BIS Bank for International Settlements. A club for central bankers where they can meet and tut-tut about any impending crisis and reminisce over how they made the last one worse.

Blue chip A share in a large, safe, prestigious company. British Telecom is a blue chip, so is the Hong Kong and Shanghai Bank Corporation. Many of the shares making up the **FTSE 100** are blue chips.

Bond A bond is essentially a loan which you, the investor or 'bondholder', agree to give to a company (or a government) for a fixed period. In the return, the company pays you a fixed rate of interest. At the end of the bond's term, you then get your original investment back. In the meantime, you can sell your bond on to someone else if you wish. If interest rates generally are going up, the price of the bond will fall. Effectively, this offers new buyers a higher return on their money. Conversely, if rates are falling, bond prices rise, but the holder will still get the same interest income. Interest rates vary depending on the quality or reliability of the bond issuer. Government bonds, or gilts, for example, carry little risk and thus offer lower interest rates. Company bonds offer higher interest rates, with the riskiest companies (or governments') bonds offering the highest of all and being called junk bonds.

Bonus issue Or, in the US, a stock split. Whenever a company believes that the price per share of its stock has risen to a point where investors may wrongly perceive it as 'expensive,' they will split the stock, reducing the price but increasing the number of shares outstanding. For instance, if Huge Fruit PLC trades at £60 a share with 3 million shares outstanding and decides to split its stock two-for-one, this means that each share will now trade at £30 but there will be 6 million shares outstanding.

Book value What the accountant says a business is worth. It often bears no relationship to what the owners (shareholders) think the business is worth. It is calculated by adding **retained profits** to the initial share capital and is a purely arithmetic calculation. It can be grossly distorted by inflation. It is 100 per cent accurate and often totally useless as a way of valuing a business.

Broker One who sells financial products. Be it in insurance, pensions or shares, most brokers work under compensation structures that are at direct odds with the greatest good of their clients. (Also see **Independent Financial Adviser, execution-only stockbroker, advisory stockbroker, stockbroker.**)

Brother Male sibling. See **debtor.**

Building Society A mutual organization, owned by the people saving with and borrowing from it. Increasing numbers have converted to banks in recent years, paying windfall profits to the owners. See **demutualization.**

Bull Are your glasses rose-coloured? Do you see nothing but blue skies ahead for the stock market or a particular security? Then you're a bull – an optimistic investor – as opposed to a **bear.**

CAC 40 French index of – wait for it – the 40 major French companies.

Capital A business's cash or property, or an investor's pile of cash.

Capital employed The total value of all the assets being used by the business to make money. Usually calculated as total assets less current liabilities. See **Return on capital employed.**

Capital expenditure What the company has to spend to stay in business and grow. If everyone else is using computers while you are using typewriters you probably haven't spent enough.

Capital gain You bought a share and later sold it. If you made a profit, that's your capital gain. If you lost money, it's a capital loss. If you make enough of a capital gain outside your tax-sheltered accounts (PEPs, ISAs), you'll be liable for Capital Gains Tax (CGT). The amount of profit you can make without paying CGT is £7100 for the 1999/00 tax year.

Cash flow This term gets used rather vaguely. Operating cash flow is the cash generated by the business after changes in **working capital.** Free cash flow is this figure less what you have to pay the taxman and the bank for the money you borrowed. Net cash flow is how much the piggy bank has changed at the end of the year.

Chief Executive The Chief Executive is the highest executive officer in a company, rather like the captain of a ship. He or she is accountable to the company's Board of Directors and is frequently a member of that Board. The Chief Executive participates in setting strategy with the Board and other officers and is responsible for the tactics in meeting the company's goals. Known in the **US** as the Chief Executive Officer or CEO.

Churn Churning is the unconscious or conscious

over-trading by a stockbroker in a customer's account. Stockbrokers are paid on a **commission** on the consideration of a trade. The consideration is the number of shares traded multiplied by the price. As commissions have stabilised the only way brokers can make more money is to trade more shares. There is therefore a natural temptation to trade for the sake of it. It's illegal, but hard to prove.

The City London's financial district, which encompasses the square mile of the old City of London, bounded on the south by the Thames, on the west by the Law Courts, on the east by the Tower of London and in the north by Islington.

Commission The way a **stockbroker** or an **Independent Financial Adviser** is compensated. When he or she makes a transaction for a customer, the customer pays a commission. In the Fool's opinion this is a Bad Thing, as it sets up a situation where the customer's and the broker's interests are not the same.

Common stock A US term for shares.

Compound Interest The investor's best friend. One hundred pounds invested in the stock market in 1918 would be worth just over £1,000,000 today. (No, that's right. Not a misprint.)

Consultant Someone who borrows your watch and tells you the time in return for a fee.

Cookie A piece of software that gets downloaded into your computer when you register with a web site. It can provide the web site with details of how you use the site.

Cookie cruncher Something that knows what a cookie is and eats it.

Cookie monster Something which eats cookie crunchers, naughty children, stray dogs and **day traders**. Cookie monsters also like honey.

Correction A decline, usually short and steep, in the prevailing price of shares traded in the market or an individual share. Any time that commentators cannot find a reason for an individual stock or the entire market falling, they call it a correction. It sounds better than a 'Crash'.

Creditor Someone you owe money to, like the Inland Revenue. See **debtor**.

CREST Introduced in 1996, this is a computerised system to settle up share purchases. No more bits of paper passing hands any more.

Cum-dividend 'Cum' means 'with' in Latin. If you buy shares cum-dividend, you are buying them at a time when you will be entitled to receive the next dividend. This is as opposed to **ex-dividend**. If restrictions on entitlement to dividends didn't exist, people would simply buy shares the day before the dividend was due, collect it and then sell them the day after.

Cyclical Not a bicycle missing a wheel, but a description of a company, such as a steel maker, that is ultra-sensitive to the business cycle. Some investors enjoy buying and selling cyclicals according to which way they think the cycle is going next. Like any form of market-timing, this is a tricky exercise.

Dax German index of major companies, broadly equivalent to the **Dow Jones Industrial Average**.

Day trader A US term. Day traders are in and out of the market many times during the course of one trading session and may not even hold a position in any securities overnight. This approach tends to generate a lot of expenses in the form of commissions and denies the day trader the ability to participate in the long-term creation of wealth through the compounding that is possible if you own the shares of a quality business. See **Cookie monster**.

Debtors People, or businesses, that owe you money. Usually it is your biggest client, or your brother.

Deflation Opposite of **inflation**. A rise in the value of money.

Demutualization The process **building societies** go through when they convert to banks and thus go from being owned by their members (the borrowers and savers of the society) to being a public limited company owned by shareholders. There are pros and cons and the arguments rage on.

Depreciation The diminution through time of the value of fixed asset. Basically it is an allowance for things wearing out. There is normally a charge in the profit and loss account to account for this. It is purely an accounting feature and has no effect on the cash flow. In a steady state the capital expenditure of a company will normally equate to the depreciation charge.

Derivatives If shares are assets, derivatives represent contracts to buy a particular **security** at a given point in the future for a particular price. Options and futures are derivatives. They can be used to lessen investment risk, but often their main attraction is that they are highly **geared** and can thus offer spectacular profits . . . and spectacular losses. We do not advocate their use.

Directors These people form the Board of Directors and are legally responsible for running a company. If they transgress they can go to jail. If they run the business properly they can make themselves, and you as a shareholder, very rich.

Disclosure Since 1995, **Independent Financial Advisers** and **tied agents** have been forced to disclose the level of commission they will earn from selling financial products to clients. It's a good thing, but the investor still isn't able to compare the levels of commission between investments. **Stockbrokers** also have to tell you of any financial interests they have in securities they are recommending.

Discount broker The US term for execution-only stockbroker.

Dividend A distribution from a company to a shareholder in the form of cash, shares, or other assets. The most common kind of dividend is a distribution of earnings. See **Dividend yield**.

Dividend yield The dividend divided by the current share price, expressed as a percentage. Different companies have different policies on the size of their dividend payouts. See **Beating the Footsie**.

Dow Jones Industrial Average The 30 companies chosen by editors of Dow Jones & Company that are supposed to epitomise the very best American corporations and reflect the landscape of corporate America, although high-tech companies are grossly under-represented.

Earnings The amount a company says it added to shareholders' funds after all the costs of delivering a product or service have been accounted for. See **Earnings Per Share**.

Earnings Per Share (EPS) Net income divided by the current number of shares outstanding. This is one of the principal elements used in determining at what value the shares should trade.

EBITDA A horrible acronym for Earnings Before Tax, Interest, Depreciation and **Amortization**.

Economic Value Added Commonly shortened to EVA. This figure is the difference between the Return on Capital Employed by a company and the Cost of the Capital Employed by a company. A simple, but flawed, analogy is to compare the annual cost of your mortgage with the annual increase in value of your house. If your house has risen in value by 10 per cent and your mortgage is only costing 6 per cent, then you are ahead. The same logic applies with a company. If it gets more out of its capital than it is paying for it then it is adding value.

Endowment A life assurance and savings and investment policy, classically sold to back an interest-only mortgage. The key word here is 'sold'. No-one in their right minds would 'buy' one of these overcharging and underperforming abominations these days. See **with profits insurance** and **surrender value**.

Endowment assurance An assurance policy that pays a specified amount of money on an agreed date or the death of the life assured, whichever is the earlier.

Enterprise Value The sum total of the market value of a company's debt and equity. It represents an open market valuation of the business or enterprise that supports it. In other words, how much a company is actually worth. It has no direct relation to **book value**. Commonly shortened to EV and divided by **EBITDA** to give a useful ratio.

EPIC An abbreviation for a company's name which is used as shorthand by share quote reporting services and various online sites. Known in the US as a ticker symbol.

Equities A concept that comes from 'equitable claims'. Equities are essentially shares of stock. Because they represent a proportional share in the business, they are equitable claims on the business itself.

Ex-dividend A share sold without the right to receive the dividend payment which is marked as due to those shareholders who are on the share register at a pre-announced date. These shares have "xd" next to their price listings in *The Financial Times*.

Exceptional items These are features in the profit and loss statement that are not expected to occur regularly. They are typically profits or losses recorded by selling businesses, or charges incurred in closing activities down. They make interpreting of accounts, especially **earnings per share**, quite tricky. It is one reason why companies also produce adjusted figures to show the underlying performance of the company.

Execution-only stockbrokers Stockbrokers who offer fewer of the services championed by advisory stockbrokers, but charge cheaper transaction fees. Basically, you tell them to buy or sell a particular share and they get on and do it with no frills and no hassles. Often they hold your shares in a nominee account. Execution-only brokers are ideal for do-it-yourself investors – that's you. They are called discount brokers in the US.

Exit charge A sales charge paid for redeeming a unit trust or other investment. See **front-end loading**.

Fair value The theoretical price at which a company is 'fairly valued', meaning that it would not be reasonable to assume that the shares will rise. Fair value at any given point is derived from a number of qualitative and quantitative aspects of the business.

Financial Services Authority (FSA) The top investment watchdog. Contact them on 020 7638 1240, but if you have a problem with a financial adviser or insurance company, contact the **Personal Investment Authority**. If you have a problem with a stockbroker, contact the **Securities and Futures Authority**.

Fixed asset Something solid a company owns that hurts your shin if you fall over it; like a factory.

Flotation See **new issue**.

Flow Ratio Also known as the Foolish Flow Ratio or the Flowie. This tells you how well a company manages its assets and liabilities and is a useful indicator of financial health. You'll find the formula on p. 129.

Flying freehold A term used to describe that part of a freehold property which is built above land which is not part of the property freehold, e.g. a bedroom built over a common access passage-way.

Flying trapeze Circus act involving high levels of skill, courage and sequins.

Fool One who exhibits a high degree of **Foolishness**.

Foolish Four The US Fool's variation of the Beating the Footsie strategy.

Foolishness The state of being wry, contrary, canny and capable of looking after your own investments. Fools believe in shares as the long-term path to wealth creation and believe in buying and holding good companies for the long haul based on their fundamental financial and business strengths. Also see **Wisdom**.

Front-end loading A sales charge paid when a **PPP**, **AVC**, endowment or other investment is purchased. It can amount to the whole of the first two years' contributions.

FT 30 For many years the FT 30 was the index most often quoted in relation to the London Stock Exchange. It was originally conceived as being the UK equivalent to the Dow Jones Industrial Average, but is little quoted now. (Except by Fools intent on Beating the Footsie.)

FTSE-All Share Index (FTSE-ASI) An index containing the 800 largest companies on the London Stock Exchange. Either the FTSE-ASI or the FTSE 100 are the indices generally tracked by index trackers.

FTSE 100 An index containing the 100 largest companies by market capitalisation on the London Stock Exchange. Came into being in 1984 and largely superseded the FT 30.

FTSE 250 An index containing the 250 largest companies by market capitalisation on the London Stock Exchange, created in 1992.

Full-service broker The US name for an advisory stockbroker.

Futures A type of **derivative** that allows you to bid for the right to pay a future value on either an index option or a commodity. Futures are a great way to lose 100 per cent, or possibly even more, of your investment, because if they expire worthless, you get nothing. Futures have a fixed duration and normally only last for one year at the most.

GAAP 'Mind the . . . ' No, nothing to do with the tube at Embankment station, this is an acronym for Generally Accepted Accounting Principles.

GDR Global Depositary Receipt. Similar to an **ADR** but used for international stocks traded in London as well.

Gearing Buy a house for £100,000 with a deposit of £10,000 and the rest as a mortgage. Six months later, sell it for £150,000 and you've made 400 per cent profit on your original profit: that's gearing. Of course, it can work the other way too: see **negative equity**. Gearing can be expressed as the ratio of debt to shareholders' equity and is used by companies and investing individuals to enhance their profits, as well as homeowners to allow them to buy a home.

Gilts When the government needs to borrow money, it sells you these. They are government bonds and as a rule the interest is paid gross (i.e. free of tax). They are very safe and their US equivalent is the Treasury bill, or "T-Bill". See **risk-free rate of return**.

Goodwill The difference between what a company pays for another company and the **book value** of that company. In the unlikely event of the **book value** being higher than the purchase price then you get Badwill.

Gross The payment of any form of income (interest or dividend payout) without the prior deduction of tax. Also, see **net profit**.

Gross profit The profit declared after the costs of making your product are deducted from turnover. See page 113 for a more detailed explanation.

Independent Financial Adviser A financial adviser who is not employed by a particular company to market their products. They may be paid by commission, which in our view amounts to a conflict of interest, or else by agreed fee. We like to call these people Independent Financial Advisers (salespeople). See **Personal Investment Authority**.

Index Groups of shares mathematically reworked to be representative of the current level of the market or of different sub-groups of companies within the market. See **FTSE 100, FTSE-ASI, FTSE 250, FT30**.

Index-linking Something which increases at the rate of inflation is index-linked. Some gilts are index-linked and the old age pension is index-linked.

Index tracking unit trust The only type of unit trust that makes sense to us. While most unit trusts are actively (mis-)managed, index trackers are generally computer-driven and designed to mimic the performance of a given stock market index, such as the FTSE 100 or the FTSE-All Share Index.

Individual Savings Account (ISA) ISAs started in April 1999 and replace PEPs and TESSAs. In the first year you can invest £7000 and thereafter £5000 per year into a wide variety of investments. They are very attractive to Fools. There's more information on the different types of ISA in Chapter 4.

Inflation A fall in the value of money.

Initial Public Offering (IPO) The US name for a company's first sale of shares to the public. In the UK we call it a **new issue**.

Inland Revenue Come on, you know who these people are! You probably don't know their very helpful web site, though: **http://www.open.gov.uk/inrev/irhome.htm**

Insider dealing This is when you buy or sell a share and at the same time possess privileged information which would move the price if it were widely known. It's illegal, but is also widespread and there are few prosecutions for it.

Institutions Institutional investors include pension funds, unit trusts and insurance companies. These are the big players in the stock market as they have a lot of money to invest and as major shareholders they often have a say in company decisions.

Intangible asset An asset in thin air that someone thinks is valuable. Typically this could be a brand name, the rights to a process or a publishing title.

Interest-only mortgage Monthly payments to the lender are made up simply of interest. You don't pay off any of the capital of the mortgage during the term of the mortgage, but do so at the end, having accrued a large enough amount of money in an investment fund. Classically, these investment funds have always been endowments, but increasingly they are ISAs.

Intestacy A licence for lawyers to print money. If you die without making a will (dying 'intestate'), the law dictates how your estate will be passed on and lawyers have a great time. The law aims, in the first instance, to protect your immediate family – husband, wife and children. This might mean that unmarried partners lose out. Your husband or wife is entitled to all your personal chattels (i.e. personal possessions, such as clothes, furniture, your car, etc.) If your estate is valued at £125,000 or less, the surviving spouse also inherits the whole estate irrespective of whether there are any children. If there are children, the surviving spouse is entitled to £125,000 and the household contents and personal effects of the deceased. The rest of the estate is then divided up into two equal parts. One of which will go to the children. The other half goes into a trust. The income from this legal entity will go to the surviving spouse, but the asset will on the death of the surviving partner become entirely the possession of the children. Moral: Make a will.

Investment club Group of investors which meets regularly to discuss which shares to buy and sell out of a common fund.

Investment trust A public limited company which makes investments into a variety of other companies. Notwithstanding several important differences to unit trusts, these are also pooled stock market investment funds. Unlike unit trusts they can take on debt that can amplify the underlying movements. See **gearing**.

ISEQ The Irish stock market index.

Large-cap See **market capitalization**.

Leverage The US term for **gearing**.

Libor The London interbank fixing rate. A benchmark used to define a particular interest rate.

LIFFE This is not a typographical error but the name of a futures market in London. See **futures**.

Life insurance See **term life insurance** and **whole of life insurance**. (By the way, life insurance means the same as life assurance. It is just that life **as**surance lasts until your death, which is a guaranteed event. Life **in**surance is for a defined period that might, if you are lucky, not include your death.)

Liquidity The easier it is to turn an asset into cash, the more liquid it is. Shares are very liquid as they can be sold any weekday at any brokerage. Works of art and homes are not nearly as liquid because you need to find an interested buyer. Since every buyer needs a seller and vice versa, penny shares, which are very thinly traded, are more illiquid than larger capitalization shares.

Listed Company A Public Limited Company (PLC), listed on a Stock Exchange.

Margin 1. Borrowing money to use specifically for buying securities of any kind in a brokerage account. 2. A measure of profitability of a company, like profit margin, operating margin or gross margin.

Market Capitalization The total market value of all of a firm's outstanding shares. Market capitalization is calculated by multiplying a firm's share price by the number of shares outstanding. Large-cap, medium-cap, small-cap refer to shares in decreasing order of market capitalization.

Medium-cap See market capitalization.

Message board stroller A surfer who gets paid for patrolling Internet message boards.

MIG Mortgage Indemnity Guarantee. If you borrow more than 75 per cent of the value of your house, you'll probably get stung with one of these. It insures the lender against you being unable to pay. Even though it's you that pays this premium, it still won't stop you ending up at the Salvation Army soup kitchen.

Minorities Profits due to the outside shareholders of a subsidiary company. It is also that element of a company's balance sheet that is funded by outside equity interests.

Mortgage A loan to buy a home, where you put up the property as a security against your paying back the loan.

Mutual Fund The US equivalent to our unit trust.

Mutual society An organisation set up and owned by its members and run for their benefit. Building societies, friendly societies and some life insurers are examples of mutual societies.

Nasdaq National Market A national US stock market where trades are made exclusively via computers. The second largest market in the country, the Nasdaq is home to many high-tech and newer firms, including Microsoft. It now has its own web site for UK investors http://www.nasdaq.co.uk

Negative equity Bought a house for £80,000 and now it's only worth £60,000? Bad luck – that's £20K of negative equity you're sitting on there. See **gearing**.

Net profit Usually enough to support the Chairman's gross habits. What's left for the shareholder after everyone else has taken their cut.

New issue The first time a company is floated on the stock market. Selling your company, or a part of it, to outside investors is a way to raise money for expansion plans. Also known as an **initial public offering**, or **IPO**.

New York Stock Exchange (NYSE) The largest and oldest stock exchange in the United States, this Wall Street haunt is the one frequently featured on television, with hundreds of traders on the floor staring up at screens and answering phones, ready to trade stocks upon command from their firms.

Nil paid Shares on which no payment has yet been made but which are being dealt in on a stock market. These shares usually arise from a new issue or a rights issue. Because the price at which a rights issue is made is at a discount to the market price of the existing shares, the rights issue shares have a value in their own right.

Nominee account A type of account in which execution-only stockbrokers tend to hold shares belonging to clients, to make buying and selling of those shares easier. It does mean, however, that any shareholder perks are unlikely to be enjoyed by the investor.

Occupational pension scheme Contribute to your firm's pension scheme and get a maximum of 40/60ths of your final salary. Few, very few, get this much, though. Your occupational pension may well not be enough for your retirement.

OEIC See **Open Ended Investment Company**.

Open Ended Investment Company These are replacing unit trusts and indeed many unit trusts are already converting to them. Ostensibly, they will be simpler for investors to understand and the charges will be lower as there will not be a bid-offer spread between the buying and selling prices. In practice this will likely be replaced by a "Dilution levy". *Plus ça change* . . .

Operating profit The same as for gross profit but after administration, marketing and research and development expanses have been charged as well.

Options Contracts that give a person the right to buy or sell an underlying share or commodity at a set price within a set amount of time. The majority of options expire worthless.

Orphan assets Assets which are no longer required by life assurers to satisfy their future liabilities to policyholders and shareholders. Some life companies which have been going for many years have accumulated surplus funds, the precise ownership of which may be obscure and can be a matter of contention. Others may suffer the reverse problem, in which case they go bust.

Penny share A share of very low market capitalization (often a few million pounds) trading in multiples of just a few pence. They are very volatile, subject to extreme price fluctuations on the flimsiest of rumours and not at all the thing for the long-distance Fool. See **liquidity**.

Personal Equity Plan (PEP) Started in 1987. Up to April 1999 you were able to put up to £9000 per year into equity-based investments in one of these and allow it to grow tax free. They have been replaced by ISAs, but existing PEPs can continue to grow in their tax-free state.

Personal Investment Authority The people who regulate Independent Financial Advisers and indeed anyone marketing retail investment products to the general public. You can contact them on 020 7538 8860.

Portfolio management Give all your money over to the stockbroker and say 'Here, go manage this.' It's one step up even from an advisory service. See **advisory stockbroker**. You can of course manage a portfolio on your own, for zero cost.

Preference shares Shares issued by companies that have additional rights, normally in terms of dividends.

Price/Earnings Ratio (P/E) A measure of a share's price in relation to its trailing twelve months earnings per share. Often the higher the sustainable growth rate of a company, the higher its price-to-earnings ratio.

Profit and loss statement The most important of the three key financial statements to equity investors. It explains how the balance sheet has changed over the year and gives a figure for the profits reported. It does not necessarily reflect the cash the company has made or lost during the year.

Profit Before Interest and Tax (PBIT) As for **operating profit**, but adding in any income from associates. This number is divided by **capital employed** to calculate **ROCE**.

Prospectus A prospectus must be issued by any company before issuing shares to the public.

ProShare A special interest group representing the interests of the private investor. They publish a magazine called *The Investor*, and also have a useful information pack on how to set up an investment club. Contact them on 020 7600 0984.

Provisions A charge made against the assets of a company for some event that is known will happen in the future, but has yet to be paid out. This could be taxes for next year, or the cost of cleaning up old industrial sites.

Public Limited Company (PLC) As opposed to private, a company is public after it issues partial ownership of itself, in the form of shares, to the public. Only PLCs can be listed on the **London Stock Exchange** or the **Alternative Investment Market**.

Quarterly reporting In the US, after each quarter year a company is required to file a report providing investors with juicy details on how the company is doing. In the UK equivalent reports are seen only every six months. See **10-Q**.

Red herring The slang term for a pathfinder prospectus prepared for a US issue and used in pre-marketing. It contains all the details of the issue except the price. The front page is covered in red ink warning potential investors of all sorts of dire consequences if they were to invest in this company.

Retained profits The profits left in the business each year, if any, after all charges have been paid and dividends declared. This number is added, or subtracted if it is a loss, to shareholders' funds at the end of the year.

Return on Capital Employed Often shortened to ROCE. This ratio is a measure of how effectively the company is using its **capital**. The formula looks like this:

Profit before interest and tax ÷ (total assets − current liabilities)

This measures the return on all the assets the company is using.

Revenue The money a company collects from a customer for a product or service. Also known as 'sales' and 'turnover'.

Rights issue When a public company creates new shares. Existing shareholders are generally offered the right to purchase a certain number, usually at a discount to the market value. In the US, a rights issue is a form of secondary offering.

Risk Something it pays to take. See **risk-free rate of return**.

Risk-free rate of return The interest rate you get on **gilts**. Because the British government is reckoned to be one of the least likely entities in the world to default on a loan, this rate of interest is reckoned to be about as close to risk-free as you can get. The equity risk premium is the average amount by which share returns are higher than gilt returns. In the UK this century, it has been about 5.6 per cent per year and is effectively the bounty Fools get paid for taking the risk of investing in shares.

Rule Breakers Maverick companies which radically reshape a market, causing others to have to imitate them. Some Rule Breakers are great investments and eventually go on to make the rules they once broke. More on this in *Rule Breakers, Rule Makers* by David and Tom Gardner. Amazon, the online bookshop, is a good example of a Rule Breaker.

Rule Makers Companies which so dominate a market that they make the rules. Microsoft is the classic example. More on this in *Rule Breakers, Rule Makers* by David and Tom Gardner.

Securities 'Securities' is just a blanket way to refer to any kind of financial asset which can be traded.

Security and Exchange Commission (SEC) The United States agency charged with ensuring that the US stock market is a free and open market. All companies with stock registered in the United States must comply with SEC rules and regulations, which include filing quarterly reports on how well the company is doing.

Securities and Futures Authority (SFA) The people who regulate your stockbroker. Phone number: 020 7378 9000.

Securities and Investments Board (SIB) Now called the **Financial Services Authority**.

SETS The Stock Exchange Electronic Trading Service (SETS) is the formal name for the electronic trading order book introduced October 1997.

Share A security which represents part ownership of a company.

Shareholder If you buy even one share in a company, you can proudly call yourself a shareholder. As a shareholder you get an invitation to the company's annual meeting, and you have the right to vote on the members of the Board of Directors and other company matters.

SIPP Self Invested Pension Plan. Like a **PPP**, but the plan holder calls the shots in terms of which investments fill the plan.

Small-cap See **market capitalization**.

Stag A short-term, Wise trader who subscribes for new issues in the hope of selling them immediately they are listed for a quick profit.

Stamp duty A tax you pay on buying shares (0.5 per cent) or buying properties (1 per cent). In the latter case, stamp duty starts to be charged at £60,000.

Standard and Poor's 500 Stock Index (S&P 500) An index of 500 of the biggest and bestest companies in American industry.

Stock The same as a **share** and used more commonly in the US. A share of stock (confusing, yes – just use the two interchangeably, everyone else does) represents a proportional ownership stake in a corporation. Investors purchase stock as a way to own a part of a publicly traded business.

Stockbroker Woody Allen described a stockbroker as someone who invests your money until it has all gone. Normally it is a middleman who buys and sells shares on your behalf and earns commission on the transactions. Considered by many to be the fifth-oldest profession after prostitutes, pimps, tax collectors and accountants. See **execution-only stockbroker**, **advisory stockbroker**, **portfolio management** and **Securities and Futures Authority**.

Stock exchange A place where stocks and shares

are bought and sold. The London Stock Exchange serves this function in the UK.

Stock split US name for a **bonus issue**.

Subsidiaries A company where between 50 and 100 per cent of its shares are held by another is deemed to be a subsidiary. It is normal practice to assume that the parent controls the subsidiary. It is important for accounting and analysis because 100 per cent of the revenue and profits down to the pre-tax level are ascribed to the parent company. The amount of profit due to the other shareholders is deducted at a line called **minorities**.

Surrender value Accurately reflects what you get if you cash in your endowment before its time. On average, it takes more than seven years for the surrender value to equal the money you've put in.

Tax-deferred When you invest in something like an **AVC** or **PPP**, you receive an initial tax refund from the government and are then deferring taxes until you withdraw money in the form of annuity payments, when you will be liable to income tax.

Tax-efficient investments PPPs, AVCs, ISAs and formerly **PEPs** and **TESSAs**.

Tax relief Usually this refers to some allowance that the tax authorities allow companies. It can also apply to personal allowances.

TESSA Tax Exempt Special Savings Account. Being phased out after 1999 and replaced by the **Individual Savings Account**. Keep your money in this bank deposit account investment for five years and you won't pay any tax. For the truly long-term investor, TESSAs are an irrelevancy, as the stock market provides much greater returns.

Tied agent Less independent even than an Independent Financial Adviser. These are company sales persons, trying to sell you the products of the company they work for. Buying from them is a fool's, not a Fool's game.

Total return What investors are most interested in. The total amount of growth in value – in whatever form – which something provides. For shares, this is made up from price **appreciation** and **dividends**.

Treasury The government's finance department. They have a natty little web site **http://www.hm-treasury.gov.uk/**

Underwriter/underwritten The stockbrokers who help a company come public in a new issue. They underwrite (vouch for) the stock. When a company has been brought public, the shares have been underwritten.

Unit trust Your money is invested with thousands of others in one pooled fund. Presiding over the fund is a manager or managers responsible for achieving the fund's stated investment objective. Most unit trusts underperform the index and have high charges. They are to be replaced by **Open Ended Investment Companies**. Index trackers are the only form of unit trusts we advocate.

US Spiritual heartland of capitalism. Home, among others, to Motley Fool Global HQ, the Empire State Building, California and Alistair Cooke (bless him).

Valuation The determination of a fair value for a security. If you don't use some reasonable method, then you have what is technically called a 'guess' or a 'hope'.

Volatility The degree by which a share price tends to move. The more the price jumps about, the more volatile the share.

Wall Street Also known as 'The Street' in US cocktail-party patter, this is the main drag in New York City's financial district.

Widget A widget is universal catch-all name to describe things that factories make and, hopefully, sell for a profit. They are solid things that hurt if you drop them on your toe. Things like fridges.

Wisdom The state of being **Wise**. These are the people who seek to sell you inherently underperforming investments, hobbled even further by heavy charges. See **Independent Financial Adviser, tied agent, endowments** and **foolishness.**

With profits insurance Insurance policies which have both an insurance cover element and an investment element. Endowments are a form of 'with profits' policy often sold to back interest-only mortgages. Here's a quote from the *Daily Telegraph* about endowment mortgages in 1991: 'It cannot be said too often that the advantages to the householder of an endowment mortgage are as nothing compared to the gain to the policy salesman, that life assurance has nothing to do with house purchase, and that savings-related life assurance is a waste of money.'

Working capital The amount of money tied up in a company just to keep it running. This usually means stocks of widgets it has made but not yet sold, debtors, creditors and cash in the bank.

The World Bank Another collection of bankers that gives money to countries to prove they are uncreditworthy and thus justify the existence of the IMF.

WTO The World Trade Organisation. A body of important people that meets regularly to try and stop the **US** and Europe arguing about bananas, with limited success.

Yield See dividend yield.

Yield curve A graph illustrating the projected yield from government securities over the next ten years or so. It stretches from overnight money to the 10-year bond. In a normal market money costs more in the future. But when an economy is approaching a recession it is common to see short-term costing more than long-term money. This is a long-winded way of saying it might affect your mortgage.

Yield gap Also often expressed as the yield ratio. It is the difference between yields on 10-year bonds and **dividends** on the **FTSE All Share Index**. Typically, bonds yield twice as much as equities because they have no growth. The yield gap is watched closely by many "value investors".

Zamboanga A dance performed by joyous Fools at midnight on the night of the full moon closest to April Fool's Day. Also, a town in the Southern Philippines, bordering the Sulu Sea and renowned for piracy.

Acknowledgements

'I love deadlines. I like the whooshing sound as they fly by.'
Douglas Adams

Thanks first and foremost to David and Tom Gardner for the inspiration behind this book, in the form of the original *Motley Fool Investment Workbook*, and also for bringing to life such an amazing ethos and out-of-this-world company. Thanks also to the other Foolish collaborators on the *US Investment Workbook*.

Gabrielle Loperfido, our literary editor at the Fool, was as ever a calm, soothing voice amidst a flurry of deadline fever: 'You know, guys, I think we're in pretty good shape.' Alan Oscroft, one of the UK Fool's most extraordinary finds and possibly the most ardent supporter of A.F.C. Bournemouth we have in Fool HQ, wrote the majority of the Rule Breakers, Makers and Shakers chapter. Not only did he do an excellent job on that, but also on proof-reading the entire manuscript. (He always seems to draw the short straw.) Rob Davies attacked the 'Fool's Guide through the Jargon Jungle' like a trooper. Many thanks, Rob. Other Fools a-plenty have variously had their original works copied, modified, plagiarised or simply stolen and twisted in the process of writing this book. Isabel Berwick's writings on ISAs and specifically her joke about the Austin Maxi being useless (well, it was, wasn't it?) spring to mind, as do the message board contributions of Petrea and JKew. George Row sorted out the graphs for us and came up with the quotation at the front of the book during one hilarious and rather Foolish company meeting in the opium den.

James Kraft, Chief Business Fool, was extraordinarily solicitous for our writing welfare. If he could have bathed us in ass's milk to get the words flowing more freely, he would have. Ginger Huang, StyleMeister from the US Fool, gave great advice on the cover design.

Clare Hulton and Mark Wallace, our editors at Boxtree, were tolerance itself throughout and a joy to pick up the phone and talk to. Mark kept his cool as, relentlessly, one deadline after another came and went. Not only were we impressed at his *sang froid*, but mightily relieved!

Adrian Sington's hands at Boxtree were closely on this project, although we regret to report the divine Sington Karaoke Experience was not forthcoming during the writing phase on this occasion. Truly, no-one should die without having seen him perform Alice Cooper after midnight. The cover design by Richard Evans is, well, outstandingly Foolish. Thank you! Gill Coleridge, our UK agent, steered us through the legal ins-and-outs in her usual efficient and helpful manner. Without her, we'd be lost.

Tim Bond of Barclays Capital kindly agreed to allow us to reprint the graph of stock market performance over this century from the 1999 *Barclays Capital Equity Gilt Study*.

David would like to thank his wife Carol for putting up with a quite unacceptable degree of absence and remaining good-natured and wonderful in spite of it. Also, his son Max, for crawling for the first time as the final chapter was being written and providing the boost to get him over the hump. What a thoroughly Foolish baby! He would also like to thank James and Angie Kraft for serial hospitality and a very comfy sofa. Bruce, too, made his flat freely available and, by the by, has been a terrific partner these last two years (that long . . . already?).

Bruce would like to start by thanking his parents, Verna and Keith, who gave him the best upbringing a child could ever hope for. It wasn't their fault that he almost flunked school and university, finding every excuse and distraction humanly possible to avoid studying. The same could almost be said of writing half this book, except his distractions have been confined to World Cup Cricket, Max the Cat and the back lawn of his Kilburn Village manor. To the Fools who've kept the site going while I've been penning this tome, a big thanks. Also to David, who has been a great friend and colleague over the past two years. Thanks to him for editing my bit of the book, and injecting some much needed humour and wit where required. Finally to Julie. Thanks for her love, support and understanding. She's put up with a lot (that's me!) over the past few months, not to mention the past few years. Here's hoping for the future.

Finally, we'd both like to thank all the corresponding Fools out there who through their support in emails, on the message boards and in person have provided the inspiration and put in much of the hard graft which has grown the Motley Fool to what it is today.

Fool on, friends!

David Berger
Bruce Jackson